Energy and Development in Latin America

Energy and Development in Latin America

Perspectives for Public Policy

Nazli Choucri
Massachusetts Institute
of Technology

LexingtonBooks
D.C. Heath and Company
Lexington, Massachusetts
Toronto

Library of Congress Cataloging in Publication Data

Choucri, Nazli.
  Energy and development in Latin America.

  Bibliography: p.
  Includes index.
  1. Energy policy—Latin America. 2. Latin America—Economic policy.
I. Title.
HD9502.L32C48   333.79'098   81-47741
ISBN 0-669-04799-6   AACR2

Published simultaneously in Canada

Printed in the United States of America

International Standard Book Number: 0-669-04799-6

Library of Congress Catalog Card Number: 81-47741

Contents

List of Figures

List of Tables

Preface

This book, the third in a research program on energy and international development, examines energy profiles and prospects of Latin America, economic problems posed by the oil price increases of 1973, and attendant political dislocations. A particular emphasis is placed on the transportation sector as one of the major claimants on energy use. The individual countries' policy responses to new constraints are outlined both with respect to transport policy and to development policy more broadly defined. It is my belief that the policy issues identified in the Latin American context will assist our understanding of developmental problems and processes for the 1980s, as the international community as a whole confronts the challenges posed by new energy constraints.

The strength of Latin America is predicated on the economic and political diversity within the region, its enormous potential for energy development and expansion of alternative sources of energy, and the importance of the region's initiative internationally in addressing the new developmental problems of the 1980s.

International Politics of Energy Interdependence: The Case of Petroleum (Lexington Books, D.C. Heath, 1976), the first in the series on energy and international development, examined the political and economic factors that led to the consolidation of OPEC in 1960 and the initial price increases in 1973 and to the subsequent interdependence between producers and consumers of oil. The second, entitled *International Energy Futures: Petroleum Prices, Power, and Payments* (The MIT Press, 1981), presented a simulation model of the world oil market and the decision processes of producers, consumers, and international oil companies. A set of forecasts were presented about the effects of alternative oil prices, and their consequences delineated accordingly. The third study focuses specifically on developmental issues in Latin America.

I am grateful to many colleagues and graduate students for their contributions to this book. In particular, I would like to express my appreciation for the research assistance provided by Peter Haas, Lily Ling, Elizabeth Leeds, Warren Van Wicklin, and Nancy Wright who assisted in the various stages of data compilation and interpretation. I am also grateful to Diane Beth Hyman, research associate, MIT Technology Adaptation Program, and Michael Lynch, research specialist at the MIT Energy Laboratory, for their assistance on the analysis of issues pertaining to state energy enterprises. Finally, I would like to thank Phoebe Green who patiently typed numerous versions of the manuscript, and Dana Andrus whose sharp pencil eliminated unnecessary detail.

Part I
Energy

1

Energy and Development

Parameters for Policy Planning

The oil price increases of October 1973 and subsequent market adjustments have drawn attention to immediate and long-term effects of changes in petroleum prices and availability. Traditional patterns of supply and demand and lower prices in the 1950s and 1960s were no longer sustainable in a market where prices, set by oil-exporting countries, departed so fundamentally from previous levels. The price increases of 1973 and beyond have had critical impacts on the economies of both developed and developing worlds.

For developing countries the most immediate consequences of oil price changes commonly are seen in terms of the import bill and attendant needs for borrowing from international institutions or commercial markets. Adjustments of economic targets must take place, as must a reassessment of priorities, involving reappraisal of investment strategies and infrastructure development. The potential for expanding alternative energy sources and exploiting indigenous resources in both conventional and nonconventional forms is now being examined, as are new responses to the constraints imposed by changes in the world oil market.

Changes in energy prices and availability have already affected public policy in developing countries. The energy situation highlights a wider structure of constraints that define the bounds of economic performance and provide the context for government policy. These constraints, of course, have a broader international base, creating the context for national policies in the 1980s.

The structure of the world oil market, and roles of individual countries within that market, have contributed to the present-day international constraints, affecting economic activity of developing countries and official definitions of growth objectives. Energy policy is by necessity embedded in this hierarchy of constraints. Even in developed countries nothing of substance can be done without explicit recognition of the limits of social, political, and economic parameters. Energy use everywhere is tied to population growth, industrialization, expansion of urban centers, and development of industrial and infrastructural facilities. Roads and transport networks are among the most energy-intensive of such facilities. In countries where development planning has become a tradition—regardless of its effectiveness or implementation—development pro-

3

grams provide a good record of official policies. The use of government machinery in public sector enterprises constitutes an essential corollary of planning programs in developing countries. While traces of policy are manifested through planning programs and institutions for implementation, in the last analysis macroeconomic factors and government intents define the parameters for public policy.

The full effects of the new energy situation on policy planning for developing countries are not yet known. There is little specific information on new energy parameters for sectors of their economies. Even less information is available about long-term effects of policies designed to alleviate immediate strains, or impacts of longer-term policies designed to reorient development strategies. No one knows for certain what impacts institutional, social, or political adjustments will have on growth rates. The impact of changes in oil prices on the balance of payments of developing countries is well documented and, together with statistical estimates of impacts on growth, comprise the extent of data we have for these countries. Beyond that, however, what we can use to examine energy impacts on the developing world comes from existing analyses of industrial economies.

Clearly, changes in price or availability of this critical input to industrial processes already have had distinctive macroeconomic effects for all countries. This is especially true for countries that are high users of petroleum and do not have readily available substitutes, or cannot easily make adjustments in demand in response to changes in prices or quantities. Nowhere are constraints as apparent as in the transportation sector, where the impact of higher oil prices is immediate. The transport sector's hold on the entire process of development may well be deeply circumscribed by new scarcities, in both the general economy and among individual sectors, providing new sets of problems for government and new concerns for public policy.[1] The transport sector holds the most important key to future changes in patterns of energy use.

This book examines parameters for energy policy in Latin America and policy responses to new constraints on energy use and, by extension, on economic growth. It seeks to pull together both evidence and speculations regarding the effects of changes in the world oil market for the developing countries of Latin America, in particular to identify their critical effects for policy planning. It is tempting to consider all developing countries of the region in the same guise, but the fact remains that there are fundamental national and regional differences within Latin America which in many ways make energy policy planning in the hemisphere so distinctive. This book considers the effects of changing energy environments on individual countries and regional tendencies as policy planning for development in the 1980s begins to take shape.[2]

Development in the 1980s

In its most fundamental guise, development entails four distinct but inter-related processes that lead to improvements in human conditions.[3] These are:

1. *economic growth*, due to greater productivity and increasing overall national output;
2. *structural change*, due to transformations in employment patterns, distribution of economic activity, rates of urbanization, and overall industrialization;
3. *social equity and welfare*, due to the allocation of resources and attention to social services, education, health, and other aspects of social well-being;
4. *institutional development*, due to the establishment of government agencies to allocate and manage resources for development.

These processes reflect the complexity and comprehensive nature of development. An underlying objective for most developing countries is to exercise national autonomy; this generally means exercising greater self-reliance and autonomy in decision making. But for all developing countries, the search for national autonomy has emerged as a driving force in public policy debates. These debates in turn have guided both the nature and the content of development planning. Economic growth and social equity and welfare are principal *goals* of development, entailing institutional development and structural change as the principal *means* by which they can be attained. Over the past two decades advances in all four areas have led to an improvement in human conditions for many countries. The fundamental issue for development in the 1980s is therefore to discover how these advances can be sustained and how further improvements can be made.

Economic Growth

Economic growth comes from an increase in national output through greater productivity in the use of labor, capital, and other resources. It is measured in terms of either total gross domestic product (GDP) or gross domestic product per head of population (GDP per capita). In this area the main achievements and expected trends are as follows.[4]

Despite some regional lags developing countries have rapidly improved their economic growth over the past two decades. Real income per capita increased 5.4 percent between 1970 and 1975, and the average annual rate of increase in GDP stood higher than ever before. Between 1967 and 1974 the average annual rate of increase in GDP was 6.2 percent, and, although this figure declined to 4.9 percent in the difficult years between 1974 and 1977, it remained commensurate to the average GDP growth rate for industrialized countries over the time period, with an average GDP per capita growth rate of 2.8 percent (compared to 2.7 percent for the industrialized world).

Behind these encouraging figures, however, lie some profound and critical distortions that cloud an otherwise optimistic picture. The fact that industrialized countries start out from a higher economic base than developing countries shows that, no matter how superficially impressive statistical comparisons may seem, the gap between industrialized and developing countries is increasing in absolute terms. Differences between developing countries, particularly between the oil rich and the oil poor, show that the overall economic growth rate is pushed artificially high by abnormally inflated increases toward the wealthier end of the spectrum. Oil-rich developing countries enjoyed an annual growth rate exceeding 10 percent between 1975 and 1976, whereas other developing countries achieved only 4.3 percent, thus falling short of the 6 percent annual growth-rate target set by the International Development Strategy. Once these factors are taken into account, it becomes clear that the continuing economic processes of developing countries leave no room for complacency.

A powerful case can be made that suggests bleak economic prospects for the coming decade. Developing countries are especially vulnerable to changes in the international economic climate and to factors that influence the well-being of industrialized nations. They are also vulnerable to being undermined economically by increases in their own domestic population level, which threaten to nullify improvements in economic growth rates.

Social Equity and National Welfare

Social equity and welfare result from contributions to social services and other aspects of human well-being, including equity, leisure, education, and health. The goal of development in this area is not merely to improve conditions for the poor but to provide better services for the citizenry as a whole. Social equity and welfare together comprise an aspect of development for which the governments of all developing countries are concerned, even though their degree of commitment and resources vary greatly from case to case.

Progress in social equity and welfare has been sustained over the past two decades and is likely to continue into the 1980s if economic conditions permit. Many developing countries have tried to raise their standards of living by directing investment to depressed areas, but the evidence shows that their favorite approach has been to combat poverty directly by providing social services for their populations. This approach is now expected to change. Policies for the 1980s are likely to combine greater emphasis on investment in depressed areas with increased governmental planning in the sphere of employment, to expand agricultural and rural productivity while reducing inequities in access to government services.

In order to reduce poverty and other forms of human deprivation, the governments of developing countries have assumed a far greater responsibility for the provision and maintenance of social services than did the governments of industrialized countries when their populations were at comparable levels of development. Governments of developing countries have increasingly devoted their efforts to improving qualitatively those social services, and many countries are showing a greater appreciation of the need to deliver social services to rural areas as well. Increasing governmental intervention and the growing role of the state do not, in themselves, guarantee improvements in the conditions of the more deprived sectors of the population.[a]

Structural Change

Structural change is assessed in terms of alterations in employment patterns, extent of urbanization, distribution of economic activity, and overall industrialization. Although it differs in rate and type from country to country, there are some features that are almost universal. In general, and despite possible exceptions in the case of high-income agricultural countries like New Zealand and Denmark, structural change in developing countries follows the path already traversed by the industrialized West. Growing industrialization leads to changes in employment patterns as agricultural production declines and the rate of rural-urban migration increases.

The lower-income countries of Africa and Asia are in the earliest part of this transformation relative to middle- or high-income countries. Their ratios of agricultural to total employment are maximal. The role of industry and services in their economies is small; employment in rural areas is highest relative to employment in cities, and agriculture generates the major share of their total economic output. By contrast, the middle-income countries of Latin America, the Mediterranean, and parts of East Asia exhibit the type of change that, when persistent, generates the structural profile common in

---

[a]The expanding role of government in the development process is one of the major themes underlying the record of the 1960s and 1970s. Despite growth of the private sector in many developing countries, and irrespective of political orientation, the public sector assumes the role of ultimate decision maker and regulator of societal transactions.

the industrialized West. Per capita income is high in these countries; their service sectors continue to grow, and their industrial and agricultural sectors are stabilizing.

Institutional Development

Institutional development is commonly viewed as the creation of national and international agencies to assist in planning, implementing, regulating, and monitoring economic progress. Whenever new economic activities are initiated, new social services delivered, and new sections of the population mobilized for work, institutional development is regarded as a necessary prerequisite for putting plans and programs into effect. In the longer run it is the most central and permanent legacy of development.

Over the past few decades institution building in developing countries has been due largely to the work of central governments acting either as regulators or as investors. There has been an expansion of government agencies directly concerned with economic growth and the allocation of resources, and also a high degree of government control in major state enterprises, in particular among those with large-scale, capital-intensive activities such as steel, petrochemical, and industrial products. The creation of government agencies or authorities to regulate these industries emerged as a natural by-product of the expansion of the public sector. By far the most typical feature of institution building in developing countries until the 1970s was the closeness of its connection to central government.

During the 1970s, however, two diversifying trends occurred that seem likely to continue into the 1980s. First, favorable economic and political climates in several developing countries that encouraged the formation of private manufacturing and smaller industries resulted in these entrepreneurs using individual and organized means of influencing their governments' developmental policies. Second, greater public awareness and political concern led to an increase in the number of autonomous and semiautonomous local agencies organized at the grass roots or community level. The 1980s are expected to witness increasing recognition of the fact that development entails greater public participation in defining the direction of economic activities.

As ever more governments have made explicit development plans to budget and target their industrialization, the role of public financing and management has become increasingly important. Public enterprises in large-scale industries are endemic to all developing countries and as government-owned institutions are designed to capture the full benefit of industrialization for the state. How the state captures and then distributes these benefits is often the most fundamental issue of domestic politics.

Energy and Development

By now, the relationship between energy consumption and economic growth is familiar to everyone: it is an almost perfect positive correlation which appears across time and in crossnational comparisons. Figure 1-1 shows the relationship between energy consumption and GNP in 1973 for select countries at different levels of development. The robustness of this relationship will necessitate macroeconomic adjustments due to oil price increases of 1973 and subsequent changes in the world oil market. Low fuel prices, which were instrumental in enabling rapid economic growth rates in the industrial West, can no longer be counted upon for growth in the developing world. While considerable ambiguity remains regarding the direction of causation—whether from energy to economy or the other way

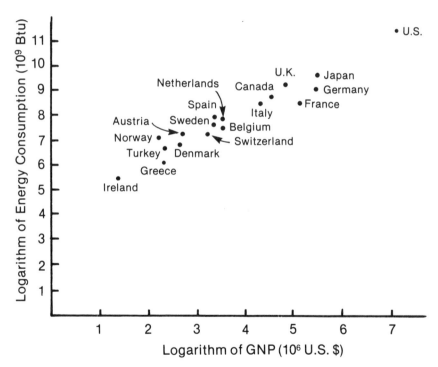

Source: OECD, *Statistics of Energy* (Paris: OECD, 1974). United Nations, *Statistical Yearbook* (New York: United Nations, 1974). Presented in James M. Griffin, *Energy Conservation in the OECD: 1980 to 2000.* Copyright 1979, The University of Pennsylvania. Reprinted with permission from Ballinger Publishing Company, Cambridge, Mass.

Figure 1-1. Relationship between Energy Consumption and GNP in 1973 for Select Countries

around—the robustness of energy-economy interactions is not at issue: energy use, a necessary input for economic growth, is also a function of growth. Figure 1-2 shows the energy-GNP association over time for the United States.

Despite this close tracking, for the developed countries there is no correlation between constant ration of energy and gross national product. The relationship varies over time and across countries, as shown in figures 1-3 and 1-4. Per capita income does not seem to affect the energy-GDP ratio. Sweden and Portugal, for example, with fundamentally different levels of GDP, have similar ratios. Note that these figures indicate only association of energy with economic growth, not the interaction of energy and economic activity within different sectors of the economy.[5]

The role of technological change has always confounded any simple assessment of energy-economy linkages. With energy price hikes and potential constraints in supply availability, technological changes will appear

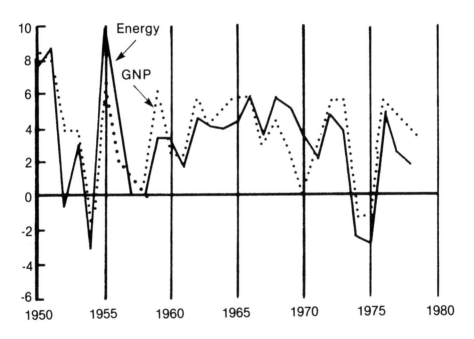

Source: Data for GNP changes from the *Economic Report of the President* (Washington, D.C.: Government Printing Office, January 1979); energy data from the Bureau of Mines for 1950-1974 and from the Department of Energy for 1974-1978. Presented in Hans H. Landsberg et al., *Energy: The Next Twenty Years.* Copyright 1979, The Ford Foundation. Reprinted with permission from Ballinger Publishing Company, Cambridge, Mass.

Figure 1-2. Changes in Primary Energy and GNP in 1950-1978

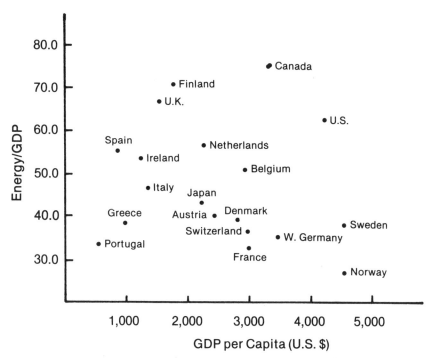

Source: Data for 1973 from OECD, *Statistics of Energy* (Paris: OECD, 1974); United Nations, Statistical Yearbook (New York: United Nations, 1974). Presented in James M. Griffin, *Energy Conservation in the OECD: 1980 to 2000.* Copyright 1979, The University of Pennsylvania. Reprinted with permission from Ballinger Publishing Company, Cambridge, Mass.

Figure 1-3. Relationship between Energy Consumption and GDP in 1973 for Select Countries

increasingly as a panacea for the problem at hand. Historically, technological breakthroughs enabling the introduction and utilization of new forms of energy have expanded utilization patterns and rates of consumption, and the use of new fuels has increased the overall resource base and labor productivity. But today these related changes are no longer predictable. Experience in the past provides only the roughest gauge for the future.

Since World War II industrial countries have witnessed major changes in fuel consumption—in total magnitude and in types of fuel. Coal, the dominant source of energy in the nineteenth century, remains important only in the United Kingdom and has dropped sharply in final consumption. Today no industrial country exhibits a share higher than 15 to 18 percent. Yet it remains unclear whether this means that in a broader historical context coal consumption is adversely affected by industrialization or whether

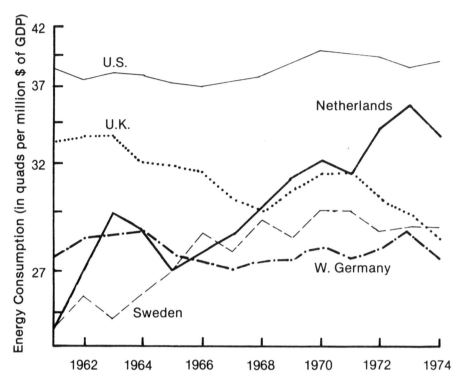

Source: From J. Darmstadter et al. *How Industrial Societies Use Energy: A Comparative Analysis* (Baltimore: The Johns Hopkins University Press, 1977). Presented in Hans H. Lansberg et al., *Energy: The Next Twenty Years.* Copyright 1979, The Ford Foundation.

Note: The data were converted to Btus per dollar of 1978 GDP by using 0.04 quadrillion (10^{15}) Btus per million tons of oil equivalent (see Darmstadter et al., p. 15) and the U.S. GNP deflator. See also L. Schipper and A. Lichtenberg, "Efficient Energy Use and Well Being: The Swedish Example," *Science* (December 1976), p. 194. Reprinted with permission from Ballinger Publishing Company, Cambridge, Mass.

Figure 1-4. Energy-Output Ratios for Five Selected Countries in 1961-1974

this decline is idiosyncratic. Gas, both natural and manufactured, maintains a positive correlation with per capita income. Heavy fuels and derivatives are dominant in all industrial countries. Finally, we note that the share of electricity in final demand has ranged between 9 and 20 percent, with the exception of Norway (42 percent) due to abundance of hydroelectric power. There is no consistent relationship between electrical energy utilization and per capita income; it also appears that interfuel substitution for some usages may not always fluctuate with price: for countries with low electricity prices, substitution possibilities may exist; for those with high prices, these possibilities do not.[6]

The economic growth rate in almost all countries has been adversely affected by increases in the price of oil over the past few years. Against the background of a worsening position in international trade, the demand for petroleum products has dampened somewhat. Although there has been a slight recovery and improvement after each round of price increases, developing countries have been burdened by an increased and economically weakening reliance on foreign resources to meet their domestic energy needs. This situation cannot change overnight. Energy balances are expected to remain tight in the industrial West, with consumption outstripping production until well into the 1990s.

With increasing oil prices, developing countries will continue to be faced with a diminishing availability of conventional development resources. There are some grounds for optimism, however, in that the more petroleum prices rise, the more politically desirable and economically plausible it will become for developing countries to exploit and develop their own indigenous resources. Latin America stands at the forefront of such developments. Experimentation with nonconventional fuels holds promise. Already policy debates about alternatives to petroleum are taking into account the nonconventional sources, with these countries exemplifying willingness to invest in broadening the alternatives available.

The Role of Transportation in Development

The transportation sector is critical to any economy for two reasons: first, it provides the basic infrastructure for communication and mobility; second, it is frequently the largest consumer of energy. On both counts investments in transportation and the disposition of transport facilities shape and constrain a country's future policy options for development and energy use.[7]

For developing countries, in particular, investments in transportation are critical to the establishment of a basic industrial and communications infrastructure. Transportation is seen both as a mechanism for national integration—connecting geographical regions and often disparate communities—and a necessary prerequisite for integrating market structures and commercial networks. It is customary to acknowledge the special role of agriculture in development, which employs often over 50 percent of labor and is generally responsible for the same proportion of GDP. It is also customary to stress the special role of construction as an investment sector, buttressing infrastructure and delimiting the rates of investment, overall capital formation, and economic growth. So, too, the manufacturing sector is regarded as a vehicle for industrialization. Yet most important is the impact of transportation on the development of these sectors. The criticality of transportation goes beyond the simple provision of infrastructure facilities or vehicles for movement. As transmitters of goods, materials, and people tied to the networks in place, the transportation sector determines basic parameters of physical communication and mobility for a nation.

Investments in transportation become effectively realized as investments for facilitating trade, movement of people, and communications between regions. In the modern world physical networks of communications define the basic parameters of statehood. These parameters must be set in place to enable the exercise of governmental authority and affirmation of national cohesion. The political impacts of transportation networks in developing countries are as critical as their economic implications.

Modes, costs and prices, and the number of units transported are the essential features of any transportation network. In developing countries, modes in place, rather than competitive prices or cost factors, determine the robustness of an existing network. Transportation is more a social service, often subsidized by government policy, rather than a cost-effective means of meeting the mobility requirements for passengers or materials. As in industrialized countries energy use was not a critical element in determining the nature of the networks until the oil price increases of the 1970s.

In all societies transport facilities provide mechanisms for moving inputs into individual economic sectors and outputs from these sectors. Patterns of mobility are often assumed to be consistent with the sectorial distribution of the economy and the loads on the networks. In fact, major disjunctions can exist between networks in place and demand for transport facilities, often creating distortions in the transport sector that are reflected in the overall economy.

Despite the essential nature of this sector, it is only recently that its importance has been officially acknowledged in the development programs of industrializing countries. Few developing states formally delimit their investments or goals with respect to the expansion of the transportation sector, and fewer still have acknowledged the special role of energy inputs into shaping future decisions on communication and transportation.

The railroad has conventionally been the backbone of a transportation network, historically in the industrial countries and more recently in the developing world. Railways necessitate certain infrastructure investments tying the nation's network to this specific mode and thus making substitutions difficult if not impossible. Subsequent shifts due to changing price and cost structures often evolve alongside this basic mode. In the United States the development of a transportation network has been in terms of the sequential replacement by alternative modes, with railways giving way to trucking as the basic commercial means of moving material. Rail, both as a technology of mobility and a type of social infrastructure investment, constitutes today the primary mode of transportation in many developing countries. Intermodal shifts are occurring as a by-product of overloads on existing networks. Changing prices of energy inputs are accelerating incentives for modal shifts.

Energy in Transportation

Estimates of energy use in the transport sector vary widely. For the lowest income countries the transport sector is the largest consumer of energy, in some extreme cases even accounting for as much as 70 percent of total energy consumption.[8] More generally, however, in developing countries transportation accounts for 10 to 20 percent of total energy consumption. This wide range reflects strong variability among countries. Distribution of energy usage by transport mode is approximately as follows: highest consumption is in road transport (70 to 85 percent), followed by air (5 to 10 percent) and rail (3 to 5 percent).[9] Except in a few countries where railways utilize coal or are electrified, this sector relies almost entirely on petroleum.

Oil-based fuels provide the entire commercial requirements for energy in these countries. The use of electricity is mainly for illumination and generator drive. Since economic growth inevitably leads to greater energy consumption in all sectors, including household use, generic processes of development—economywide and sectorial—will result in greater energy consumption. Since transportation is central to economic productivity and social mobility, constraints in energy utilization for that sector will generate multiplier effects throughout the economy.

The transportation sector generally expands as per capita income grows, and with it the demand for automotive and air travel. In industrial countries transportation accounts for 15 to 25 percent of final energy consumption.[10] Fuel use in this sector is tied to the mode of transportation. Once the transportation mode is established, interfuel substitution possibilities are limited. But choices do exist in both mode usage and intermode changes if they can be correctly identified. Table 1-1 gives energy usage in transportation for industrial countries. The constraints on interfuel substitution are embodied in equipment, technology, and infrastructure. Fuel economies may be attained by decreasing utilization or by energy and communications substitutions.

Gasoline, the dominant fuel for transport, accounts for 29 to 78 percent of consumption in transportation for industrial countries—a wide range indeed. The use of fuel for highway transport ranges from 6 to 38 percent. Together these two fuels account for 70 to 80 percent of fuel consumed in this sector. Other transportation fuels—coal, residual fuel oil, gas, electricity—are used largely in rail transportation, and they are typically only a small component of fuel use. There are some exceptions, such as Norway (35 percent), Turkey (35 percent), and Japan (29 percent), where alternative fuel uses are higher.[11] These exceptions reflect the pre-1973 patterns of usages, which the changes of the past few years have not substantially transformed. On balance, substitution among fuels for transportation usages is limited to gasoline/diesel fuel substitutions to date. But it is

Table 1-1
Energy Usage in Transportation

	Canada	Six West European Countries[a]	Japan
Total energy consumption per capita (Index, U.S. = 100)	100.5	42.7	34.8
Passenger transport	66.8	24.7	13.4
Freight transport	101.1	27.7	31.6
Total energy consumption per unit of GDP (Index, U.S. = 100)	119.7	66.8	57.4
Passenger transport	79.7	38.5	22.1
Freight transport	121.1	44.0	52.3

Source: Joel Darmstadter et al., *How Industrial Societies Use Energy: A Comparative Analysis* (Baltimore: The Johns Hopkins University Press, 1977). Presented in Alan Altshuler with James P. Womack and John R. Pucher, *The Urban Transportation System: Politics and Policy Innovation* (Cambridge, Mass.: The MIT Press, 1981), p. xxiii. Reprinted with permission.

[a]France, West Germany, Italy, United Kingdom, Sweden, Netherlands.

estimated that there is considerable leeway for adjustments to nonfuel utilizations.

Energy demand is more fundamentally dependent on an energy-consuming stock of capital in the transportation sector than in the industrial or residential sectors.[12] For example, in the short-run demand for motor gasoline directly depends on the stock of cars and degree of utilization. Consumption patterns can be determined more specifically than for other transport modes. Since automobile use reflects economic activity and growth, it provides useful insights about possible demand patterns in developing countries, despite differences between developed and developing economies.

Over the past twenty-five years per capita consumption of gasoline in developed economies has increased dramatically. The average price of regular gasoline consumption, however, has shown a steady downward trend, with marginal upward adjustments following the oil price increases of 1973. Until then the real price of gasoline had been steadily declining, while per capita consumption increased at an average rate of 7 to 8 percent per year. The relationship between gasoline price and demand as a ratio of GDP is noted in figure 1-5. Crossnational comparisons indicate that the lower the price of gasoline, the higher has been the demand for motor gasoline. This relationship, now obvious to all, defines the immediate energy problem in the transport sector. Price elasticity of demand in transport is relatively high; yet fuel costs are generally a small portion of total transport costs, thereby dampening the overall effects due to energy savings.

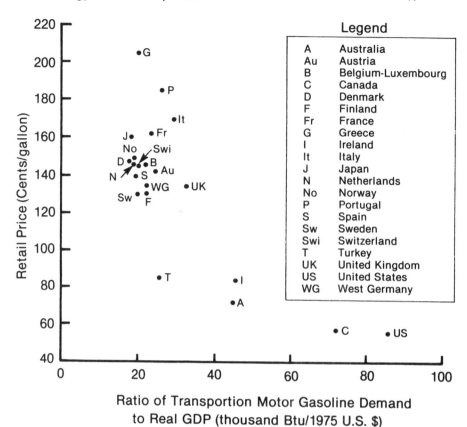

Ratio of Transportion Motor Gasoline Demand
to Real GDP (thousand Btu/1975 U.S. $)

Source: Data from *Economic Report of the President* (Washington, D.C.: Government Printing Office, 1978). Presented in Hans H. Landsberg et al. *Energy: The Next Twenty Years.* Copyright 1979, The Ford Foundation. Reprinted with permission from Ballinger Publishing Company, Cambridge, Mass.

Note: The conversions to 1975 U.S. dollars apparently based on the then prevailing exchange rates, not purchasing power priorities. Price is not the only explanation for the consumption differences; for example, the highest consumption is in countries with longest travel distances.

Figure 1-5. Cross-National Comparison of Motor Gasoline Demand in 1975

Intercountry differences for energy consumption in industrial economies are only broadly instructive for the developing world. Differences are due less to income than to geographical characteristics, transport modes, and networks in place. It is estimated, however, that the growth rate of gasoline consumption in industrial countries will rise by 2.5 percent per year from 1980 to 1985. While still an upward trend, the increase is substantially lower than previously exhibited.[13] Even smaller increases have been forecast by other studies, notably by the OECD in 1977.[14]

In the United States, the textbook case of the advanced industrial syndrome, the stock of cars doubled from 1960 to 1979, vehicle miles of travel increased from 588 billion to 1172 billion in 1978, and gasoline consumption grew from 4.1 million barrels per day in 1960 to 7.4 million in 1978. In 1979 a downward trend was discernable, dropping to 7.1 million barrels per day.[15] These trends reveal potential energy savings that might yield some insights for developing economies. In the main, demand for energy will vary according to different modes of transportation, the nature and efficiency of services, and differences in costs of increasing fuel efficiency.

In sum, the impact of changes in fuel prices and availability on the transport sector has wide implications that strongly affect public policy. The development experience of the 1980s will invariably necessitate policy adjustment, innovation, and social adaptation to new stringencies and opportunities. Latin America elucidates energy-development interactions relevant to all developing countries, anticipating and even resolving problems that will inevitably arise.

Energy, Economy, and Policy

Part I of this book looks at the changing international environment and considers the implications for Latin America as a region and for individual countries, presenting both energy profiles and future energy possibilities in Latin America. An assessment of energy-related characteristics, devoid of economic content or policy, is the bare profile with which policymakers and economic planners must work.

Part II focuses on the economic dimension in analysis of demographic characteristics and the structure of economic activity. Energy use in different sectors is examined, data permitting, with special emphasis on transportation. The results show the economic parameters of Latin America bearing on future energy use and the short-run economic and societal problems created by a changing energy environment. Conventional macroeconomic problems, distorted and aggravated by oil price increases, are producing new constraints for policy planning and new opportunities for change.

Part III assesses policy, synthesizing government responses and prospects for policy innovation in Latin America. Historical tendencies in development planning are reviewed, providing a formal definition of, and response to, the challenges of growth, as are changes in government assessments over time.

Part IV gives a concluding account of the challenges and opportunities for Latin America in the 1980s. Overall, the development process in Latin America reveals a distinctive pattern—with allowances for variations in profiles—that has been adapting to new international constraints. The example of Latin America's public policy will provide important insights for development elsewhere.

Notes

1. For a review of international and developmental issues, see Nazli Choucri, *International Politics of Energy Interdependence: The Case of Petroleum* (Lexington, Mass.: D.C. Heath, 1976).

2. This book expands upon Nazli Choucri, *Energy in Latin America: Transportation, Development, and Public Policy*, prepared for the Seminario "Impacto del Costa del Energia en el Sector Transporte," 1-3 December 1980, Bogota, Colombia.

3. Adapted from The World Bank, *World Development Report*, 1979 and 1980 (Washington, D.C., 1979, and 1980).

4. Ibid.

5. James M. Griffin, *Energy Conservation in the OECD: 1980 to 2000* Cambridge, Mass.: Ballinger, 1979), pp. 5-8.

6. Ibid., p. 13.

7. Brookhaven National Laboratory Developing Countries Energy Program, *Energy Needs, Uses, and Resources in Developing Countries* (March 1978), p. 84.

8. The World Bank, *Energy in the Developing Countries* (Washington, D.C., August 1980), p. 56.

9. Ibid.

10. Griffin, *Energy Conservation in the OECD*, p. 181.

11. Griffin, *Energy Conservation in the OECD*, p. 183.

12. Robert S. Pindyck, *The Structure of World Energy Demand* (Cambridge, Mass.: The MIT Press, 1979), p. 225.

13. See Pindyck, *The Structure of World Energy Demand*, pp. 226-227, for comparative trends.

14. Pindyck, *The Structure of World Energy Demand*, p. 235. See also, Organization for Economic Cooperation and Development, *Energy Prospects to 1985* (Paris, 1974).

15. Alan Altshuler with James P. Womack and John R. Pucher, *The Urban Transportation System: Politics and Policy Innovation* (Cambridge, Mass.: The MIT Press, 1979).

2 Energy Prices and Market Structure

Pressure for Change

In October 1973 the oil-exporting countries announced an increase in oil prices from $3.11 to $5.12 per barrel. The move was viewed as bold, unwarranted, and unreasonable. It unleashed a variety of reactions in the West, ranging from those who maintained the move itself was a crisis to those who feared its ramifications might unleash longer-term changes in the market. But everyone regarded the oil price increases with horror. Since then, the oil-exporting countries have effectively increased the market price of crude ten times, reaching $32-36 a barrel by mid-1981 for 34° crude. In today's context the 1973 price increases were moderate. Their importance lies perhaps less in their immediate economic impacts than in their longer-term economic and political implications. The events of 1973 created irrevocable changes in the market, in relations between producer and consumer countries and, more important, in the power structure of international relations.[1]

In retrospect it is now clear that changes in the world oil market were long in coming. The oil price increases of 1973 were a reaffirmation of more fundamental transformations in economic relations and in power politics. The long-term pressures of the oil-exporting countries upon the international oil companies—seeking changes in the concession arrangements and in the nature of government take—came to fruition in October 1973. Yet the roots of these pressures date as far back as the end of World War II. Latin America's main producer, Venezuela, urged cooperation among oil-exporting countries by extending advice to Iran and to Saudi Arabia, then negotiating with their concessionaires. The establishment of the Organization of Petroleum Exporting Countries (OPEC) in 1960 marked the end of a decade of trial and error, the beginning of cooperation and attempts to coordinate activities and policies. For thirteen years the organization appeared inconsequential in the wider scheme of things. The world oil market was effectively controlled and managed by international oil companies, often with little regulation or interference from industrial countries.[2]

But economic relations do not exist in a vacuum: power politics, then as now, provide the broader context within which the oil market operates and define the bounds of what each participant can or cannot do irrespective of market conditions. The concession system itself was a by-product of imperialist policies in the Middle East. The policies of Britain and France during the interwar period—and eventually of the United States—were aimed at maintaining control over the area and created a political environment within which international oil companies imposed systems of oil concessions.

The companies introduced advanced technology, management skills, and attendant requisites for developing viable national petroleum industries. Their hosts were by all counts technologically inferior, economically disadvantaged, and politically dependent on the good will of imperial powers. The resulting exchange between company and host government was not one among equals. This basic inequality generated hostilities, dissatisfaction, and discontent—eventually manifested in the establishment of OPEC. The impetus had come from Latin America whose experience with the United States had long established the uneasy relationship between countries of vastly unequal power. The giant in the North had already fully established hegemony over the entire hemisphere, and any efforts to change the status quo would inevitably be regarded as a source of threat and provoke a reaction accordingly.

With the benefit of hindsight it appears somewhat surprising that the establishment of OPEC evoked comparatively little interest and had little immediate impact in the world oil market or in more broadly defined international politics. The oil companies were well in control of the market, they regulated the oil industry, and all seemed in good order.

Yet the convergence of a set of circumstances resulted in the consolidation of changes that had been brewing over a long period of time. When Venezuela suggested cooperation to Iran in 1949 at the time of that country's negotiations with its concessionaire, the Anglo-Iranian Oil Company, the roots of OPEC were set. The information on its own tax arrangements given by Venezuela to Iran, Saudi Arabia, and the "host" governments at the time was in part responsible for changing the general method of payments from the oil companies. The first formal agreement among exporters was concluded in 1953, prescribing the exchange of information and frequent consultation regarding oil prices and policies between Iran and Saudi Arabia. Twenty years later the exporters were successful in influencing the market. During this period changes in the oil market were gradually developing, as were changes in relations among the producer countries.

Again, with the benefit of hindsight the development of OPEC as an organization can be traced to three factors: (1) a persistent fear of the oil companies' ability to cut prices without consulting the "host" government, (2) the realization among more established exporters that entry of new producers with lower prices might cut into their established markets, (3) an increased sense of technological competence among oil-exporting countries and therefore a willingness to exert pressure to protect their interests and to incur the displeasure of both major oil companies and major powers of the West. This threefold process took time to consolidate. For twenty years—between 1949 and 1969—the oil exporters were gradually developing the basis for cooperation and for a modicum of consensus.[3]

There were two sources of pressure. In the Western Hemisphere Venezuela had already taken the lead in mobilizing the exporters and in opposing the price cuts announced by the companies in 1959. During that year posted prices in the Middle East were reduced by about 8 percent. The cut was initiated by British Petroleum (BP). Venezuela protested to the British government, but the latter would not (or could not) intervene in company policy. During the same year, Shell Oil Company of Venezuela reduced posted prices by $.05 to $.15 according to the type of oil. These reductions were adjustments to the market in the United States and, more generally, worldwide. In 1959 more drastic price cuts were announced by BP for its operations in Kuwait, Iran, and Qatar. Similar reductions were posted in Venezuela to meet the Middle East price cuts. The First Arab Oil Congress met that year. No action was taken. But a second source of pressure was taking shape in the Middle East. Two parallel sets of events were occurring: consultation among the Middle East exporters regarding oil company policies and critical cooperation, however erratic, in the development of the Arab League, its functional agencies, and the establishment of institutionalized means of political communication. Not to be underestimated, of course, was the then pervasive anti-imperialist sentiment in the area, and the rejection of western military presence in the region. By 1960 these events had consolidated. Venezuela's repeated efforts for cooperation were beginning to pay off. In August of that year the majors reduced posted prices again, by about 6 percent (or $.10 per barrel). That meant a loss for the exporter governments of about $300 million in revenue. Following these price cuts, representatives of Iran, Iraq, Kuwait, Saudi Arabia, and Venezuela met in Baghdad. OPEC was announced in September of that year.

This history is important. It points to country-company pressures too numerous to record here. The majors until recently exerted formidable political and economic influence. This was demonstrated, for instance, during the 1951 nationalization in Iran. At that time the majors were willing to freeze out producers who tried to raise prices significantly and, until Occidental broke the unwritten rules in Libya, prevent them from marketing their oil at all. In addition, in cases where the companies had long-term concessions (seventy-five years in Iraq, for example), they threatened to sue any buyer who purchased oil from a nationalized oil company. Thus until the mid-to-late 1960s, the major international oil companies did wield great power over the producers.

While the specific events can be interpreted differently—particularly the motives behind corporate price cuts for Venezuela in 1959—the fact remains that the creation of a formal organization in 1960 was the product of trial and error, probes and failures, and eventual success. The same must be said of the oil price increases of October 1973. It was not the first time the oil exporters, together, tried to increase the price of crude. In 1967 the first major effort was made, with no success. In 1970-1971 Libya challenged the independent companies operating in the country, with some success. In 1973 the same convergence of political events in the Middle East occurred again, repeating the 1967 scenario but with one important difference. The world oil market had changed substantially during those intervening six years. Conditions for successful cartelization had converged.

Between 1967 and 1973 demand for petroleum by three main consumers, Western Europe, Japan, and the United States, grew by 5 billion barrels per year, while production in these three areas increased by less than a tenth of that amount. As a result imports grew by 95 percent, from 4.9 billion barrels to 9.5 billion barrels. Virtually all of this increase was met by higher OPEC production, nearly 80 percent of which occurred in the Middle East.

But the success of OPEC cannot be viewed in economic terms alone. Its role is fundamentally political: OPEC transformed power relations in the world oil market and changed both the decision-making process and the locus of decision. Critical decisions pertaining to the oil market are no longer made by the majors alone. Governments of oil-exporting countries control not only prices but, by extension, economic adjustments to these prices. Low elasticity of demand in effect makes producer countries final arbiters of economic policies in the West. It is perhaps a final irony that political power rests in immutable laws of supply and demand. When alternatives to critical industrial commodities are not commercially available, the sellers' policies determine the buyers' reactions. In 1973 the dominant view in the West was to accuse OPEC of undue interventions in the market—as if the market had normally been a competitive one—and that restoring normalcy was necessary for economic stability. Yet price determination in the world oil market has never been governed by the mechanisms of a competitive market. Even prior to 1973 competitive market relations did not govern world prices. With the benefit of hindsight, today almost everyone agrees that there remain some possibilities for further price increases—but at potentially high costs for everyone—producers, consumers, and international oil companies.

Supply and Demand

A dramatic rise in world petroleum consumption over the past decades provides the single most important element underlying current global energy transactions.[4] Figure 2-1 illustrates the magnitude of the increase. Since the mid-1960s petroleum has been the world's largest single source of energy and also the basic raw material for almost all the organic chemical products. For most important uses there are as yet no commercially viable substitutes. Coal, the dominant fuel of the nineteenth century, receded in importance and reached something of a plateau well before the oil price increases of 1973. The major advance in use of other energy sources was for gas, growing notably since the mid-1960s. Recently, increased use of nuclear energy and hydroelectric power is noticeable. The most immediate effect of the 1973 oil price increase has been a clear drop in demand for oil. The subsequent recession (1974-1975) required demand adjustments which appear as notable cuts in consumption. The upward swing from 1976 on reflects both an improved economic environment and an increased use of petroleum in developing countries.

The world petroleum market—defined by patterns of supply and demand, production and consumption, imports and exports—has undergone a marked transformation over the past two decades, both in the magnitude of trade and in major actors and influence of various groups. The situation has changed from one in which international oil companies dominated the

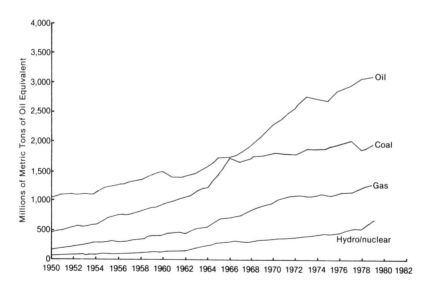

Source: U.N. Statistical Office, *1950-1974 World Energy Supplies*, series J, no. 19 (New York: United Nations, 1975); U.N. Department of International Economic and Social Affairs, *1979 Yearbook of World Energy Statistics* (New York: United Nations, 1981); British Petroleum, *BP Statistical Review of the World Oil Industry* (London: British Petroleum Company, 1977, 1978, 1979).

Figure 2-1. World Consumption of Major Energy Sources

petroleum industry to one in which national governments of producing countries have become major actors, coordinating their policies and actions; where governments of consumer countries have become directly involved; and where oil companies provide services to both. There have been changes in the patterns of alignment among producers and consumers, as well as a heightened awareness of the problems of production and transportation and the virtues of conservation. Table 2-1 gives some comparative data for the world oil market.

Demand

Of total energy consumed by the world in 1950, 25.34 percent was in the form of liquid fuel. By 1977 this figure increased to 45.48 percent. This steady trend in energy consumption toward petroleum is explained by the fact that Middle Eastern and North African oil is relatively cheap to produce in comparison with other fuels. In addition, given present technology, petroleum is much "cleaner" than coal, its technology is more developed than that of nuclear power, and hydroelectricity is not commercially feasible in many areas.

With one exception, all industrialized nations have increased their use of petroleum in relation to total energy consumed over the past twenty years. Only the United States has maintained a relatively stable proportion of oil consumption to total energy consumption, due to a relative abundance of coal, natural gas, and hydroelectric power, and there is some evidence of decline in the use of oil. However, these differences in consumption have interjected new tensions into the Western alliance. Japan and Western Europe have become concerned by the rate of increase in U.S. reliance on imports at a time when the availability of supplies to meet their own demand is in question. The issues of strategic vulnerability and of insecurity of supply are looming large for both the United States and other oil-importing countries (see figures 2-2 and 2-3).

In the United States growth in imports has been most notable since 1970, with imports more than doubling between 1970 and 1974. Today the United States continues to be a net importer, although import levels have declined since 1977. Projected growth of oil imports in Western Europe and the Far East is substantially greater than in North America. It is anticipated that Europe will remain the leading market for petroleum from the Middle East and North Africa. It was also anticipated that imported oil will account for over 80 percent of European energy consumption by 1990, but this projection did not take sufficient cognizance of the North Sea discoveries and their expected pace of development. Subsequent drops in Europe's oil imports reflect demand adjustment, due to economic recession

Table 2-1
World Petroleum Market
(in million barrels)

	1980 Reserves	Percentage of World Reserves	1980 Crude Production	Percentage of World Production	1979 Demand	1980 Demand	1979 Imports (Crude and Products)	Percentage of World Imports	1980 Production-Demand Ratio
Algeria	8,200	1.26	365	1.68	39.0	43.9			
Canada	6,400	0.99	520	2.40	644.2	633.2	101.1	0.87	0.82
China	20,500	3.16	772	3.56					
Ecuador	1,100	0.17	74	0.34	24.5	27.5			
France	40	0.006			769.0	719.2	879.3	7.56	
Gabon	450	0.07	59	0.27	3.3	3.7			
West Germany	450	0.07	34	0.16	972.4	862.3	1,035.9	8.90	0.04
Indonesia	9,500	1.46	576	2.65	131.8	144.6			
Iran	57,500	8.87	607	2.80	284.0	208.6			2.90
Iraq	30,000	4.63	918	4.23	67.5	78.7			11.70
Japan	52	0.008			1,887.4	1,711.4	1,946.2	16.72	
Kuwait[a]	64,900	10.00	604	2.78	45.6	45.8			
Libya	23,000	3.55	652	3.00	31.4	33.0			
Nigeria	16,700	2.58	750	3.46	58.0	75.0			
Oman	2,340	0.36	103	0.47					
Qatar	3,585	0.55	172	0.79	3.3	3.7			
Saudi Arabia[a]	165,000	25.40	3,614	16.65	169.0	195.8			18.46
U.A.E.	30,410	4.69	624	2.88	24.5	29.3			
U.K.	14,800	2.28	592	2.73	616.9	520.5	159.1	1.37	1.14
U.S.A.	26,400	4.07	3,137	14.46	6,757.2	6,224.2	3,045.6	26.17	0.50
U.S.S.R.	63,000	9.71	4,278	19.71					
Venezuela	17,950	2.77	791	3.64	117.2	133.6			5.92
Mexico	44,000	6.78	707	3.26					
World	648,525[b]	100.00	21,701	100.00	23,806	22,880	11,637.3	100.00	

Source: *International Energy Statistical Review* (Washington, D.C.: Central Intelligence Agency, June 30, 1981); *Statistical Review 1981* (Berkshire, United Kingdom: Energy Economics Research Ltd.); *Oil and Gas Journal*, January 1, 1981.

[a]Total crude productions of Kuwait and Saudi Arabia include half the total production of the neutral zone.
[b]Total world reserves gives the total reserves of all countries in the table plus others.

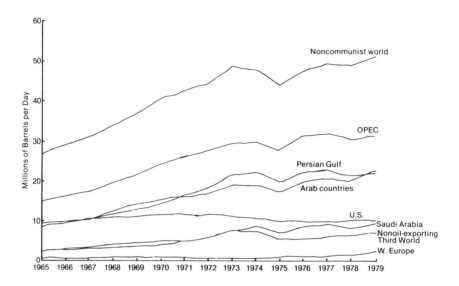

Source: British Petroleum, *BP Statistical Review of the World Oil Industry* (London: British Petroleum Company, 1975, 1979, 1980).

Figure 2-2. World Production of Oil

and government policies toward curtailing imports. Japan's petroleum needs are supplied primarily by the Middle East, although new offshore discoveries in Indonesia and the South and East China Seas may modify this assessment. In any case Japan's dependence on imported oil will remain, despite the government's ability to stabilize imports. Clearly, Western Europe and Japan do not have the option of relying on domestic sources of petroleum, nor are alternative sources of energy commercially feasible in the near future.

Supply

There are marked changes in patterns of petroleum production over the past twenty years, only one of which is the exponential rise in output. In 1950 world production of crude petroleum was dominated by the United States, whose production was 52.5 percent of the world total. By 1972 the centers of production were no longer in the Western Hemisphere. Although the United States was still a major producer, it accounted for only 21.16 percent; in 1980 that figure was 16.45 percent. The single most critical factor in the production of petroleum since World War II has been the extensive development of Middle Eastern and North African fields. In 1980 these fields

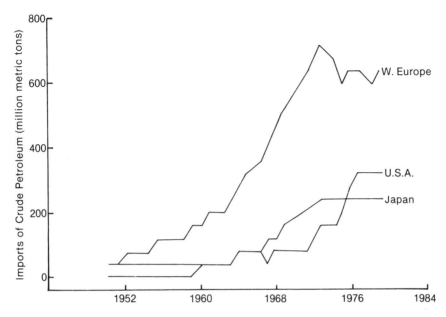

Source: U.N. Department of International Economic and Social Affairs, *1979 Yearbook of World Energy Statistics* (New York: United Nations, 1981).

Figure 2-3. Imports of Crude Petroleum

accounted for 46.4 percent of the non-Communist world's total production. Figure 2-4 illustrates recent changes in the production of crude petroleum.

The general trend toward increased production, however, has been accompanied by periodic declines in the output of individual states, particularly in 1970 to 1972. The largest declines were in Libya and, to some extent, in Algeria. For different reasons, and with different impacts, Venezuela, Iraq, Oman, and even the United States also experienced noticeable declines. From 1972 to 1975 Kuwait also cut back significantly, by about 40 percent throughout the period, and all of it voluntarily. These cuts are attributed variously to the desire to maintain the OPEC price, to domestic political problems, to internal or international conflicts that inhibit production increases, to the existence of unstable prices, to national security concerns, and/or to a concern for the exploitation of a critical nonrenewable resource.

Between 1955 and 1970 total world exports of crude petroleum increased by 358 percent. In 1980 trade in petroleum accounted for over 10 percent of total world trade in all commodities. There has been a transformation from the Western Hemisphere as the focal point of petroleum exports to other areas of the world, most notably the Middle East. In 1980 Persian Gulf

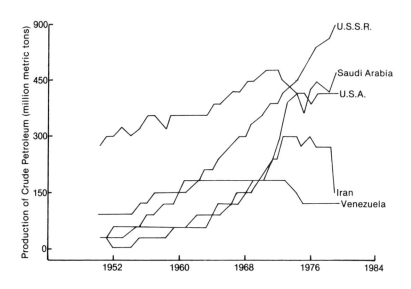

Source: U.N. Statistical Office, *1950-1974 World Energy Supplies*, series J, no. 19 (New York: United Nations, 1975); U.N. Department of International Economic and Social Affairs, *1979 Yearbook of World Energy Statistics* (New York: United Nations, 1981).

Figure 2-4. Production of Crude Petroleum

sources controlled 63.7 percent of exports. But no one state had a preponderant position, although Saudi Arabia clearly had the reserves and the attendant production capacity to exercise significant influence on the market. With the demise of Iran as a major exporter, Saudi Arabia has clear predominance. Venezuela, the major Latin American producer and exporter, has witnessed notable declines of output since the early 1970s. These declines largely reflect reserve constraints and government efforts to regulate production while increasing investments in exploration and development.

New Sources of Supply

Discovery of new reserves outside traditional areas of supply may change the situation in the years to come. But the effects, if any, will not be immediate. Major producers of today remain the largest sources of future reserves, and aside from Mexico, the North Sea, and China the potential of newer sources is still speculative. (Table 2-1 includes recent evidence on ultimate discoverable reserves.) Few of the new sources can be considered as likely to have substantial export capacity in the immediate future. There are inevitable time lags between exploration and development of any new oil field, difficulties in raising sufficient capital and obtaining adequate equipment, and obstacles in the development of the necessary pipelines and transportation facilities. While everyone acknowledges the potential impact of these new finds upon the world petroleum market in the years to come, no one has yet offered a definite schedule or a clear statement concerning the expected nature of these impacts. Smaller producers, like Egypt, have benefited strongly from oil-price increases since 1973. Today Egyptian oil exports account for about $2 billion, the largest single contribution to the country's balance of payments. Smaller producers in Latin America, Guatemala, Trinidad and Tobago, and Peru may have potential for expansion. Ecuador, one of the oldest producers, is already reaching production limits. Venezuela reached its limits on light crudes long ago.

Prices

While the initial shocks of 1973 were due to the increases in petroleum prices, it is now clear that there were fundamental market changes at work.[5] Figure 2-5 shows delivered price of energy for industrial countries over a twenty-year period. Note the steady decline to 1973. Figure 2-6 presents both OPEC and spot market prices to 1980, which created the obvious upward swing in energy prices for industrial countries.

Changes in the official price of Saudi Light Crude, a convenient indicator of oil prices internationally, reflects both impetus for market change and consequence of such change. Note the sharp jump from 1979 to 1980, relative to the smooth increase from 1973 to 1979. Doubling of per barrel price of gasoline during this period highlights principally the major costs confronting the transportation sector in all countries.

Official prices of crude oil for individual countries are presented in table 2-2. Traditionally, differences were due largely to crude types. Changes in prices reflect the countries' adherence to OPEC directives in addition to their own adjustments.

These price trends must be viewed in the context of world gasoline prices, by regions and in different countries. Table 2-3 presents the price per gallon of regular gasoline in U.S. dollars. The discrepancy between Saudi price and final price to the consumer reflects, of course, not only transportation costs but the end-use taxes of the consumer countries. This gap motivates the oil-exporting countries to argue for the necessity of focusing debates on the "just" price of refined products, rather than the price of crude.[6]

Within Latin America itself there are significant variations in gasoline prices. The lowest prices have consistently been in Venezuela, for obvious

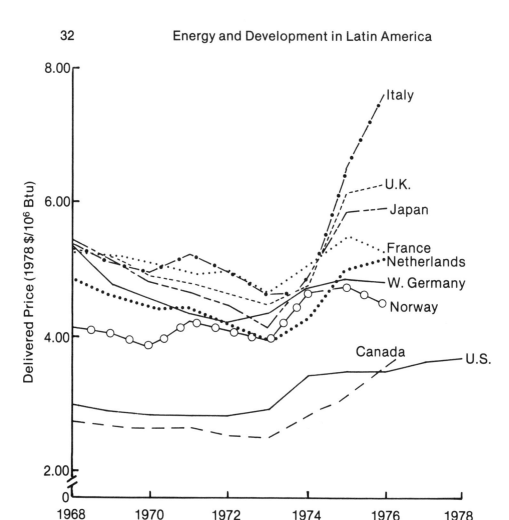

Source: Price data primarily from Robert S. Pindyck, *The Structure of World Energy Demand* (Cambridge, Mass.: The MIT Press, 1979). See W. Hogan, "Dimensions of Energy Demand," in *Selected Studies on Energy: Background Papers for Energy: The Next Twenty Years* (Cambridge, Mass.: Ballinger, 1979), for a description of data sources and updates. From Hans H. Landsberg et al., *Energy: The Next Twenty Years.* Copyright 1979, The Ford Foundation. Reprinted with permission from Ballinger Publishing Company, Cambridge, Mass.

Figure 2-5. Price of Energy Delivered for Select Industrial Countries

reasons. The price of gasoline in Colombia and Ecuador has also been low relative to other countries. Brazil, Jamaica, and Paraguay have had higher prices relative to other Latin American countries. The price of gasoline is one of the most direct policy instruments available to these governments, and considerable public debate exists regarding the extent to which it can or

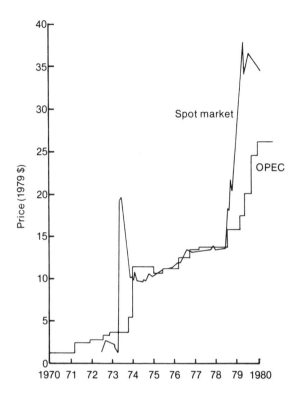

Source: Nazli Choucri, *International Energy Futures: Petroleum Prices, Power, and Payments*
(Cambridge, Mass.: The MIT Press, 1981), p. 205. Reprinted with permission.
Figure 2-6. Oil Prices in 1970-1980

should be used. Development plans for many countries in the region make
explicit promises for use of such instruments.[7]

Market Structure

Price increases and adjustments in supply and demand relationships created
fundamental structural changes in the world oil market. Shift of market
power toward the suppliers of the Middle East became apparent. However,
broader trends included a marked increase in demand for petroleum, an increase in U.S. demand from Gulf sources, increasing controls of supply-
related decisions in the governments of the oil-exporting countries, and new
cohesion among the members of OPEC. While the interventions of 1973

Table 2-2

Government Official Sales Prices of Crude Oil

(in current U.S. dollars)

Country/Petroleum	Gravity (in degrees)	1970	1974	1975	1976	1977	1978	1979	1980	1981
Abu Dhabi/Murban	39	1.88[c]	11.88	10.87	11.92	12.50	13.26	14.10	29.56	36.56
Algeria/Saharan	44	2.65[c]	14.00	12.00	12.85	14.30	14.25	14.81	33.00	40.00
Ecuador[b]			13.70[c]	13.70[c]	11.45	13.00	12.65	13.03	36.41	
Indonesia/Minas	35	1.70[b]	10.80	12.60	12.80	13.55	13.55	13.90	27.50	35.00
Iran/Iranian Light	34	1.79[c]	11.16	10.67	11.62	12.81	12.81	13.45	30.37	37.00
Iraq/Basrah Light	35	1.72[c]	10.97	10.48	11.45	12.65	12.60	13.29	27.96	35.96
Kuwait/Kuwait	31	1.59[c]	10.85	10.36	11.30	12.37	12.27	12.83	27.50	35.50
Libyan/Zuetina	40.5	2.23[c]	16.00	11.86	12.32	14.00	14.05	14.74	34.72	41.00
Nigeria/Bonny Light	37	2.17[c]	14.69[c]	11.66[c]	12.72	14.33	14.33	14.82	29.99	40.02
Qatar/Dukhan	40	1.93[c]	11.67	11.17	11.85	13.19	13.19	14.03	29.42	37.42
Saudi Arabia/Arabian Light	34	1.80[c]	10.95	10.46	11.51	12.09	12.70	13.34	26.00	32.00
Venezuela/Tiajuana Light	31	2.19[a]	12.10[a]	12.65[a]	12.30	13.54	13.54	14.22	26.90	36.00

Source: Data from Middle East Publications, *International Crude Oil and Product Prices* (Beirut, Lebanon: January 1981, except where noted).

[a]Minimum tax export values (excluding freight and sulphur premiums) from *Annual Statistical Bulletin 1979* (Vienna: OPEC).

[b]*Annual Statistical Bulletin 1979*, (Vienna: OPEC).

[c]Posted or tax reference price from *Annual Statistical Bulletin 1979*, (Vienna: OPEC).

Table 2-3
World Prices of Regular Gasoline
(in U.S. dollars per gallon)

	1973	1974	1975	1976	1977	1978	1979[b]
OECD							
Athens	0.881	1.701	1.659	1.591	1.811	1.991	2.79
Bonn	1.180	1.265	1.246	1.386	1.443	1.682	2.09
Brussels	1.136	1.427	1.310	1.430	1.663	1.852	2.27
London	0.780	1.250	1.270	1.251	1.183	1.153	2.16
Madrid	0.783	1.160	1.136	1.210	1.390	1.530	2.29
New York	0.419	0.599	0.639	0.639	0.664	0.710[a]	0.91[a]
Oslo	0.841	1.470	1.391	1.512	1.682	1.864	2.10
Ottawa	0.567	0.572	0.597	0.626	0.692	0.757	0.71
Paris	1.062	1.318	1.559	1.400	1.696	2.148	2.43
Rome	0.988	1.690	1.671	1.698	2.058	2.154	2.44
Sydney	0.534	0.591	0.693	na	0.707	0.926	1.34
Tokyo	0.832	1.361	1.361	1.361	1.625	2.066	2.27
Vienna	0.851	1.190	1.210	1.380	1.530	1.700	2.02
Third World							
Accra	0.542	0.80	1.015	1.015	1.015	0.793	0.90
Addis Ababa	0.895	1.162	1.180	1.187	1.213	1.213	1.38
Beirut	0.470	0.510	0.530	na	0.730	0.775	na
Jiddah	0.224	0.122	0.113	0.118	0.113	0.247	0.19
New Delhi	0.712	1.747	1.599	1.424	1.424	1.642	1.97
Rabat	0.893	1.290	1.390	1.460	1.600	1.800	2.57
Singapore	0.880	0.967	1.040	1.040	1.070	1.176	1.29
Tehran	0.297	0.336	0.336	0.322	0.456	0.538	0.54
Latin America							
Asuncion, Paraguay	0.570	1.500	1.500	1.500	1.500	1.500	2.34
Bogota, Colombia	0.143	0.133	0.111	0.211	0.274	0.308	0.61
Buenos Aires, Argentina	0.604	1.282	1.442	0.966	0.826	0.910	1.14
Caracus, Venezuela	0.086	0.132	0.138	0.138	0.132	0.132	0.13
Kingston, Jamaica	0.376	1.025	1.008	1.067	1.717	1.480	1.75
Lima, Peru	0.210	0.210	0.350	0.770	0.930	0.740	0.78
Mexico City, Mexico	0.242	0.420	0.64	0.65	0.460	0.470	0.47
Montevideo, Uruguay	0.850	1.290	1.280	1.400	1.57	1.56	na
Panama, Panama Republic	0.468	0.800	0.800	0.950	1.00	1.00	1.45
LaPaz, Bolivia	0.170	0.170	0.170	0.278	0.278	0.278	0.28
Quito, Ecuador	0.180	0.180	na	na	0.152	0.164	0.16
Rio de Janeiro, Brazil	0.292	0.606	1.110	1.507	1.512	1.512	1.55
San Salvador, El Salvador	0.520	0.932	0.79	0.86	0.976	0.976	1.25
Santiago, Chile	0.567	0.637	0.840	0.870	0.907	0.907	1.53

Source: Data adapted from *International Petroleum Annual 1978*, Energy Data Report (Washington, D.C.: Government Printing Office, 1978), U.S. Department of Energy, pp. 24-31.

Note: na = not available.

were economic in nature, the success of the move relative to earlier attempts, notably in 1967, indicated new changes in power relations.

First, clearly there will be in the near future greater competitiveness in the world oil market. This does not imply a reduction in the dominance of OPEC or in the consumer world's reliance of Gulf supplies, rather greater diversification among the suppliers and new changes in patterns of demand.

Second, there will be greater government-to-government deals and greater imperatives for direct interactions among governments over the buying and selling of petroleum. This trend will cast the international oil companies in yet another role, possibly one that reduces their dominance in the market.

Third, these trends have been buttressed by the growing importance of national oil companies in the producer countries—state enterprises. The emergence of national companies in the oil market is significant on several grounds: for the producer countries it reflects the growing capacity to make decisions in the industry, to regulate and manage national industry, and to act as an agent for the government in international transactions. State enterprises in consumer countries, where they are prominent, have emerged as direct replacements for the dominance of transnational enterprises, again buttressing the role of national governments vis-à-vis the international companies and legitimizing direct government-to-government deals. .

Fourth, debates and guesses about the future price of oil are now being supplemented by debates regarding the prospects of changes in patterns of production and concerns regarding the future production policies of the exporter countries.

Fifth, more critical for the longer run in the world oil market are the incentives for investments in exploration and development. The prospects of expanding non-Gulf reserves, or finding new reserves in developing countries, becomes increasingly attractive on political, if not economic grounds.

Finally, international institutions—both regional and global—will become more active in energy. The initial concern for assistance in alleviating payments problems is developing into concerns for expanding investments in new sources of petroleum and alternative sources of energy in different areas of the world.

These trends consolidated growing politicization of trade in oil and the increasingly governmental nature of these transactions. The oil market itself no longer reflected economic forces alone but represented immediately changing power relations and creation of new institutions in that market.

Structural changes encompass a prominent set of important trends, namely new entrants in the oil market, such as Mexico and the North Sea, which indicate the potential of non-Gulf supplies to respond to changing prices and market conditions. The prospective diversification of the oil exporters, while still a longer-term trend, if a trend at all, nonetheless reveals potential for further changes in the export market.

The second half of 1980 revealed greater competitiveness in the world oil market among the buyers and sellers. These shifts occurred simultaneously with yet another development, namely direct deals between the independent oil companies and producer governments. This development, in conjunction with the proliferation and aggressiveness of small traders, though relatively unimportant on a worldwide scale, nonetheless, poses some problems for the multinational oil companies.

In the 1980s the critical issues in the market pertain less to oil prices—although these are undoubtedly important—than to the production schedules of the exporting countries, and specifically production capacity and capacity utilization. For the OPEC countries the major issues of the future pertain to production policies. But for non-OPEC countries—the new suppliers—the principal concerns are investments in exploration and in development.

The price of oil has two distinct impacts on producer countries: for established producers it serves as a signal for moderating production and even planning for cutbacks as a means of sustaining prices. For new entrants price serves as a signal to allocate resources for investments in exploration and in development. Investment decisions emerge therefore as the most critical decisions for new producers.

Yet another facet of a changing world market structure is the formal institutional context. The creation of OPEC in 1960 was largely unnoticed internationally. By 1973 it became a major force to be reckoned with. By 1980 it had assumed the role of an established international institution, signaling the ability of developing countries to establish formal means of communication, to cooperate on broad policies, and to establish mechanisms for transferring technical information among the members. The response in consumer countries—notably the establishment of the International Energy Agency—was precisely that: a *response* rather than a well-reasoned institutional development in a clearly changing international context. In Latin America the establishment of the Organizacion Latinoamericano de Energia (OLADE) reflects the importance of coordination in both the regional and the international context.

These trends will create a new world oil context that is significantly different from that prevailing in the 1970s. Latin America will play a central role in all of these respects. Clearly, the emergence of Mexico, as a major producer will increase the region's bargaining power and the role of OLADE internationally. Thus the prospects of attracting investments in oil and other sources of energy appear excellent. Latin America's energy profile as an innovator in the development and commercial viability of alternative energy sources offers important prospects for both the industrial and developing world.

Notes

1. See Nazli Choucri, *International Energy Futures: Petroleum Prices, Power, and Payments* (Cambridge, Mass.: The MIT Press, 1981), for an analytical representation of the world oil market and the dynamics of change.

2. For a historical review, see Nazli Choucri, "OPEC: Calming a Nervous World Oil Market," *Technology Review* (MIT), 83 (October 1980), pp. 36-45.

3. Nazli Choucri, *International Politics of Energy Interdependence: The Case of Petroleum* (Lexington, Mass.: D.C. Heath, 1976), chapter 2.

4. This section draws upon data presented by the United Nations, governments, and international oil companies. See especially U.N. Statistical Office, *1950-1974 World Energy Supplies,* series J, no. 19 (New York: United Nations, 1975); British Petroleum, *BP Statistical Review of the World Oil Industry,* 1977, 1978, 1979; Central Intelligence Agency, *International Energy Statistical Review* (Washington, D.C., June 30, 1981); *Oil and Gas Journal* (January 1981); and *Oil and Energy Trends, Statistical Review 1981* (Berkshire, United Kingdom: Energy Economics Research Ltd.), among others.

5. See Hans H. Lansberg, et al., *Energy: The Next Twenty years* (Cambridge, Mass.: Ballinger, 1979) for a good review of price-related issues. For data series see Middle East Petroleum and Economic Publications, *International Crude Oil and Product Prices* (Beirut, Lebanon, January 1981); *OPEC Annual Statistical Bulletin 1979* (Vienna).

6. Debates within OPEC and OAPEC are illustrative. See, for example, various issues of *OPEC Review,* issued by the Organization of Petroleum Exporting Countries, Vienna; and *Oil and Arab Cooperation,* published by the Organization of Arab Petroleum Exporting Countries, Kuwait.

7. See chapter 7 of this volume for a review and analysis of development plans in Latin America.

3

Energy in Latin America: Profiles and Prospects

In 1979 the World Bank reviewed the energy situation in developing countries and classified these countries according to the extent of their oil imports.[a] Table 3-1 reproduces the classification for Latin American countries and indicates net imports as a percentage of commercial energy demand. The exporters are listed as either OPEC or non-OPEC countries. This classification, while essentially useful, obscures the overall picture in Latin America, where substantial changes in energy supply and demand have occurred over the past thirty years and where alternatives to petroleum are increasingly plausible.

Energy Profile

While the demand for primary energy in Latin America has doubled over the past ten years, from 1.46 billion barrels of oil equivalent in 1970 to 2.34 billion barrels of oil equivalent in 1979, the share of energy utilized by different sources has not changed substantially.[1] Petroleum, which accounted for 69.2 percent of all primary energy consumed in 1970, declined to 66.2 percent in 1979. Consumption of natural gas decreased from 15.1 to 13.7 percent, while that of coal increased marginally from 4.8 percent in 1970 to 5.1 percent in 1979. Notable changes in consumption patterns are in hydroelectricity, from 10.3 percent of total energy consumed to 14.5 percent, and nuclear energy, from a negligible proportion in 1974 to some slightly greater reliance in 1979 (about 0.26 percent). Although these changes are marginal, they do indicate increased diversification of shares of primary petroleum consumption. Table 3-2 presents comparative energy shares for Latin America as a whole. While the decline in petroleum consumption is perhaps too small to consider as evidence of a definitive trend, it does point to substitution possibilities. The relationship between energy consumption and GNP, noted in chapter 1 for industrial countries (figure 3-1) is closely replicated for Latin America, reaffirming the role of energy in development.

---

[a]There are few comprehensive analyses of energy problems in developing countries. The World Bank report, *Energy in Developing Countries* (Washington, D.C., August 1980), is one of the most informative in terms of coverage. However, none of the issues is examined in any depth. See also *Latin America and Caribbean Oil Report*, prepared by *Petroleum Economist* (London: Nichols, 1979); and Peter R. Odell, "Energy Prospects in Latin America," *Bank of London & South America Review*, 14 (May 1980), pp. 98-112.

Table 3-1
Energy Classification of Latin America and the Caribbean in 1978

Net Oil Exporters		Net Oil Importers as Percentage of Commercial Energy Demand			
OPEC	Non-OPEC	0-25	26-50	51-75	76-100
Venezuela	Mexico	Argentina	Chile	Brazil	Bahamas
Ecuador[a]	Peru	Boliva			Barbados
	Trinidad	Colombia			Costa Rica
	Tobago				Dominican Republic
					El Salvador[a]
					Grenada[a]
					Guatemala
					Guyana
					Haiti[a]
					Honduras[a]
					Nicaragua
					Panama
					Paraguay
					Uruguay

Source: Data adapted from The World Bank, *Energy in Developing Countries* (Washington, D.C.: August 1980), p. 5.
[a]Countries with actual or potential firewood shortages.

Latin America accounted for 7.4 percent of total world oil consumption in 1980, 9.4 percent of world production, and 10.5 percent of known reserves.[2] These figures, seemingly small, obscure the emerging importance of Latin America in the world oil market, both as a growing claimant on petroleum resources and as a source of production with a growing reserve position internationally. In 1970 the region exhibited the same reliance on oil as did Japan. Subsequent reduction of percentage of oil consumption to total energy consumption shifted the area's position globally.

Latin American countries increased their exports of petroleum (crude and products) from 1969 to 1979, as they did their imports. However, exports of petroleum products, by volume, were during this period considerably greater than exports of crude. Indeed, in comparison with other regions Latin America exhibits a fairly balanced proportion of crude and products in exports of petroleum, while imports are almost uniformly of crude with only little direct import of products.

Although oil production remained fairly steady over this period, the productivity of producing wells is relatively high in comparison with other regions. Well productivity is about the level of Communist bloc wells (notably U.S.S.R. and China) and considerably higher than Canada, the United States (as to be expected), and Western Europe.

Recent revisions of Latin American reserves are noteworthy when compared to previous estimates. The region's proven petroleum reserves

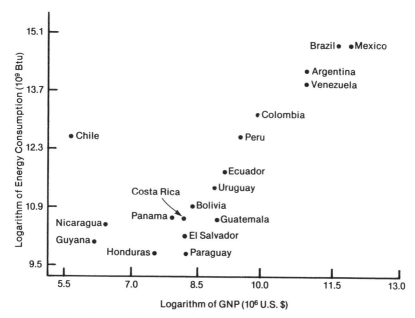

Source: U.N. Department of International Economic and Social Affairs, *1979 Yearbook of World Energy Statistics* (New York: United Nations, 1981); International Monetary Fund, *International Financial Statistics* (Washington, D.C.: August 1981).

Figure 3-1. Relationship between GNP and Energy Consumption in 1979

expanded from 29.3 billion barrels in 1974 to 69.5 billion barrels in 1980. Almost all of these new reserves were in Mexico. Oil production in Latin American countries for 1980 reveals the dominance of Venezuela and Mexico (at 793 million barrels and 788 million barrels, respectively). Other major producers in 1980 were Argentina (179 million barrels), Ecuador (82 million barrels), and Trinidad (79 million barrels). Latin America as a whole produced 2.133 billion barrels of crude petroleum last year.[3] The oil-refining capacity of Latin America has grown steadily during this period, although it still lags behind other major regions (with the exception of Japan whose refining capability had stabilized, even tapered off, by 1975).

Producers of natural gas are principally Mexico, Venezuela, and Argentina, each revealing an increase in output over the past ten years. For the region as a whole, total production of natural gas jumped from 1.095 trillion cubic feet in 1970 to 2.599 trillion cubic feet in 1980. For only two countries in the region, Bolivia and Chile, is production of natural gas greater than domestic consumption. For other consumers of natural gas, domestic consumption equals or exceeds production.

The coal situation is even more precarious. Only in Colombia is domestic production even marginally greater than consumption. But coal accounts for 24 percent of total energy consumed in the country, rendering that positive balance more significant than it might otherwise be.

Latin America's predominance in hydroelectric power stands in sharp contrast to other regions in the world. Latin America continues to be one of the largest consumers of hydroelectricity in the world. During 1979, the latest year for which data are available, the 14.7 percent share of energy consumption in the region accounted for by hydroelectric power was notably higher than for any other region or area. This percentage is more than double the world average. There are some clear possibilities for expanding hydroelectric usages. A comparison of Latin America's electricity generation to per capita energy consumption is shown in figure 3-2.

National Energy Balances

Broad generalizations inevitably obscure critical variations among individual countries, and, although most of the countries rely on petroleum and petroleum derivatives for over 50 percent of their total energy consumption, there are exceptions. Trinidad, for example, relies on oil at about 39 percent level of total consumption, and Colombia 46.75 percent. Only eight countries reveal a favorable balance, with domestic production exceeding consumption. Ecuador, Mexico, Venezuela, Peru, and Trinidad show a clear excess of production in relation to consumption. The proportionate share of energy utilization patterns within Latin America reveal some important differences among the individual countries and some critical distinctions (tables 3-3 through 3-6).

Demand

The two dominant consumers for all types of energy are Mexico and Brazil, accounting for 27.70 and 24.41 percent, respectively, of the region's consumption in 1979, followed by Argentina (13.48 percent) and Venezuela (10.86 percent).[4] The other countries utilized less than 4 percent each, with the exception of Colombia (5.53 percent).

Mexico accounts for 38.31 percent of Latin American consumption of natural gas (as opposed to 1.90 percent for Brazil), 23.82 percent of coal, and 13.7 percent of vegetable fuels (in 1975). Mexico claimed 26.74 percent in 1979 of the region's entire petroleum and petroleum derivatives consumption. Only one other country reflects this type of pattern for all sources of energy.

Brazil has the national profile closest to that of Mexico. Brazil remains distinctive in its heavy utilization of hydroelectricity (in comparison with

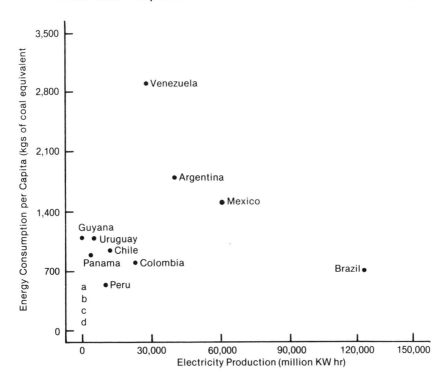

Figure 3-2. Energy Consumption per Capita in Relation to the Production of Energy in 1979

Source: U.N. Department of International and Social Affairs, *1979 Yearbook of World Energy Statistics* (New York: United Nations, 1981).

[a] Costa Rica, Ecuador.

[b] Bolivia, Nicaragua.

[c] El Salvador, Guatemala.

[d] Honduras, Paraguay.

other countries) at about 55 percent of the region's overall use of hydroelectric power. Brazil also accounts for close to 37 percent of Latin American utilization of vegetable fuels as a source of energy (in 1975), 26.48 percent of petroleum and derivatives, and 36.65 percent of coal consumed in Latin America. These shares of regional consumption summarize the major role of Brazil in the area as a whole.

Among dominant consumers Argentina utilizes 18.14 percent of Latin American natural gas, while its share of the region's other non-oil sources of energy is less than 7 percent. Venezuela, a major producer of petroleum, consumes 26.48 percent of the region's natural gas, but only 7.90 percent of its petroleum derivatives. The Venezuelan share of coal consumed within

Table 3-2
Energy Consumption in Latin America
(billion barrels of oil equivalent[a])

	1970	1971	1972	1973	1974	1975	1976	1977	1978	1979
Primary	1.46	1.56	1.64	1.76	1.86	1.92	2.04	2.14	2.24	2.34
Petroleum	1.01	1.08	1.11	1.20	1.26	1.28	1.36	1.42	1.48	1.55
Share (%)	69.2	69.2	67.7	68.2	67.7	66.7	66.7	66.4	66.1	66.2
Natural gas	0.22	0.24	0.27	0.27	0.28	0.29	0.30	0.29	0.31	0.32
Share (%)	15.1	15.4	16.5	15.3	15.1	15.1	14.7	13.6	13.8	13.7
Coal	0.07	0.08	0.08	0.09	0.10	0.10	0.11	0.10	0.11	0.12
Share (%)	4.8	5.1	4.9	5.1	5.4	5.2	5.4	4.7	4.9	5.1
Hydro	0.15	0.16	0.18	0.21	0.23	0.25	0.26	0.32	0.34	0.34
Share (%)	10.3	10.3	11.0	11.9	12.4	13.0	12.7	15.0	15.2	14.5
Nuclear	0	0	0	0	0.001	0.005	0.005	0.003	0.005	0.006
Share (%)	0	0	0	0	0.05	0.26	0.25	0.14	0.22	0.26

Source: British Petroleum, *BP Statistical Review of the World Oil Industry* (London: British Petroleum Company, 1979), pp. 20-32.
[a]Errors due to rounding.

Table 3-3
Distribution of National Energy Production and Consumption by Energy Type in South America in 1979

	Coal and Lignite	Crude Petroleum and Natural Gas Liquids	Natural Gas	Hydro and Nuclear Power	Total
Percentage of total national production					
Argentina	1.28	74.99	20.31	3.42	100
Bolivia	0	47.44	49.70	2.86	100
Brazil	11.13	40.26	4.37	44.24	100
Chile	15.02	31.82	38.13	15.04	100
Colombia	23.99	47.16	21.00	7.85	100
Ecuador	0	98.86	0.49	0.65	100
Mexico	3.29	77.32	17.43	1.96	100
Nicaragua	0	0	0	100	100
Panama and Canal Zone	0	0	0	100	100
Paraguay	0	0	0	100	100
Peru	0.21	89.08	5.67	5.05	100
Uruguay	0	0	0	100	100
Venezuela	0.03	90.26	8.95	0.76	100
Percentage of total national consumption					
Argentina	3.14	68.83	24.76	3.28	100
Bolivia	0	86.90	7.33	5.72	99.95
Brazil	8.96	75.12	1.43	14.49	100
Chile	13.75	66.21	11.98	8.06	100
Colombia	24.04	46.75	21.25	7.96	100
Ecuador	0	96.14	1.65	2.21	100
Mexico	5.12	66.67	25.37	2.83	99.99
Nicaragua	0	97.74	0	2.26	100
Panama and Canal Zone	0	96.27	0	3.73	100
Paraguay	0	89.85	0	10.15	100
Peru	2.02	80.61	9.19	8.18	100
Uruguay	0.52	91.88	0	7.60	100
Venezuela	0.95	50.39	44.87	3.79	100

Source: U.N. Department of International Economic and Social Affairs, *1979 Yearbook of World Energy Statistics* (New York: United Nations, 1981).

Table 3-4

Distribution of National Energy Production and Consumption by Energy Type in Central America and the Caribbean in 1979

	Coal and Lignite	Crude Petroleum and Natural Gas Liquids	Natural Gas	Hydro and Nuclear Power	Total
Percentage of total national production					
Bahamas	0	0	0	0	100
Barbados	0	83.87	16.13	0	100
Costa Rica	0	0	0	100	100
Cuba	0	88.58	8.12	3.05	99.75
El Salvador	0	0	0	100	100
Grenada	0	0	0	0	100
Guatemala	0	60.71	0	39.29	100
Guyana	0	0	0	0	100
Haiti	0	0	0	100	100
Honduras	0	0	0	100	100
Jamaica	0	0	0	100	100
Dominican Republic	0	0	0	100	100
Trinidad and Tobago	0	82.30	17.70	0	100
Percentage of total national consumption					
Bahamas	0	100	0	0	100
Barbados	0	96.39	3.61	0	100
Costa Rica	0	86.60	0	13.40	100
Cuba	1.07	98.59	0.24	0.09	99.99
El Salvador	0	86.68	0	13.32	100
Grenada	0	100	0	0	100
Guatemala	0	97.87	0	2.13	100
Guyana	0	100	0	0	100
Haiti	0	89.84	0	10.16	100
Honduras	0	90.69	0	9.31	100
Jamaica	0.04	99.47	0	0.50	100
Dominican Republic	0.04	99.73	0	0.23	100
Trinidad and Tobago	0.02	39.01	60.97	0	100

Source: U.N. Department of International Economic and Social Affairs, *1979 Yearbook of World Energy Statistics* (New York: United Nations, 1981).

Table 3-5
Distribution of Regional Energy Production by Energy Type in South America in 1979

	Coal and Lignite	Crude Petroleum and Natural Gas Liquids	Natural Gas	Hydro and Nuclear Power	Total
Percentage of total regional production					
Argentina	4.13	8.79	14.17	6.87	9.29
Bolivia	0	0.50	3.14	0.52	0.84
Brazil	22.35	2.94	1.90	55.37	5.78
Chile	5.98	0.46	3.28	3.73	1.15
Colombia	33.69	2.41	6.38	6.88	4.04
Ecuador	0	3.91	0.12	0.44	3.13
Mexico	33.21	28.37	38.05	12.33	29.06
Nicaragua	0	0	0	0.10	0.00
Panama and Canal Zone	0	0	0	0.34	0.02
Paraguay	0	0	0	0.32	0.01
Peru	0.24	3.70	1.40	3.59	3.29
Uruguay	0	0	0	0.96	0.04
Venezuela	0.40	44.86	26.46	6.46	39.36
Percentage of total regional consumption					
Argentina	7.09	13.39	18.14	6.91	13.48
Bolivia	0	0.73	0.23	0.52	0.58
Brazil	36.65	26.48	1.90	55.39	24.41
Chile	6.81	2.83	1.93	3.73	2.96
Colombia	22.25	3.73	6.38	6.89	5.53
Ecuador	0	1.78	0.12	0.45	1.28
Mexico	23.82	26.74	38.31	12.33	27.77
Nicaragua	0	0.40	0	0.10	0.29
Panama and Canal Zone	0	0.80	0	0.34	0.58
Paraguay	0	0.21	0	0.25	0.16
Peru	0.95	3.26	1.40	3.59	2.80
Uruguay	0.07	1.09	0	0.97	0.82
Venezuela	1.72	7.90	26.48	6.45	10.86

Source: U.N. Department of International Economic and Social Affairs, *1979 Yearbook of World Energy Statistics* (New York: United Nations, 1981).

Table 3-6
Distribution of Regional Energy Production by Energy Type in Central America and the Carribbean in 1979

	Coal and Lignite	Crude Petroleum and Natural Gas Liquids	Natural Gas	Hydro and Nuclear Power	Total
Percentage of total regional production					
Bahamas	0	0	0	0	0
Barbados	0	0.01	0.01	0	0.01
Costa Rica	0	0	0	0.77	0.04
Cuba	0	0.09	0.05	0.05	0.08
El Salvador	0	0	0	0.65	0.03
Grenada	0	0	0	0	0
Guatemala	0	0.01	0	0.14	0.02
Guyana	0	0	0	0	0
Haiti	0	0	0	0.11	0.01
Honduras	0	0	0	0.28	0.01
Jamaica	0	0	0	0.06	0
Dominican Republic	0	0	0	0.03	0
Trinidad and Tobago	0	3.95	5.05	0	3.80
Percentage of total regional consumption					
Bahamas	0	0.49	0	0	0.34
Barbados	0	0.10	0.01	0	0.07
Costa Rica	0	0.46	0	0.77	0.37
Cuba	0.63	5.00	0.05	0.05	3.51
El Salvador	0	0.39	0	0.65	0.31
Grenada	0	0.01	0	0	0.01
Guatemala	0	0.59	0	0.14	0.42
Guyana	0	0.35	0	0	0.25
Haiti	0	0.09	0	0.11	0.07
Honduras	0	0.25	0	0.28	0.19
Jamaica	0	1.08	0	0.06	0.75
Dominican Republic	0	0.99	0	0.03	0.69
Trinidad and Tobago	0	0.86	5.05	0	1.52

Source: U.N. Department of International Economic and Social Affairs, *1979 Yearbook of World Energy Statistics* (New York: United Nations, 1981).

the region as a whole is negligible, while its share of hydroelectricity amounted to 6.45 percent.

Supply

Patterns of production of energy within Latin America differ considerably from consumption patterns, yielding different degrees and forms of dependence on external sources. Some features stand out.

The dominant producer of all forms of energy is Venezuela, accounting for 39.36 percent of all Latin American energy production, 44.86 percent of the region's entire production of petroleum, and 26.46 percent of natural gas production. Venezuela contributes, however, only 6.46 percent of the area's production of hydroelectric power (included in this figure is a marginal contribution of nuclear-generated electricity from a research reactor in Venezuela). Venezuela clearly leads in petroleum production.

Brazil produced only 5.78 percent of the region's total energy production (not including vegetable fuels which would double this figure) but 55.37 percent of its hydroelectric power and 22.35 percent of its coal production. Brazil is making distinctive gains in the production and consumption of vegetable fuels.

Given Mexico's new position as a major producer of oil, it is often overlooked that in 1979 the country produced 33.21 percent of the region's coal, 12.33 percent of its hydroelectric power. The only estimate for vegetable fuels is for 1975, when 13.67 percent of the region's production originated from Mexico. Mexico also provides 38.05 percent of Latin American natural gas. By 1980 Mexico ranked about sixth among world petroleum producers with a ratio of proven crude oil reserves to production of 56 years.

The only other notable producer of energy in Latin America, Argentina, accounts for 9.29 percent of the region's energy production. The country produces a fairly well-distributed, though small, share of the region's different sources of energy. Argentina's oil production has risen sharply in the past two years, due largely to reopening of exploration and development to private capital. The military takeover of 1976 initiated a change in oil policy that substantially transformed the country's supply profile.

The role of vegetable fuels in Latin America is critical. For example, if vegetable fuels were to be taken into account, Brazil would outrank Argentina in percentage of the region's energy production. Since vegetable fuels are not included, Argentina outranks Brazil.

Among other countries of the region which are negligible producers of energy of any type, thus depending mostly on external sources, Peru increased its oil reserves dramatically in the past decade. In 1971, when

Petroperu signed a thirty-five year contract with Occidental Oil, Peru was importing $1 million worth of oil a day.[5] This year, oil reserves amount to a total of $22.4 billion (using $32/b as a base price). Put another way, Peru has gone from a $200 million a year importer to a net exporter. Over the past four years Peruvian oil production has more than doubled. Eight years ago the price of a barrel of crude oil was $2. Now individual nations are contracting for sales pegged at $34/b for marker crudes. As a result of the sharp turn about in Peruvian resources, foreign oil companies are suddenly showing great interest in Peru's crudes.

Petroleum Production and Consumption

Comparisons of patterns of crude oil production reveal critical distinctions: Venezuela produced 70.67 percent of the region's petroleum in 1970, 53.40 percent in 1975, and declined to 37.18 percent in 1980. This reflects major changes in the distribution of production and the entrance of new producers. For example, Mexico produced only 9.29 percent of Latin American petroleum in 1970, jumping to 18.34 percent in 1975, and placed at close to 37 percent in 1980 (36.94 percent, to be precise, not including a minor contribution of natural gas liquids to Mexico's percentages of petroleum production).

Brazil's share of regional production has remained remarkably steady throughout the ten years in question, at 3.18 percent in 1970 and 3.28 percent in 1980. Yet within the context of Brazil's distinctive energy profile this small share of oil production—both in terms of consumption and production—has remarkably diverse possibilities for that country. However, its petroleum endowments may be negligible at best. Table 3-7 shows production figures for 1979.

There have been notable changes in the consumption of refined products in Latin America. For example, Brazil consumed 19.55 percent of the region's refined product consumption in 1970 and increased it to 25.34 percent five years later and 26.56 percent in 1978. Mexico's share of refined products consumed increased more modestly during these years, from 19.37 percent of the region's consumption of refined products in 1970 to 21.5 percent in 1975 and 23.21 percent in 1978. Argentina's share, on the other hand, declined, from 16.27 percent in 1970 to 13.29 percent in 1975 and 11.9 percent in 1978. Many smaller consumers of refined products in Central America and the Caribbean exhibited some declines in consumption between 1970 and 1975, while those of South America revealed a more general upward trend. These figures are marginal in a worldwide context, of course. Only Mexico and Brazil account for more than 1 percent of the

Table 3-7
Petroleum Production in Latin America
(in billion barrels per year)

	1970	1971	1972	1973	1974	1975	1976	1977	1978	1979	1980
Argentina	0.142	0.155	0.159	0.154	0.151	0.145	0.145	0.158	0.165	0.172	0.179
Bolivia	0.009	0.014	0.016	0.017	0.017	0.015	0.015	0.013	0.012	0.011	0.011
Brazil	0.061	0.064	0.063	0.064	0.066	0.065	0.066	0.061	0.061	0.063	0.070
Chile	0.012	0.012	0.011	0.010	0.008	0.007	0.007	0.007	0.006	0.008	0.011
Colombia	0.080	0.079	0.072	0.067	0.062	0.057	0.053	0.050	0.048	0.046	0.046
Ecuador	0.002	0.002	0.029	0.076	0.065	0.059	0.069	0.067	0.074	0.078	0.082
Mexico[a]	0.178	0.177	0.185	0.192	0.237	0.294	0.340	0.383	0.486	0.590	0.788
Peru	0.026	0.023	0.024	0.026	0.029	0.027	0.028	0.033	0.057	0.070	0.071
Trinidad and Tobago	0.052	0.049	0.050	0.058	0.065	0.079	0.078	0.084	0.084	0.080	0.079
Venezuela	1.354	1.295	1.179	1.229	1.086	0.856	0.840	0.817	0.791	0.860	0.793
Others[b]	neg	neg	neg	neg	neg	neg	neg	neg	neg	0.001	0.002
Total Latin America	1.916	1.869	1.786	1.891	1.786	1.603	1.640	1.672	1.783	1.979	2.133

Source: Oil and energy trends, *Statistical Review 1981* (Berkshire, United Kingdom: Economics Research Ltd.). Reprinted with permission.
[a]Includes natural gas liquids.
[b]Negligible.

world consumption of refined products (and in each case less than 2 percent). Recall that Latin America as a whole claimed 5.69 percent of total world consumption of refined products in 1970 and 6.46 percent in 1975, decreasing only slightly to 6.31 percent in 1978.

Overall, future prospects in the petroleum sector are not encouraging. Other than Mexico's new finds, the expectations for Bolivia, Brazil, Peru, and Ecuador are uncertain, given present knowledge and existing technology. Venezuela will begin importing light crudes for use in internal combustion engines, and the Orinoco tars which appear to have some potential for the future may necessitate the return of multinational companies—involvements that run contrary to the country's autonomy concerns.

The Five Giants

The five countries that stand out in the energy picture in Latin America— Argentina, Brazil, Colombia, Venezuela, and Mexico—also account for the vast extent of infrastructure and transportation facilities in that region. Together they accounted for 82 percent of total energy consumption during 1979 and 88 percent of total energy production. They make up 87 percent of Latin American crude oil production and 73 percent of refined products consumption. These countries dominate also in other types of energy, representing 93.8 percent of the region's coal production in 1979, 87.9 percent of total hydroelectric power, and 64 percent of energy produced from vegetable fuels (in 1975). The four largest—Mexico, Venezuela, Brazil, and Argentina—dominate the Latin American energy scene.

These four countries alone accounted during 1979 for 76.5 percent of Latin American energy consumption, 83.5 percent of energy production, and 85 percent of crude oil production. This is not to belittle the role of Colombia, which ranks fifth among the Latin American countries in these categories. Colombia is the largest coal producer, the third in hydroelectricity production, and higher than both Argentina and Venezuela in vegetable fuel production. Nevertheless, heavy reliance on petroleum products underscores the predominance of the other four. In contrast, Colombia is a country with significant energy resources but without an equally well-developed infrastructure and transportation network. The growth of energy consumption for the five giants is presented in table 3-8.

Energy Alternatives: New Directions

Despite claims that Latin America will remain dependent on petroleum for the rest of the century,[6] both the Organization for Latin American Energy

Table 3-8
Growth Rates of Energy Consumption
(in thousand metric tons of oil equivalent)

	1969	1979	Percentage of Annual Growth Rate
Argentina	26,198	34.541	2.8
Brazil	29,177	62,561	7.6
Colombia	8,229	14,164	5.4
Mexico	32,523	71,188	7.8
Venezuela	14,991	27,829	6.2
Total	111,118	210,283	6.4

Source: U.N. Statistical Office, *1950-1974 World Energy Supplies*, series J, no. 19 (New York: United Nations); U.N. Department of International Economics and Social Affairs, *1979 Yearbook of World Energy Statistics* (New York: United Nations, 1981).

Development and a recent report of Argentina's Fundacion Bariloche are optimistic that nonconventional energy will play an important role in Latin America.

The OLADE study of the nonconventional energy sources in Latin America undertaken in connection with the United Nations has drawn an energy development plan for the region.[7] The study claims that, by implementing the plan, the continent could save 3 billion barrels of oil by 1995. By then 11 percent of the region's energy would come from non-conventional sources. The environmental benefits would be substantial: a 24 percent drop in deforestation and an increase in energy supplies for the low-income and rural populations. Moreover the study predicts that by 1995 adoption of nonconventional energy strategies would increase total energy supplies by 5 to 15 percent without increasing the use of conventional sources. The Bariloche Report claims that by 1985 nonconventional energy sources will provide more than 10 percent of Latin America's energy requirements.[8] Hydroelectric power has long been a crucial energy source and is expected to increase in importance. Many observers agree that the key issue is how best to exploit the indigenous resources that exist in virtually all countries.

Vegetable Fuels

The development of alternative sources of energy is a high priority in Brazil. The National Energy Commission, composed of key ministers and heads of state and industrial enterprises, is directing an accelerated energy program to increase use of coal, alcohol production, and expansion of shale oil and hydroelectric resources. One of the most important programs is production of alcohol from sugar cane.[9] Table 3-9 gives comparative shares of vegetable fuel production and consumption for the region.

Brazil's gasohol project is designed to contribute up to 49 percent of the fuel needs of Brazilian cars by 1985-1986. The vulnerability of Brazil's foreign oil supplies has stimulated both a surge in the sales of alcohol-powered cars and government action to halt sugar exports to provide resources for alcohol production. The price of a liter of alcohol is currently less than half that of petroleum. However, competition from the export sales of sugar suggest that alcohol prices will have to be raised to four times the current price in order to compete with the return on sugar from exports. In 1979 Brazil made its first international contract for its national alcohol program with a U.S. $1.2 billion loan extended in London by a consortium of fifty-one banks, headed by the Morgan Guaranty Trust.[10] Production of alcohol is projected at 6 billion liters for 1981, enough to power 1.4 million cars. A target of 10.7 billion liters has been set for 1985. This would be the equivalent of only 160,000 barrels of oil per day out of the current 1 million barrels per day that Brazil now consumes. Perhaps alcohol will eventually account for 40 percent of consumption and petroleum for 60 percent.

To reach the 1985 goals, some 2 to 3 million extra hectares of land will be needed to grow the necessary sugar cane, an approximate 7 percent increase a year until 1985. Conflicts over land in the competition between alcohol production and food production are likely to occur. For example, in the Sao Paulo state, where most of the new sugar plantations have been recently established, there is already considerable pressure on small producers who are currently growing subsistence crops, such as maize and beans.[11] The World Bank has recently offered Brazil $1 billion for the alcohol program, on the condition that provision of equipment be opened up to international competition.[12]

Brazilian authorities are also looking into alternative types of oil, as fuel plans now call for the production of an extra 2 to 2.5 billion liters of vegetable oil to substitute for diesel in approximately 16 percent of consumption. Among the crops to be used are soy (despite relatively low yields of 350 to 400 kg per hectare) and higher yielding crops such as rape, sunflower, groundnuts, and dende palm oil, which might prove to be the highest yielder of oil per hectare. The Amazon region is the site of a proposed new palm plantation (50,000 hectares per year).[13] One fear of concentrating too heavily on vegetables as alternative fuel production is that ultimately it might lead to a scarcity of food crops, thus require importation of food. Moreover some of the crops being cultivated under the energy program, particularly sugar, rapidly exhaust the soil. In July 1981 the World Bank agreed to lend Brazil $250 million to assure production targets for sugar cane. Brazil's National Alcohol Commission pledged to assist the alcohol-fuel industry with an additional $244 million in 1981. Energy planners are skeptical about prospects for meeting 1981 targets.[14]

Table 3-9
Vegetable Fuels in 1975

	Percentage of Country's Consumption	Percentage of Country's Production	Percentage of Region's Consumption	Percentage of Region's Production
Argentina	5.31	4.93	4.03	4.03
Bolivia	43.40	13.41	2.07	2.07
Brazil	20.18	31.39	37.40	37.40
Chile	6.79	5.26	1.37	1.37
Colombia	17.30	14.75	6.65	6.65
Ecuador	38.46	14.54	3.37	3.37
Mexico	9.81	7.54	13.67	13.67
Nicaragua	34.25	77.21	0.99	0.99
Panama	13.70	86.19	0.44	0.44
Paraguay	54.00	74.34	0.11	0.11
Peru	17.86	20.07	4.17	4.17
Uruguay	4.97	23.13	0.25	0.25
Venezuela	3.42	0.48	1.85	1.85
Bahamas	0.71	100.00	0.01	0.01
Barbados	27.59	100.00	0.15	0.15
Costa Rica	23.52	43.87	0.72	0.72
Cuba	34.87	93.96	9.21	9.21
El Salvador	42.39	81.98	1.32	1.32
Grenada	42.86	100.00	0.04	0.04
Guatemala	51.68	92.65	2.56	2.56
Guyana	32.83	100.00	0.74	0.74
Haiti	90.38	96.38	2.77	2.77
Honduras	47.96	79.68	1.19	1.19
Jamaica	16.49	90.69	0.92	0.92
Dominican Republic	43.81	97.61	2.66	2.66
Trinidad and Tobago	5.63	1.01	0.36	0.36

Source: CEPAL, *Energy in Latin America: The Historical Record* (New York: United Nations, 1978).

Colombia, as well, is investigating the use of ethyl alcohol, as shown in studies made by the Empresa Colombiana de Petroleos (Ecopetrol) and the Federacion Nacional de Cafeteros, and reported in the Colombian magazine *Estrategia*. The studies have calculated the cost of producing alcohol from a variety of materials, including cassava, sugar cane, potatoes, maize, and rice. They estimate a minimum production of 15,000 barrels a day, which could easily be combined with normal fuel. In addition to reducing petroleum dependency, the project has been seen as a good opportunity for providing a stable market for increased agricultural production. To produce sufficient quantities of alcohol, it would be necessary to plant 220,000 hectares of sugar cane or 140,000 hectares of cassava at an investment of 11 billion pesos.[15]

These programs are notable but will only help countries with large uncultivated lands—clearly not the case for the Caribbean, Chile, and El Salvador. The rapid rates of urbanization call into question the large-scale possibilities of switching to vegetable residues. Nevertheless, the region's endowments of vegetable residues as a major source of fuel place it in a distinctive position, and, although there is some talk of expanding local production of methane, it cannot be done on short order.

Biogas

OLADE has set up a pilot project for small-scale production of methane in Ecuador. Based on a system extensively used in China, the practice involves feeding human and animal excrement and vegetable waste matter into a digesting tank for the generation of methane. This is seen as a potentially important alternative to wood for cooking and heating water, since deforestation is becoming a serious problem in many rural areas. It is particularly appropriate for warmer climates, where crops produce large quantities of vegetable waste as a by-product. It is expected that OLADE's methane program will extend to rural areas of Guyana, Honduras, and Jamaica.

Nuclear Power

Nuclear energy, a marginal source of power in Latin America, is an option only for Argentina, Brazil, Cuba, and Mexico. These are the only countries apparently planning to generate electricity in that way. Given concern for national autonomy prevalent in Latin America, prospects of technological dependency emanating from decisions to expand nuclear power capability emerge. Argentina's decision to control its own fuel cycle through utilization of natural uranium is a case in point: cost factors are essential. The third nuclear power plant in Brazil, for example, will cost U.S. $2,800 per installed kilowatt, in comparison with the initial estimate of U.S. $2,000 which was regarded as plausible for Brazil's nuclear power.[16] The government has postponed the completion date of the nuclear power program from 1995 to 2000. The first nuclear power plant, Angra I, was to begin operation in May 1981.[17]

During 1980 Argentina had the only plant on-line in the region, producing 335 net MW, and two plants under construction with a total of 1,300 net MW. Brazil had three plants with a total of 3,116 net MW under construction, and Mexico was building two plants with a total of 1,308 net MW. The precise program for Cuba could not be found.[18]

Argentina and Brazil are also pushing ahead with plans for nuclear development, both individually and jointly. The two countries have been discussing the formation of a regional body for nuclear development comparable to Euratom. Both countries have received technological assistance from West Germany, but Argentina would like to form a united front with Brazil to avoid problems of technological dependency. They are particularly interested in exchanging their own technological resources, such as Argentinian expertise in uranium processing and nuclear engineering, in exchange for the Brazilian experience in detecting uranium deposits. Technological collaboration would also be involved in the areas of radio isotopes, particle acceleration, reactor management, nuclear plasma, and joint training facilities for scientists and technicians.[19]

Despite a poor history in nuclear energy production (for example, the Laguna Verde project in Veracruz State which is six years behind schedule), the Mexican government has placed great emphasis on the development of this resource. It is confident that Mexico has the reserves to become one of the world's greatest uranium producers. The state uranium company, Uramex, has grown from a staff of 900 to 2,000 in an eighteen-month period and is expected to grow by 1,000 in the coming year, an indication of the importance placed on the development of nuclear power. Mexico has enlisted the technological assistance, in the form of feasibility studies, of Canada, Sweden, and France. In an effort to avoid technological dependence, Mexico is expected to make use of a wide range of expertise from industrialized countries. Energy plans currently call for the construction of fifteen to twenty nuclear plants over the next twenty years, with the aim of achieving the production of 20,000 MW by the end of the century.[20]

Coal

With respect to coal Colombia stands out as a country with important long-term prospects. At present, however, coal is being shipped out of Latin

America to regions where the installed capacities for efficient use are already in place. The Colombian state coal corporation, Carbocoal, has signed a contract with Exxon, calling for the investment of U.S. $3 billion in exploiting the El Cerrejon coal deposits in the La Guajira Peninsula, which are estimated at 1.6 billion tons of good quality steam coal. The agreement calls for production to begin in 1986, with expectations of reaching 15 million tons a year. The operating company will be the Exxon subsidiary, Intercor. Carbocoal will own 50 percent of the shares. Part of the project includes construction of a 90 mile railroad to the Caribbean coast and expansion of port facilities Exxon began. The agreement stipulates Exxon to pay a 15 percent royalty fee on its half of the production and taxes based on a sliding scale of profits.[21]

For Brazil, the government's energy plan is to replace 30 percent of present consumption of fuel oil with wood, charcoal, and coal. However, to provide the necessary wood and charcoal, an extra 1.4 million hectares of forestry will have to be planted each year. As with vegetable oils and sugar, the program is limited by land availability. It has been established that 230 hectares of land on the central plateau of Brazil would be required to produce the equivalent of 1,000 tons of oil.

Natural Gas

The recent evolution in the international energy market has had a profound impact on the prospects for natural gas in the region. The discovery of natural gas reserves in Latin America is usually a by-product of oil exploration, since the two are often found together. Few projects have been undertaken in the region in search of natural gas simply because the amount of proven gas reserves has usually been far more than what was required to meet demand. In the past governments have preferred to invest limited capital in the search for and development of oil deposits rather than in the development of expensive systems of gas transmission and distribution needed to release gas reserves for consumption.

Latin American interest in natural gas production has increased in recent years and can be expected to continue growing with the desire to find alternatives to petroleum.[22] Recent development plans associated with natural gas bear out this point. A major pipeline project is being planned to carry gas from Bolivia's gas fields all the way to the industrial center of Sao Paulo in Brazil, a distance of 1,200 miles. In 1975 the cost of this project was estimated at $3 billion dollars. Mexico has made plans to construct gas pipeline projects, and in Chile interest has been shown in shipping gas from its southern gas fields to central and northern centers of energy consumption in the country, as a substitute for the imported oil on which these centers now rely heavily. In general the high price of oil in world markets promises a widespread review of the potential for exploiting Latin America's wealth in natural gas, as the region seeks to diminish its quantity of imported oil.

Hydroelectricity

Hydroelectricity is undoubtedly the most essential alternative source of energy for Latin America. Although operational costs are low, these will rise over time, accentuating the cost calculations of building new dams and the installations of turbines. But prospects seem good. While Brazil exhibits the largest usage of hydroelectric power, the harnessing of rivers has already been done in many regions of the country. The Amazon provides important possibilities that remain fraught with technical and environmental difficulties. Argentina has more unexploited rivers than Brazil, but their location far from population centers accentuates problems of development. Close to $12 billion is expected to be allocated for expansion of hydroelectric power to 38 percent of power generated by 1985 and 73 percent by 1995.[23] Some countries, like Colombia, have "massive potential" which is only marginally exploited.[24]

Geothermal Energy

Hot springs down the whole length of the Andean range are possible sources of thermal energy. Beyond, however, only Mexico and El Salvador actually operate geothermal power stations. Mexico has two units of 37.5 MW. each which together supply 1 percent of Mexico's electricity supplies.[25]

Issues for the Future

Energy development in Latin America clearly has tremendous potential. Three specific problems, however, interact to reinforce the difficulties of expanding the region's alternative sources of energy. These include the magnitude of capital expenditures required, access to technology, and resolution of potentially critical environmental problems. In the past the multinational companies served as the major source of capital and technology. A return of external corporate domination of the region would signify a change in national policy for almost all countries. Powerful sentiments exist against foreign corporate pressure, however we may regard recent protests of Mexico and Venezuela against an Argentinian proposal tha the Inter-American Development Bank guarantee transnational investments in the energy sector as an important example of the region's response to prospects of large-scale foreign corporate involvement in energy development.

Ultimately, resolution of Latin America's energy and development problems lies in the region's own capability to adapt and adjust to economic and political constraints. Underlying these constraints is the area's peculiar demographic characteristics. Chapter 4 begins with a look at the region's demography and ends with an assessment of energy use in economic activity.

Notes

1. These data refer to commercial energy and exclude vegetable fuels which, in fact, provide a substantial contribution to the energy balance of Latin American countries. Data for commercial fuels are based on British Petroleum, *BP Statistical Review of the World Oil Industry* (1979); International Monetary Fund, *International Financial Statistics* (1981) Washington, D.C.; Department of International and Social Affairs (New York: United Nations, 1981). The most recent, comprehensive coverage of sources of energy, country-by-country for the region as a whole, is for 1975, from CEPAL, *Energy in Latin America: The Historical Record* (United Nations Press, Santiago de Chile, 1978).

2. Oil and Energy Trends, *Statistical Review 1981* (Berkshire: United Kingdom Energy Economics Research Ltd.).

3. Ibid.

4. The following assessments regarding demand and supply include vegetable fuels only for 1975, the most recent year for which crossnational data are available. See CEPAL, *Energy in Latin America,* note 1 for other sources; also *Platt's Oilgram News* (1980), all issues.

5. *New York Times,* January 1, 1980, pp. 31-32; *Petroleum Economist,* 46 (July 1979), pp. 283-286.

6. *Latin America Weekly Report,* October 17, 1980, pp. 3-9.

7. Ibid., for a description; see also *Latin American Weekly Report,* February 1, 1980, pp. 9-10.

8. Ibid.

9. *Petroleum Economist,* 46 (September 1979), pp. 383-384.

10. *Petroleum Economist,* 47 (October 1980), pp. 450-451.

11. *Latin America Weekly Report,* October 10, 1980, p. 10.

12. Ibid.

13. For a review of Brazil's program see, R.F. Colson, "Brazil: The Proalcool Programme—A Response to the Energy Crisis," *Bank of London & South America Review, BOLSA* 15 (May 1981), pp. 60-70.

14. *World Business Weekly,* July 6, 1981, p. 16.

15. *Latin America Weekly Report,* March 14, 1980, pp. 8-9.

16. "Latin America: After the Oil Crisis," *Bank of London and South America Review* 13 (December 1979), pp. 708-709. See also *Latin America Weekly Report,* February 1, 1980, p. 4.

17. Ibid., February 1, 1980 p. 4.

18. *Latin American Weekly Report,* January 25, 1980, pp. 3-4.

19. *Latin American Weekly Report,* May 16, 1980, p. 6.

20. *Latin American Weekly Report,* November 21, 1980, p. 7.

21. *Petroleum Economist,* 47 (October 1980), pp. 450-451.

22. *Latin America Weekly Report,* September 12, 1980, pp. 8-9.

23. *Petroleum Economist,* 46 (April 1979), pp. 166-167.

24. *Latin America Weekly Report,* September 12, 1980, pp. 8-9.

25. *Latin America Weekly Report,* March 14, 1980, pp. 8-9.

Part II
Economy

4 Demographic Structure and Economic Activity

Demographic features are especially important for estimating the future load on the area's transportation networks and, in turn, necessary adjustments to changing energy prices and availability. Differences in demographic characteristics among Latin American countries, however, are quite considerable. We will not only examine the general trends of Latin American demography but also look at economic activities of individual countries.

Table 4-1 ranks the countries of the region by size at five-year intervals from 1970 onward; the 1981 figure is, however, based on previous projections. Brazil clearly dominates the ranking in population number, which is especially striking with relation to Mexico, the second country in size. These two countries, in fact, account for over 51 percent of Latin America's total population. Other countries in table 4-1 can be considered as belonging to one of three groups: seven countries register a population of more than ten million; five countries from five to seven million; and eleven countries less than five million each. Table 4-2 presents some comparisons in population size and rate of growth.[a]

Basic Demographic Structure

In 1950 Latin America represented only 6.5 percent of total world population and no more than 8.2 percent in 1978, but rates of growth for the region as a whole were higher than for the world total and greater than for any other single region (except Africa).[1] Although immigration played an important role in the development of the region, the dramatic rise in the growth rate was primarily due to increases in birth rates.

Between 1950 and 1978 the total rate of growth for the region tended toward a consistent rate of over 2.7 percent. As such, it represents the most notable sustained increase in any region of the world. Even South Asia, conventionally viewed as a high-growth area, increased less rapidly than Latin America (2.3 percent). These increases, however, have been concentrated in some areas more than others. Over the past thirty years, Honduras, Paraguay, Nicaragua, Mexico, and Venezuela have consistently had

---

[a]A recent survey of economic change in Latin America by *World Business Weekly*, August 24, 1981, pp. 29-37, provides one of the most up-to-date assessments of the region's problems and economic prospects. This chapter takes account of these developments.

Table 4-1
Population Size and Growth in Latin America

	Population Size[a]				Rate of Growth		
	1970	1975	1980	1981	2000	1970-1975	1975-1981	1981-2000
Brazil	95,322	108,400	122,320	125,223	187,494	2.6	2.4	2.1
Mexico	51,187	60,102	69,752	71,817	115,659	3.2	3.0	2.5
Colombia	20,803	23,177	25,794	26,356	37,999	2.2	2.1	1.9
Argentina	23,748	25,378	27,036	27,368	33,222	1.3	1.3	1.0
Peru	13,461	15,397	17,625	18,121	30,703	2.7	2.7	2.8
Venezuela	10,962	13,109	15,620	16,155	27,207	3.6	3.5	2.7
Chile	9,368	10,196	11,104	11,294	14,934	1.7	1.7	1.5
Ecuador	5,958	6,891	8,021	8,275	14,596	2.9	3.1	3.0
Guatemala	5,353	6,243	7,262	7,480	12,739	3.1	3.0	2.8
Haiti	4,605	5,157	5,809	5,954	9,860	2.3	2.4	2.7
Bolivia	4,325	4,894	5,570	5,720	9,724	2.5	2.6	2.8
Dominican Republic	4,523	5,231	5,947	6,096	9,329	2.9	2.6	2.2
El Salvador	3,582	4,143	4,797	4,939	8,708	2.9	2.9	3.0
Uruguay	2,824	2,842	2,924	2,944	3,448	0.1	0.6	0.8
Honduras	2,639	3,093	3,691	3,821	6,978	3.2	3.5	3.2
Paraguay	2,290	2,686	3,168	3,268	5,405	3.2	3.3	2.6
Nicaragua	1,970	2,318	2,733	2,824	5,154	3.3	3.3	3.2
Jamaica	1,869	2,043	2,192	2,224	2,871	1.8	1.4	1.3
Costa Rica	1,732	1,965	2,213	2,266	3,377	2.5	2.4	2.1
Panama	1,464	1,678	1,896	1,940	2,823	2.7	2.4	2.0
Trinidad and Tobago	1,027	1,082	1,139	1,151	1,377	1.0	1.0	0.9
Guyana	709	791	884	904	1,252	2.2	2.2	1.7
Barbados	239	245	253	255	297	0.5	0.7	0.8
Totals	282,815	321,149	364,144	373,390	545,156			

Source: CELADE, *Boletin Demografico*, vol. 14, no. 27 (January 1981), pp. 10-11.
[a]Listed by size of 1975 population (in thousands at midyear).

the highest growth rates in the region (over 3.2 percent per year). Brazil has grown at a slightly lower rate. The lowest population increase is evidenced in Uruguay and Argentina.

Despite such impressive growth in population, the region as a whole did not suffer from high density. Against a total world density of 31 per square kilometer in 1978, the highest densities were found in Europe (97/sq km), and the lowest in Africa (15/sq km), North America (11/sq km), and the U.S.S.R. (12/sq km). At 17/sq km, Latin America registered a slightly higher density than the latter group.

Latin America is one of the most urbanized regions of the world and *the most* urbanized of the developing areas. Against a worldwide rate of urbanization of 35 percent in 1965, the Latin American figures were higher than 50 percent: in other words, over half the population of the region is located in cities. By 1970 the worldwide rate had risen to 36.3 percent, while Latin America's urbanization rate was 56.7 percent. The increase during this five-year period was the highest, in comparison with other regions, both developed and developing.[2] In 1975 only two countries—Uruguay and Argentina—registered 80 percent urbanization. Five years later four countries qualified: Argentina, Venezuela, Chile, and Uruguay—a dramatic feature of demographic structure in any context. Only eight of the twenty-three countries of the region are less than 50 percent urban. Table 4-3 presents the urban percentage of total population for the twenty-three countries. For example, Buenos Aires alone accounts for over 36 percent of

Table 4-2
Polulation Size and Rate of Growth in Major Regions

	Population in Millions				Rate of Increase		
	1950	1960	1970	1980	1950-1960	1960-1970	1970-1980
Total region	164	216	283	364	2.8	2.7	2.5
Andean area[a]	37	49	65	84	2.8	2.8	2.6
Atlantic area[b]	74	96	124	155	2.6	2.6	2.2
Central American isthmus[c]	9	12	17	23	2.9	3.5	3.0
Mexico and Caribbean republics[d]	38	50	68	92	2.7	3.1	3.0
Other countries and territories of the Caribbean[e]	6	7	9	10	1.5	2.5	1.1

Source: CELADE, *Boletin Demografico*, vol. 13, no. 26 (July 1980), p. 113.
[a]Bolivia, Colombia, Chile, Ecuador, Peru, Venezuela.
[b]Argentina, Brazil, Paraguay, Uruguay.
[c]Costa Rica, El Salvador, Guatemala, Honduras, Nicaragua, Panama.
[d]Cuba, Haiti, Mexico, Dominican Republic.
[e]Netherlands Antilles, Bahamas, Barbados, Virgin Islands, Guadeloupe, Guyana, French Guyana, Belize, Jamaica, Martinique, Puerto Rica, Surinam, Trinidad and Tobago, Panama Canal Zone, American Virgin Islands, British Virgin Islands, other smaller islands.

Table 4-3
Urban Concentration of the Major City as Percentage of
Total Population of Country

Country	Major City	1960	1970	Growth Rate
Argentina	Buenos Aires	34.0	36.1	0.6
Bolivia	La Paz	12.3	14.5	1.6
Brazil[a]	Rio de Janeiro	4.5	4.6	0.2
Colombia	Bogota	9.7	12.8	2.8
Costa Rica	San Jose	18.4	19.2	0.4
Chile	Santiago	25.9	30.7	1.7
Ecuador	Guayaquil	11.4	12.6	1.0
El Salvador	San Salvador	10.2	9.5	-0.7
Guatemala	Guatemala City	13.4	13.5	0.07
Guyana	Georgetown	12.5	23.4	6.3
Honduras	Tegucigalpa	7.1	10.2	3.6
Mexico	Mexico City	8.1	6.0	-3.0
Nicaragua	Managua	15.3	20.8	3.0
Panama	Panama City	25.4	30.3	1.8
Paraguay[b]	Asuncion	15.9	16.7	0.5
Peru	Lima	15.4	21.7	3.4
Uruguay	Montevideo	44.7	44.5	-0.04
Venezuela	Caracas	10.5	9.7	-0.8

Source: Economic Commission for Latin America, *Statistical Yearbook for Latin America 1978* (New York: United Nations, 1978.)

[a]The 1950 and 1960 censuses give higher figures for Rio de Janeiro; during 1970 Sao Paulo came to have a larger number of inhabitants than Rio. For the purposes of this table Rio de Janeiro with its corresponding growth rates is taken as the major city for the three years to illustrate this. The percentage of the total population of Sao Paulo and its respective growth rates are 3.9, 4.5, 5.6, 4.53, and 5.17.
[b]In 1950 and 1960 the second largest city of Paraguay was Encarnacion, while in 1970 it was Fernando de la Hora.

Argentina's population. Santiago attracts over 30 percent of Chile's population. In Uruguay over 44 percent of the population is concentrated in the capital. These estimates are for 1970 (though provided in 1978), and it is expected that today this concentration is higher still. Regionally, the Atlantic area has the highest urbanization growth (58 percent), followed by the Andean area (54 percent). The mass of the region registers an average of 40 percent urbanization growth (table 4-4).

At the same time there is increasing international migration, that is, *among* the countries of the region. The movement is composed largely of unskilled workers responding to higher wages and greater employment opportunities. There is some evidence that mobility occurs from rural areas of one country to urban areas of another.[3] According to the Centro Latino Americano de Demografica (CELADE), Venezuela, Panama, and Argentina have the highest shares of migrant populations. For Venezuela, the figure may be as high as 7.4 percent of the total population.[4] The International Labor Organization has estimated that there may be about 5 million foreign workers in South America alone.[5]

For the region as a whole there is some evidence of out-migration.[6] Only in Argentina is there a consistent pattern of in-migration from 1960 and projected to 1980, while all other countries individually register a net loss of population. For the large countries the loss is less than 1 percent per year. For smaller countries, in the Caribbean region specifically, it is much higher.[7] More critical, however, is the distance between intraregional move-' ments, and migration out of Latin America as a whole. The data are in-clusive, yet recent economic changes may motivate greater population movement within the region itself. Greater mobility will mean higher energy use.

These migration rates are projected to increase throughout the next two decades. CELADE estimates that the highest rates will be in Paraguay, the Dominican Republic, Nicaragua, Bolivia, Panama, and Mexico. Mexican migration to the United States has received considerable attention due to its magnitude and apparent number of illegal migrants.

Table 4-4
Ratio of Urban Population to Total Population

	Urban Population as Percentage of Total Population		Average Annual Growth Rate	
	1960	*1980*	*1960-1970*	*1970-1980*
Andean area				
Boliva	24	33	3.9	4.1
Colombia	48	70	5.2	3.9
Chile	68	80	3.1	2.3
Ecuador	34	45	4.5	4.5
Peru	46	67	4.9	4.3
Venezuela	67	83	4.7	4.2
Atlantic area				
Argentina	74	82	2.0	2.1
Brazil	46	65	4.8	3.7
Paraguay	36	39	3.0	3.5
Uruguay	80	84	1.3	0.6
Central American isthmus				
Costa Rica	37	43	4.2	3.3
El Salvador	38	41	3.2	3.3
Guatemala	33	39	3.6	3.7
Honduras	23	36	5.4	5.5
Nicaragua	41	53	4.2	4.5
Panama	41	54	4.4	3.6
Mexico and Caribbean republics				
Mexico	51	67	4.8	4.2
Cuba	55	65	2.9	2.2
Haiti	16	28	4.0	4.9
Dominican Republic	30	51	5.8	5.3

Source: The World Bank, *World Development Report 1981* (Washington, D.C., August 1981). Reprinted with permission.

Latin America's demographic expansion, however, cannot be matched by its productivity. A crucial factor is its principally youthful population. In 1975 over 46 of 100 individuals in the region were classified as dependents (which includes those over sixty-five years), a figure higher than the world average (42). Given this age structure, Latin America's population is one of the least economically active in the world—in terms of size of economically active age group (15-65). In years to come, the rate of entry into the labor force will be highest; meanwhile, the dependency rate places great pressure on the region's resources. The implications for future transport concerns are clear: concentration and dispersion of population is the major challenge to be met by adequate infrastructure facilities.

Projections of the rate of growth in Latin America in comparison with major regions of the world indicate that its overall rate of increase is expected to remain high at least to the turn of the century. For 1980-1985 it is expected that the region will grow by 2.38 percent per year, declining to 2.15 percent for 1990-1995, and to 2.02 percent from 1995-2000.[8] Projections of increases in the labor force are at 2.4 percent in 1965 to 2.7 percent in 2000.[9] Given the high dependency rates noted earlier, these projections may even be on the conservative side. If population growth and economic activity are determinants of energy use, then these projections point to inevitable growth in energy consumption.

But urbanization can also be a major source of economic opportunity. Density of population may not only assist the growth of wealth and productivity, but it may also provide a demographic base for the regulation and rationalization of economic investments and developmental policies. At the same time, however, urbanization heightens the priority that developmental policies should award to human welfare. Provision of housing for middle-and low-income families, improved transportation, power and water supplies, and waste disposal facilities are all areas in which greater improvements can be made. In an era when it is recognized that it is important to provide a more viable urban environment, to improve the quality of life and to absorb new migrants and render them productive, the issue of energy "savings" becomes particularly poignant. This cannot be achieved, however, without a corresponding emphasis on and restructuring of overall economic activity.

Economic Activity

The structure of economic activity in Latin America gives further insight into overall energy use. The composition of economic activity for the region is given in table 4-5. The largest sector as a percentage of GDP is manufacturing, accounting for 24.2 percent of GDP in 1970 and 25.1 percent in 1977. This fact highlights the region's stage of development in comparison with other areas of the world. Latin America is an industrializing area and can-

Table 4-5
GDP by Type of Economic Activity as Percentage of GDP Producers' Values for Latin America

Activity	1970	1971	1972	1973	1974	1975	1976	1977	Growth Rate
Agriculture, hunting, forestry, and fishing	13.8	13.4	12.6	12.2	12.0	11.9	11.6	11.7	−2.4
Mining and quarrying	4.3	4.0	3.8	3.7	3.7	3.4	3.4	3.5	−2.9
Manufacturing	24.2	24.8	25.3	25.6	25.5	25.1	25.3	25.1	0.5
Electricity, gas, and water	1.8	1.9	1.9	2.0	2.0	2.1	2.2	2.3	3.5
Construction	5.2	5.2	5.3	5.4	5.5	5.6	5.6	5.6	1.1
Transportation, communications, and storage	6.1	6.1	6.1	6.2	6.3	6.5	6.5	6.5	0.9
Producers of government services	8.2	8.3	8.4	8.2	8.2	8.6	8.7	8.6	0.7

Source: Economic Commission for Latin America, *Statistical Yearbook for Latin America 1978* (New York: United Nations, 1978).

not be regarded in the same conventional guise of a developing country. It is noteworthy that agriculture was only 13.8 percent of GDP in 1970 and declined to 12 percent in 1977. This, too, indicates the industrializing nature of the region and the strong structural change that underlies industrial growth. The annual rate of growth for the region of GDP for this period was 5.7 percent.[10]

Variation in rates of growth among the countries for the past three decades is impressive. As a general trend the decade of the 1960s saw an increase in the average annual real growth for almost all of the countries in the region. Changes during the years 1970 to 1977 were more variable. In South America high rates of growth were in Brazil (9.9 percent), Ecuador (9.2 percent), the Dominican Republic (8.0 percent), Paraguay (7.0 percent), Costa Rica (6.0 percent), Guatemala (6.0 percent), and Belize (6.0 percent). Brazil's industrial production rose by 7.5 percent in 1978. Much of this growth was concentrated in specific industries such as automobile manufacturing, which increased by 16.3 percent.[11] The slowest rates of GDP growth were in Chile (0.1 percent), Jamaica (0 percent), Guyana (1.3 percent), and Uruguay (1.6 percent). For Argentina the rate of growth in the decade of the 1970s was more modest (2.8 percent until 1977). Tables 4-6 and 4-7 give percentage contributions to GDP of each sector of the economy for individual South and Central American countries.[12]

On a per capita basis, however, the most notable increase in GDP since 1970 (to 1977) was in Ecuador (6 percent), Brazil (6.8 percent), and Belize (5 percent). Other countries uniformly reflected slower per capita growth rates. In only four cases (Jamaica, Chile, Guyana, and Honduras) does the trend from 1970 to 1977 reflect a decided, though small, decline.[13]

Turning to gross fixed capital formation, the region generally reflected growing industrialization by relatively high rates of gross fixed capital formation as a percentage of GDP. Only in Chile, suffering from major economic stagnation, did the relationship between gross fixed capital formation and GDP show a marked decline (− 9.2 percent/year for 1973 to 1979). Brazil, Ecuador, and Nicaragua declined very slightly, and all other countries reflected increasing rates of contribution of gross fixed capital formation to GDP. The greatest rates of capital formation investment were Guatemala (7.3 percent/year), Guyana (12 percent/year, only four years reported), Honduras (6.5 percent/year), El Salvador (7.2 percent/year), Paraguay (9.4 percent/year), and Uruguay (9.6 percent/year). See table 4-8.

Gross domestic investment as a percentage of GDP reveals an economy's investment demand, hence a necessary condition for growth. Brazil (12.6 percent) and the Dominican Republic (13.2 percent) stand out as reflecting consistently strong patterns. The other noteworthy trends are Costa Rica, El Salvador, Guatemala, Venezuela, Ecuador, Haiti, and Peru. The surprise, however, is Paraguay, which for the period 1970 to 1977 was 20.7

Table 4-6
Structure of Economic Activity in South America in 1977 as Percentage of GDP Producers' Values
(in constant 1970 prices)

	Argentina	Bolivia	Brazil	Chile	Colombia	Ecuador	Mexico	Paraguay	Peru	Uruguay	Venezuela
Agriculture, hunting, forestry, and fishing	12.5 (-0.6)	14.7 (-2.0)	8.0 (3.0)	8.9 (1.7)	25.4 (-1.7)	25.3 (-2.6)	9.3 (-3.4)	32.3 (-0.9)	15.1 (-3.1)	11.2 (-1.7)	6.6 (-1.8)
Mining and quarrying	1.9 (-1.4)	10.5 (-5.0)	0.9 (1.7)	13.8 (2.4)	1.1 (-9.2)	6.7 (28.7)	4.9 (2.5)	1.4 (2.0)	8.3 (-0.5)	1.4 (2.2)	8.4 (-12.3)
Manufacturing	31.3 (0.5)	13.9 (-1.1)	29.1 (0.4)	23.2 (-2.3)	18.8 (1.0)	20.1 (2.3)	24.1 (0.4)	17.1 (-0.2)	21.8 (0.8)	25.0 (1.2)	16.0 (1.0)
Electricity, gas, and water	2.8 (3.4)	1.9 (0)	2.8 (2.2)	2.1 (5.8)	1.8 (2.6)	1.8 (4.6)	1.8 (3.6)	2.4 (1.0)	1.2 (0)	1.7 (1.8)	2.4 (5.0)
Construction	4.5 (-3.4)	4.5 (0)	6.6 (1.8)	2.4 (-8.0)	4.2 (-3.9)	6.6 (5.5)	5.5 (0.3)	5.4 (8.4)	5.2 (2.1)	4.7 (3.0)	7.1 (8.9)
Transportation, communications, and storage	9.7 (-0.6)	9.6 (1.0)	5.9 (0.5)	5.6 (-2.5)	9.0 (2.8)	5.6 (-4.0)	3.2 (3.0)	4.9 (2.2)	5.0 (1.2)	9.3 (1.1)	13.6 (3.2)
Producers of government services	9.3 (0)	10.3 (1.8)	7.8 (1.4)	7.2 (1.7)	6.5 (-0.9)	8.8 (-2.8)	8.6 (4.0)	4.3 (-4.0)	8.9 (0)	12.3 (-2.3)	14.2 (2.8)

Source: Economic Commission for Latin America, *Statistical Yearbook for Latin America 1978* (New York: United Nations, 1978).
Note: Figures in parentheses represent growth in 1970-1977.

Table 4-7
Structure of Economic Activity in Central America in 1977 as Percentage of GDP Producers' Values
(in constant 1970 prices)

	Costa Rica	El Salvador	Guatemala	Guyana	Honduras	Nicaragua	Panama
Agriculture, hunting, forestry, and fishing	19.9 (-3.3)	26.4 (-2.1)	29.2 (-0.4)	17.0[a] (-2.5)	30.2 (-1.4)	26.6 (-0.2)	19.4 (-0.9)
Mining and quarrying		0.2 (0)	0.1 (0)	16.0[a] (-4.9)	1.9 (-2.7)	0.2 (-15.7)	0.3 (0)
Manufacturing	18.3 (2.7)	18.2 (0.5)	14.7 (0.1)	14.2[a] (3.0)	15.0 (0.9)	19.1 (-0.07)	14.3 (-1.4)
Electricity, gas, and water	2.2 (1.4)	2.3 (5.2)	1.1 (2.8)		1.6 (1.9)	2.2 (3.7)	3.0 (5.8)
Construction	5.6 (2.2)	4.5 (5.8)	4.9 (11.4)	7.5[a] (-1.0)	5.8 (2.1)	5.5 (6.5)	6.2 (-0.2)
Transportation, communications, and storage	6.3 (3.9)	5.9 (1.5)	4.3 (2.9)	6.3[a] (1.3)	6.8 (0.2)	5.8 (0)	7.3 (3.8)
Producers of government services	12.2 (0.2)	9.0 (1.0)	7.2 (0.4)	18.5[a] (6.8)	3.9 (2.0)	7.6 (0.2)	3.7 (2.5)

Source: Economic Commission for Latin America, Statistical Yearbook for Latin America 1978 (New York: United Nations, 1978).

Note: Figures in parentheses represent growth in 1970-1977.

[a]Because 1977 data are not available, these data reflect 1975 figures.

Table 4-8
Gross Fixed Capital Formation as Percentage of GDP
(in current prices)

	1973	1974	1975	1976	1977	1978	1979	1980	Growth Rate[a]
Argentina	19.3	24.1	24.5	22.2	23.4	20.7	21.3	17.4	1.4
Bolivia	17.0	14.8	17.8	18.3	18.5	20.5	21.5		0.3
Brazil	23.0	24.2	25.4	23.7	22.2	22.0			−1.1
Chile	13.4	12.4	10.1	8.7	9.0				−10.0
Colombia	17.5	19.4	18.8	18.2	18.8	20.2	25.1		2.9
Costa Rica	22.2	24.0	22.0	23.4	22.4	24.4	24.6	23.5	2.0
Ecuador	19.6	18.2	23.1	22.1	24.1	25.7	18.8	13.0	2.6
El Salvador	15.6	18.2	23.0	20.1	21.2	22.8	18.4		−2.6
Guatemala	13.9	14.8	15.7	20.6	19.0	20.1			4.7
Guyana	24.1	20.7	29.5	34.1					11.6
Honduras	17.4	19.8	21.9	21.3	23.0	25.9	25.7	25.6	5.5
Mexico	20.4	21.3	22.4	21.8	20.2	22.4	24.2		2.8
Nicaragua	19.3	23.5	22.5	20.2	22.9	14.2	8.3		−14.1
Panama	27.9	23.0	29.4	31.6	22.2	26.3	22.5		−3.6
Paraguay	16.3	18.4	20.8	22.8	24.1	25.2	27.0		8.4
Peru	12.7	15.2	17.4	16.6	14.6	14.0	14.2	16.6	3.8
Uruguay	9.0	10.1	12.7	12.9	15.4	14.2	16.0		9.6
Venezuela	24.5	18.6	27.6	32.2	58.8	41.5	32.2		4.6

Source: International Monetary Fund, *International Financial Statistics* (Washington, D.C.: December 1980 and August 1981).

[a]Growth rate $= \dfrac{\ln(b/a)}{T}$ where b = last year, a = first year, T = total time.

percent of GDP, while from 1965 to 1970 it was 2.7 percent, an increase from the 0.4 percent of the previous five years. Expansion of hydroelectric facilities explains much of this improvement. Chile and Panama alone witnessed a decline in gross domestic investment as a percentage of GDP over the years 1970 to 1977.[14]

Energy Use and Economic Activity

The relationship between energy consumption and GNP per capita is noted in figure 4-1 for all countries of the region. This trend is not dissimilar to that noted in chapter 1 for industrial economies.

The global economic recovery of the late 1970s led the growth rate in industrial production in developing countries generally to rise from less than 1 percent in 1975 to about 9 percent in 1976. It has now been estimated

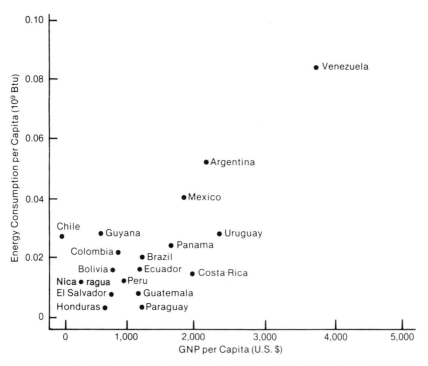

Source: International Monetary Fund, *International Financial Statistics*, August 1981; U.N. Department of International Economic and Social Affairs, *1979 Yearbook of World Energy Statistics*, (New York: United Nations, 1981) .

Figure 4-1. Relationship between GNP and Energy Consumption in 1979

that developing countries' share of total world industrial output will be close to 40 percent by 1990, with middle-income countries expected to industrialize more rapidly than those whose incomes are low. These predictions are based on assumptions regarding international economic conditions that may turn out to be invalid, but they give some idea of how industrialization is expected to increase over the coming years.

For the region as a whole it is believed that industry accounts for 40 percent of fossil fuel use, transport for 35 percent, electricity generation for 15 percent, and 10 percent use is by households.[15] Against this background table 4-9 presents the percentage distribution of energy consumed in each sector of the economy for the five energy giants of the region at a ten-year interval. The predominance of industrial and transportation usages is clear. Only in Argentina has there been a decline in energy usage in transportation, as a percentage of total energy utilization, between 1967 and 1977. Mexico increased slightly, and Colombia, Brazil, and Venezuela grew the most rapidly. The differences are most notable in Colombia, where transportation accounted for 14.91 percent of energy utilization in 1967 and increased to 20.3 percent in 1977. This trend is paralleled by the growth of

Table 4-9
Percentage of Energy Consumption by Sector

	Industry	Transportation	Agriculture	Commercial	Public Service	Residential
Argentina						
1967	27.54	37.52	0.03	na	na	9.60
1977	33.84	35.86	na	1.64	1.56	17.19
Brazil						
1967	22.04[a]	19.84[a]	0.11	1.20	na	1.51
1977	28.77[a]	25.10[a]	na	na	na	na
Colombia						
1967	2.07	14.91	na	na	na	3.82
1977	6.34	20.30	na	na	0.13	6.66
Mexico						
1967	42.69	22.99	0.89	na	na	7.90
1977	52.68	23.71	0.35	0.60	0.41	4.27
Venezuela						
1967	39.90	29.94	0.06	0.28	na	4.60
1977	38.50	35.54	0.03	0.19	na	2.26

Source: International Energy Agency, *Workshop on Energy Data of Developing Countries, December 1978*, vol. 2. (Paris: OECD, 1979).

Note: Figures do not add up to 100 percent because of nonenergy uses of petroleum products, and energy not included elsewhere; includes commercial and noncommercial uses of energy.

[a]1976 data.

the industrial sector's share of total energy consumption. Together they reflect the overall industrialization trends in Colombia over this ten-year period. Brazil and Mexico indicate similar trends, although with smaller increases in transportation's energy consumption.

More detailed data on energy in Latin America are unfortunately not readily available. The input-output table for Mexico, 1970, yields some clues as to the share of oil use in different sectors of the economy, as well as distribution of refinery costs for individual sectors. The more recent input-output table (for 1978) is not publicly available at this writing. Table 4-10 reproduces, with some adjustments of classification, the key row from the 1970 table which provides some indication of uses of refined products.

By this accounting, in 1970 Mexico exported 3.2 percent of its refined products and consumed 22.5 percent in the private sector and 2.7 percent in government agencies. The total interindustry uses were 71 percent. The major sectoral use was in transportation, with no other sector even approximating the transport level of utilization.[16] In table 4-10 the share purchased of refined products by various economic sectors is only partly comparable to table 4-9, which is due, of course, to differences in years, categories, and level of aggregation.

Besides the Mexican case little other detailed information is available. For Central America, for instance, we know only that in El Salvador the

Table 4-10
Oil Consumption by Sector

Sector	Percentage of Total Consumption
Agriculture, cattle breeding, forestry, and fishing	7.6
Oil and gas extraction	0.9
Food products	4.4
Textiles and paper	1.0
Oil refining	5.3
Chemical production	1.6
Cement and construction	7.5
Manufactures and other products	1.9
Hotels and services	3.9
Transportation	20.2
Total interindustry	71.0
Private consumption	22.5
Government consumption	2.7
Change in stocks	0.7
Exports	3.2

Source: United Nations Development Program, Secretaria de Programacion y Presupuesto, Coordinacion General del Sistema Nacional de Informacion, *Matriz de Insumo-Producto de Mexico,* ano 1970, Tomo 2, Industria Manufactura (New York: United Nations, 1970).

transport sector accounts for 57 percent of all petroleum consumption, industry for 25.4 percent, and the residential and commercial sectors for 11.4 percent of all energy consumed.[17] But these figures are approximations at best.

Some observations on noncommercial energy uses, notably bagasse, including vegetable combustibles, firewood, and charcoal, provide additional insights into orders of magnitude. A more complete view would include dung, peat, tar, wood wastes, vegetal wastes, municipal wastes, and pulp wastes. The following estimates are calculated on the basis of thousand tons of oil equivalent on the basis of initial data including all other formal sources of energy, thereby introducing additional uncertainties. A note of caution is advised in interpreting the following numbers; they represent the best approximation possible, not irrefutable fact.

The five giants—Argentina, Brazil, Colombia, Mexico, Venezuela—all revealed a *declining* percentage of noncommercial energy of total final consumption as a group from 29 percent in 1967 to 20 percent in 1977. This decrease is the result of the more rapid decrease in other sectors' consumption of noncommercial energy (66 percent to 51 percent in 1977) which more than offsets the small overall increase from 26 percent to 28 percent for the five nations during that same decade. However, the range of percentages is so great as to undermine the significance of broad changes. For example, not all the countries experienced a relative decline in the amount of energy coming from noncommercial forms, and the relative increase in industry's share of total final consumption actually breaks down into two significant increases, one major decrease, and two minor decreases, thus no overall trend.[18]

Argentina, with the second lowest overall noncommercial energy share of final consumption in 1967 (11 percent) was the single exception in increasing to 20 percent by 1977. This was due principally to the large increase in bagasse used by industry (from 1,070 th/toe in 1967 to 4,970 th/toe in 1977). None of this bagasse was used in either the iron and steel or chemical and petrochemical industries. The use of firewood/charcoal actually decreased in absolute terms, from 1,040 th/toe to 980 th/toe during the same period. All of it was consumed in residential use. Thus overall noncommercial energy nearly tripled, from 2,110 th/toe to 5,950 th/toe, a faster growth rate than either commercial energy or total energy.[19]

Brazil experienced a declining share of its energy consumption met by the noncommercial sector over this period, yet still had the highest overall usage of noncommercial energy among the five nations, 23,719 th/toe in 1967 and a slight growth to 28,088 th/toe in 1977. Brazil's growth in industrial use of noncommercial energy (from 28 to 58 percent) is similar in percentage terms to that of Argentina (20 to 48 percent), but no details are readily available on specific industries using bagasse. Firewood/charcoal use in other sectors increased slightly, from 86 to 88 percent. Nevertheless, these two areas of growth were still less than overall energy consumption growth in the economy, so their share declined from 51 percent of the total in 1967 to 32 percent in 1977. The expansion of gasohol use may extend the use of vegetal wastes, but statistics since 1977 are not detailed.[20]

Colombia has the second highest overall share of noncommercial energy but experienced the largest decline in industry's share of noncommercial energy consumption. This is more significant in percentage terms (falling from 73 to 29 percent), given the increase in real terms (197 th/toe to 310 th/toe by 1977). In other sectors, however, Colombia actually decreased noncommercial energy consumption in real terms, from 5,697 to 5,310 th/toe. Overall Colombia's noncommercial energy use went from 44 percent in total final consumption in 1967 to 32 percent in 1977.[21]

Both Mexico and Venezuela are quite similar in sharing low overall reliance on noncommercial energy, particularly in industrial sectors. Mexico had become the lowest in relative terms by 1977, declining from 9 percent overall and 5 percent in industry to 4 percent overall and 3 percent in industry. This more than offset the small real increase in industrial noncommercial energy consumption (796 th/toe to 894 th/toe), thus yielding a national decline from 3,091 th/toe to 2,937 th/toe. Needless to say, Mexico has a relatively large energy consumption figure which explains the lowest relative figures for noncommercial energy.[22]

Venezuela had the lowest rate of industrial consumption of bagasse (131 th/toe or 3 percent of total industrial energy consumption) in 1967. By 1977 it had risen to 300 th/toe and 4 percent, still a very low percentage compared to other South American nations. Firewood/charcoal consumption in other sectors was appreciably higher but still declining in relative terms (57 percent in 1967 and 43 percent in 1977). Overall final consumption of noncommercial energy grew by a third from 1967 to 1977, but in relative terms this meant going from 14 percent to 10 percent.[23]

These figures point to an important reality, namely that noncommercial energy use is decreasing as a share of final consumption in most countries. In fact, the declines are in absolute terms for both Mexico and Colombia, while noncommercial energy uses grew only very slowly in Venezuela and Brazil. Bagasse consumption seems to be growing more than that of firewood and charcoal. Residential and other sectors' use of noncommercial energy is declining more rapidly than that of industry.

Investments in experimental programs for alternative sources of energy had not yet had an effect on overall demand structure. Yet there the trends do indicate magnitude of noncommercial energy uses over the past decade or so. Success of the innovative energy programs noted in the previous chapter will be measured in terms of the share of noncommercial energy sources in total energy use. The structure of final demand would have to reflect these changes if investments in energy alternatives are to be viewed as a success.

This general review of demographic characteristics and economic activity indicates continued pressures toward greater energy use; declining use of energy for noncommercial purposes suggests greater use of petroleum rather than nonconventional sources of energy. Conversely, however, experimentation with new energy programs and efforts to expand uses of nonconventional fuels appear as a potential countervailing force mediating pressures for growing energy demand.

The following chapter focuses on transportation in Latin America, energy use in the transport sector, and critical issues for transport policy. This emphasis on transportation is due largely to our view that energy demand in the years to come will be tied to existing transport networks and related facilities and that efforts to change patterns of energy consumption are highly constrained by existing networks in place.

Notes

1. United Nations, *Demographic Yearbook* (New York: United Nations, 1978); and United Nations, *Demographic Yearbook: Historical Supplement*, Special Issue (New York: United Nations, 1979). The research assistance of Lily Ling in this chapter is gratefully acknowledged.

2. U.N. Economic Commission for Latin America, *Statistical Yearbook for Latin America, 1978* (New York: United Nations, 1979).

3. See *International Migration Review*, Mary M. Kritz and Douglas T. Gurak (eds.), *International Migration in Latin America*, 13 (Fall 1979).

4. Maria Adriana de Villegas, "Migration and Economic Integration in Latin America: The Andean Group," *International Migration Review*, 11 (1977), pp. 59-76.

5. Ibid., p. 62.

6. Ibid.

7. Ibid., p. 63.

8. Estimates provided by the United Nations Fund for Population Activities; see also CELADE, *Boletin Demografico*, 8 (July 1980), pp. 10-12.

9. These estimates have been made by the United Nations earlier and are subject to revision.

10. Based on data from United Nations, *Statistical Yearbook for Latin America 1978*, 1978.

11. Ibid.

12. United Nations, *Statistical Yearbook for Latin America, 1978*, 1978.

13. Ibid.

14. Ibid. Some of the smaller islands of the Caribbean (Barbados, Jamaica, Puerto Rico) have also experienced a decline in gross domestic investments.

15. Based on data from the International Energy Agency, *Energy Workshop on Developing Countries, December 1979* (OECD: Paris, 1979).

16. Secretaria de Programacion y Presupuesto, Coordinacion General del Sistema Nacional de Informacion: *Matriz de Insumo—Producto de Mexico Ano 1970*, vol. 2 (Mexico: Industria Manufactura, United Nations Development Program, 1970 [?]).

17. Superintendent of Energy, "Energy Analysis of the Transportation Sector in El Salvador," prepared for the Seminario "Impacto del Costa de la Energia en el Sector Transporte," 1-3 December 1980, Bogota, Colombia. Translation available at the Department of Political Science, Massachusetts Institute of Technology, Cambridge.

18. International Energy Agency, *Energy Workshop on Developing Countries*, 1979.

19. Ibid.

20. Ibid.

21. Ibid.

22. Ibid.

23. Ibid.

5

Transportation and Development

The Role of the Transportation Sector

The size, nature, and structure of the transportation sector determines patterns of use for conventional energy sources.[a] Since most of Latin America relies heavily on cars and trucks, the price and availability of gasoline is of immediate concern. Diversifying transportation networks on short order is impossible. As a result the region is faced with some immediate costs as well as with critical choices for future investments in that sector.

The size of the transport sector as a percentage of GDP is presented in table 5-1. These figures include communication and storage as well, so they do not reflect precise consumption patterns. Recall that for many Latin American countries energy consumption is considerably higher than for developing countries. This fact reinforces Latin America's unique problem: the region is rapidly industrializing; energy use follows accordingly. For the giants and some smaller countries the fundamental policy issues now pertain to the rate and nature of future structural change in the transformation to full industrialization.

Looking at transportation in relation to GDP, in figure 5-1, some important inferences can be made:

allocations to transportation increase as the level of growth in GDP increases;

there is a clear dichotomy between the five giants—Brazil, Mexico, Argentina, Venezuela, and Colombia—and the rest of Latin America;

investments in transportation appear consistent with investment in the economy generally.

This simple association between transportation and the general economy highlights the critical role of transportation in development as a vehicle for growth and as part of the essential infrastructure.

Transportation's contribution to gross fixed capital formation is seen in figure 5-2. This relationship suggests that:

---

[a]This chapter is a revised version of parts of a paper prepared for the Seminario "Impacto del Costa de la Energia en el Sector Transporte," 1-3 December 1980, Bogota, Colombia. Substantial revisions and expansion of the basic data were undertaken. See Nazli Choucri, *Energy in Latin America: Transportation, Development, and Public Policy.* Prepared for the Seminario "Impacto del Costa del Energia en el Sector Transporte," 1-3 December 1980, Bogota, Colombia.

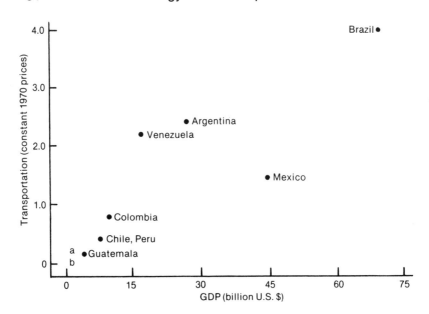

Source: U.N. Economic Commission for Latin America, *Statistical Yearbook for Latin America 1978* (New York: United Nations, 1978); International Monetary Fund, *International Financial Statistics* (Washington, D.C.: 1979).

a Bolivia, El Salvador.

b Costa Rica, Ecuador, Guyana, Honduras, Nicaragua, Panama, Paraguay, Uruguay.

Figure 5-1. Relationship between GDP and Transportation in 1977

increases in transportation accompany investments in infrastructure;

beyond a certain point investments in transportation have little effect on infrastructure or capital formation;

in such cases heavy investments in transportation result in only marginal strengthening of infrastructure;

states with higher GDP have invested a greater percentage of GDP in transportation; those with lower GDP have lower shares of transport in relation to GDP.

Parenthetically, with few exceptions the countries of Latin America have a larger transport sector relative to GDP than the United States. This reflects, of course, differences in level of development and evolution in investment priorities. In Latin America investments in transportation constitute the basis for overall infrastructure, while in the United States they reflect

Table 5-1
Transportation, Communications, and Storage as Percentage of the GDP of Latin America

	1970	1971	1972	1973	1974	1975	1976	1977	Growth Rate
Argentina	10.1	10.0	9.9	10.0	9.8	9.7	9.6	9.7	-0.6
Bolivia	8.9	8.7	8.9	8.8	9.1	9.2	9.3	9.6	1.1
Brazil	5.7	5.4	5.4	5.6	5.7	6.1	6.0	5.9	0.5
Chile	5.7	5.6	5.5	5.8	5.4	5.5	5.6	5.6	-.25
Colombia	7.4	7.5	7.6	7.7	8.3	8.6	8.9	9.0	2.8
Costa Rica	4.8	5.0	5.1	5.5	6.0	6.2	6.3	6.3	3.9
Ecuador	7.4	7.5	7.0	6.3	5.7	5.4	5.3	5.6	-4.0
El Salvador	5.3	5.1	5.1	5.1	5.5	5.6	5.7	5.9	1.5
Guatemala	3.5	3.6	3.8	3.9	4.1	4.3	4.2	4.3	2.9
Guyana	5.9	5.7	5.9	6.3	6.0	6.3			1.3
Honduras	6.7	6.6	6.7	6.8	6.9	6.9	6.8	6.8	0.2
Mexico	2.6	2.7	2.8	2.9	3.0	3.2	3.2	3.2	3.0
Nicaragua	5.8	5.8	6.0	6.1	6.0	5.8	5.8	5.8	0
Panama	5.6	6.0	6.0	6.3	7.0	7.1	7.4	7.3	3.8
Paraguay	4.2	4.2	4.3	4.4	4.7	5.0	5.0	4.9	2.2
Peru	4.6	4.6	4.8	5.0	5.0	5.0	5.0	5.0	1.2
Uruguay	8.6	8.9	8.8	9.0	9.2	9.2	9.3	9.3	1.1
Venezuela	10.9	11.2	12.0	11.6	12.1	12.7	13.1	13.6	3.2

Source: U.N. Economic Commission for Latin America, *Statistical Yearbook for Latin America 1978* (New York: United Nations, 1978).

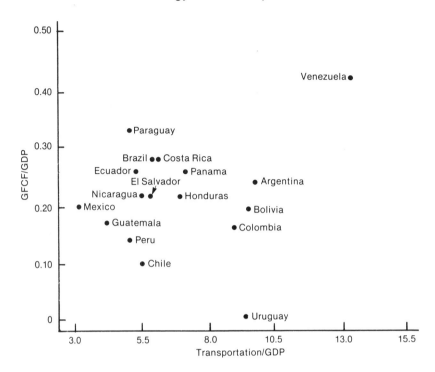

Source: U.N. Economic Commission for Latin America, *Statistical Yearbook for Latin America 1978* (New York: United Nations, 1978).

Figure 5-2. Relationship between Gross Fixed Capital Formation and Transportation in 1977

maintenance, as well as the expansion of new rather than of primary networks. Further the size of the gross domestic product in the United States masks both the magnitude and the importance of this sector. Variations among Latin American countries in the transport share of the GDP reflect both achievements to date and opportunities for further expansion. In only three countries has the transport sector exhibited some marginal declines as a percentage of GDP (Argentina, Chile, and Ecuador), and in only one case is the decline in the transport share of GDP greater than that of the United States.[1]

Transportation's role in development, however, cannot be limited to economic indicators only. The social and demographic context of each nation provides the distinctive inputs for transport planning.

Population and Transportation

Urbanization is often an important determinant of infrastructure development. Figure 5-3 shows the relationship of urbanization to transportation. Venezuela stands out as one country whose investment in transportation attempts to match its urban growth rate. Other countries following this mode are Argentina, Uruguay, and Colombia. The rest of Latin America, however, has either high transportation investment and low urban growth (Bolivia, Honduras) or high urban growth with relatively low transportation investment (Mexico, Chile, Peru).

A closer look at select components of the transport sector reveals the following: with respect to car ownership, figure 5-4 indicates the relationship

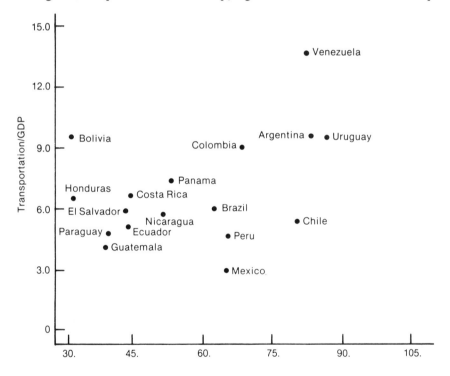

Urban Population as Percent of Total Population (current estimate)

Source: The World Bank, *World Tables, 1980* (Washington, D.C.: 1980); U.N. Economic Commission for Latin America, *Statistical Yearbook for Latin America 1978* (New York: United Nations, 1978).

Figure 5-3. Relationship between Transportation and Urbanization in 1977

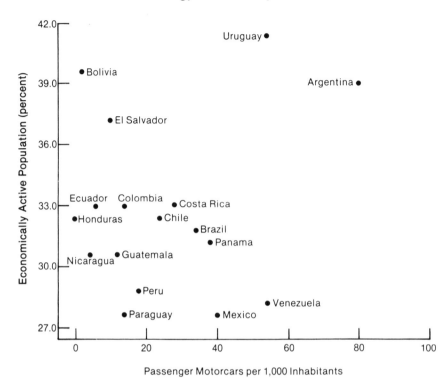

Source: U.N. Economic Commission for Latin America, *Statistical Yearbook for Latin America 1978* (New York: United Nations, 1978).

Figure 5-4. Relationship between Economically Active Population and Passenger Motorcars in 1975

between economically active populations and passenger motorcars. Bolivia and Argentina, for example, share the same level of employment but diverge to two opposite extremes where car ownership is concerned. With respect to railway traffic, figure 5-5 shows railway traffic in relation to total population. Colombia is singled out in its relative irresponsiveness of rail facilities to population size.

Latin America is one of the least dense regions of the world. The sheer dispersion of population necessitates strong transport networks. Figure 5-6 bears this out (compare figure 5-7). The lack of a general trend in both South and Central America indicates a lack of policy deliberation to correlate transportation investment (infrastructure) with general population

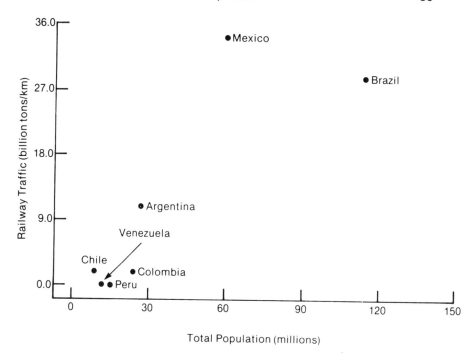

Source: U.N. Economic Commission for Latin America, *Statistical Yearbook for Latin America 1978* (New York: United Nations, 1978).
Note: Data not available for Bolivia, Costa Rica, Ecuador, El Salvador, Guatemala, Guyana, Honduras, Nicaragua, Panama, Paraguay, Uruguay.

Figure 5-5. Relationship between Population and Railway Traffic for Select Countries in 1976

growth and congestion. This incongruence is exemplified by high transportation investment and low density in some countries (Panama, Honduras, Nicaragua, Bolivia) and the reverse situation in others (Ecuador, El Salvador, Brazil, Chile, Peru). Mexico's low transportation investment will present grave problems for the country's petroleum industry. Already transportation facilities are a major bottleneck for the oil sector.

These figures convey an implicit message: the demographic structure of Latin America necessitates expansive transport facilities. These facilities place extensive claims on energy use. Prospects for energy "savings" are highly constrained by the disposition of the numbers at hand—the demography of the region—and their economic activities. Population growth, increasing cityward movement, and growing economic activity con-

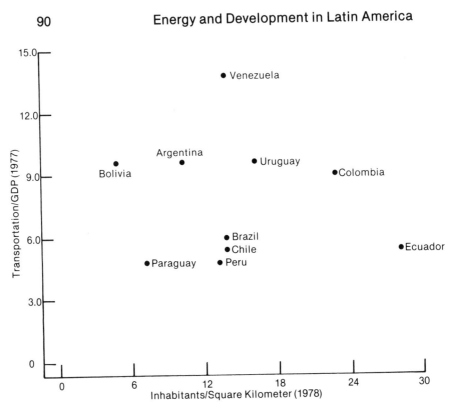

Source: UNESCO, *Statistical Yearbook 1980* (New York: United Nations, 1980); U.N. Economic Commission for Latin America, *Statistical Yearbook for Latin America 1978* (New York: United Nations, 1978).

Note: Data are for two different years; compare with caution.

Figure 5-6. Relationship between Density and Transportation in South America

tribute to higher energy use. The evidence in the previous chapter, when reviewed in conjunction with inferences presented here, points to one conclusion: in the 1980s the rate of energy consumption in Latin America will increase relative to the two previous decades. The sheer momentum of growth—at various levels of development—will force demand upward. Adjustments may well occur into the 1980s, but energy use in the next few years will be shaped by the momentum of the 1970s.

Transport Networks and Energy Utilization

In developing countries energy use in transportation, of course, is determined largely by concentration of economic activity, disposition of population,

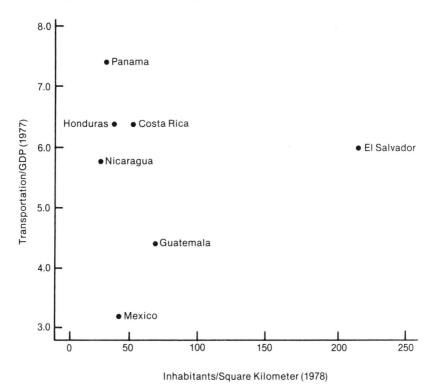

Source: UNESCO, *Statistical Yearbook 1980* (New York: United Nations, 1980); U.N. Economic Commission for Latin America, *Statistical Yearbook for Latin America 1978* (New York: United Nations, 1978).

Note: Data are for two different years; compare with caution.

Figure 5-7. Relationship between Density and Transportation in Central America

development of road and other transport networks, and growth of income. For Latin America size alone is not a notable determinant of transportation investments. If we look at the relationship between transportation's share of GDP and size (in terms of area), we find no strong association. Brazil, a clear outlier, allocates less emphasis to transportation than do many other, smaller countries. (See figure 5-8.) The interesting point here is that countries with much smaller areas (Uruguay, Bolivia, El Salvador, Ecuador) spend as much on transportation per square kilometer of land as do the much larger countries (Brazil, Argentina).

In this context four giants of Latin America—Argentina, Brazil, Mexico, and Venezuela—account for 75 percent of Latin American paved roads and

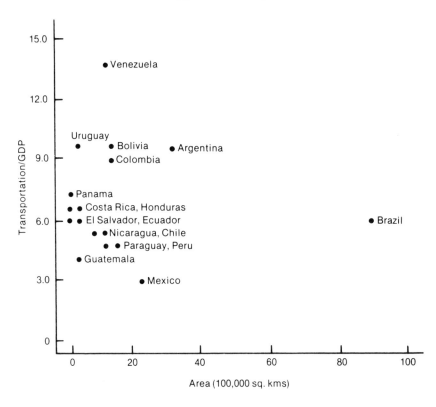

Source: UNESCO, *Statistical Yearbook 1980* (New York: United Nations, 1980); U.N. Economic Commission for Latin America, *Statistical Yearbook for Latin America 1978* (New York: United Nations, 1978).

Figure 5-8. Relationship between Size and Transportation in 1977

85 percent of total roads. Argentina, Mexico, and Brazil possess 81 percent of total South American railroad mileage and carry 94 percent of freight traffic and 88 percent of the passenger traffic. The profile of coastal and inland waterways is the same. Argentina has 74 percent of total inland waterway ship tonnage, while Brazil controls 73 percent of total coastal ship capacity. Argentina, Brazil, and Venezuela together account for 89 percent of coastal tanker tonnage, and 60 percent of all other coastal fleet tonnage. Argentina and Brazil also have the two largest overseas merchant fleets.

These four countries, in addition to Colombia, share the predominance of roads in the distribution of energy consumption among types of transportation. This share ranges from 83 to 89 percent, with a slowly decreasing trend. The greatest gains during the decade of 1967 to 1977 were made by air transportation, from approximately 5 percent of total energy consumed by transportation, up to 11 percent.

For the five giants as a group the share of energy utilized in transport by road decreased marginally over the ten-year period 1966 to 1976. The share for railroads also appeared to be declining slowly. Insufficient figures concerning inland and coastal waterways bar a clear conclusion. By contrast, air transportation's share of energy use doubled over the decade. (See table 5-2 for select trends.)

In terms of type of energy consumed, the transportation sector of all five countries is almost completely reliant on petroleum products. Railroads use some solid fuels, namely coal, and the Argentinian railroads are electrified to some extent. In addition all energy consumed is in the commercial sector, unlike the industrial or other sectors where noncommercial energy makes a contribution. While this is not surprising, it does point to the direct impacts of refined petroleum costs and availability on the transportation sector.

Brazil dwarfs the group by the fact of its geographic and demographic size. It leads in total energy consumption, and in energy use for road and air transportation. It has the largest number, *and* the largest number of kilometers, of paved roads and the fastest per capita growth rate for car ownership among the five through 1975, although Paraguay is higher through 1970. Though second to Argentina in total railroad mileage, and second to Mexico in freight traffic, it is growing far more rapidly than any other country. Its coastal fleet is the largest in Latin America in all categories except for inland waterways. In terms of energy distribution, it leads the other four in percent of energy consumed by air transportation (14 percent).

Table 5-2
Distribution of Energy Consumption in the Transportation Sector as Percentage of Total Energy Consumed

		Road	*Rail*	*Air*	*Water*
Argentina	1967	83.8	12.1	3.8	0.3
	1977	83.3	9.2	5.3	2.1
Brazil	1967	85.5	5.4	6.3	3.0
	1977	86.0	0.1	13.9	
Colombia	1967	89.8	1.8	8.4	
	1977	87.5		12.5	
Mexico	1967	90.8	4.5	4.7	
		(88.9)[a]		(11.1)[a]	
	1977	57.8		7.2	
Venezuela	1967	93.6		6.4	
	1977	86.9		13.1	

[a]With unexplained residual factor.

Source: International Energy Agency, *Workshop on Energy Data of Developing Countries, December 1978*, vol. 2 (Paris: OECD, 1979).

Argentina is distinguished by having the largest rail network and an extensive rail system (39,000 km), probably a reflection of its earlier development in an era when rails moved the bulk of goods. In Argentina government statistics indicate that passenger transport in 1977 consumed 50 percent of energy in the transport sector. Its trains carry the most passengers of any South American rail network and are behind only Brazil and Mexico in freight traffic.

Argentina also has the largest inland waterways fleet and ranks second only to Brazil in most other categories of merchant marine. Distortions within the rail network make it not well utilized, however. For example, 70 percent of the track network is over forty years old; 40 percent cannot be used; and 80 percent of traffic employs 47 percent of the system.[2] It has the second largest road network and the second fastest per capita growth rate in car ownership. In general Argentina supports a relatively high level of energy consumption, particularly in transportation. Government figures indicate an annual growth rate between 1977 and 1980 of 3.62 percent and a relative stability in the structure of demand. In 1980 road traffic accounted for 79.2 percent of transport, waterways for 6.9 percent and railways for 3.55 percent. Overall transportation leads industry in energy consumption by a greater margin than for any of the other four except for Colombia, so the share of energy consumption for transportation alone is not a definitive statistic on the state of that sector's development. In 1980 the government estimated that the annual growth rate of energy use in transportation since 1977 was 3.98 percent. Government officials argued that a 25 percent reduction of use could be made through a variety of policies, targeted at the networks as well as usage patterns. A key aspect of the policies envisaged was expansion of mass transport systems in urban areas. Expansion of such basic facilities was viewed as having a strong potential for conservation.[3]

Venezuela is the third ranking South American country in many transportation indicators. It exhibits a good convergence in transportation's and industry's shares of total energy consumption. Of the five countries it had the highest proportion of its transportation energy devoted to roads in 1967, and air transportation has made substantial gains during the past decade. Venezuela also had the fastest energy consumption growth rates during that decade for both road and air transportation. The country relies totally on petroleum in the transport sector.

Although the development of an overall energy policy and its implications for transport use remain yet to be articulated, the government has experimented with a series of increasing formalized interventions in the transport sector, including establishing "no driving day" in certain metropolitan areas (thereby inducing increased use of mass transport). In the near future gasoline subsidies might be eliminated to better reflect the true scarcities. The entire energy sector is presently being examined to determine the country's overall potential with respect to substitution possibilities.[4]

Colombia does not approximate the levels of transportation and energy consumption of the other countries, but it is rapidly growing. It ranks fifth in both types of rail traffic and has the coal resources to develop this type of transportation. Though air transportation's share of consumption is expanding rapidly, it is third after Brazil and Venezuela. As mentioned before, transportation gets the lion's share of energy resources, but Colombia is working from a smaller base than the other four nations.

Mexico is the only nation in which industry consumes significantly more energy than the transportation sector. This is somewhat surprising considering that Mexico has the third largest road network in Latin America, a relatively high rate of per capita car ownership, and the highest level of energy consumption in road transportation. This reflects either an unusually developed or an energy-intensive industrial sector. From 1967 to 1977 Mexico had by far the slowest growth in road transportation energy consumption and the second highest growth rate for air transportation, potentially signaling shifts in transportation mode.

Latin America's energy problems in the transportation sector signify a series of general structural problems that influence broader issues of public and energy policy, notably regional development, industrial policy, and infrastructure planning, in addition to energy consumption.[5] Overriding dependence on trucks and cars for transport ties transportation to petroleum. With the exception of Argentina railways play a relatively small role in transport networks. While Brazil's gasohol program provides some relief to petroleum shortages, it remains limited at best. Only countries with large expanses of uncultivated agricultural land can even envisage such options. Lack of developed infrastructure constrains industrial development, repeatedly creating bottlenecks, as in the Mexican steel industry which was hampered by the inability to transport raw materials rapidly.

To place these observations in context, figure 5-9 relates number of passenger motorcars per thousand inhabitants (often a good indicator of economic development and urban life) to consumption of petroleum. The distribution of the Latin American countries is illustrative of their urbanization as well as their utilization of energy in this one critical mode of transportation.

On the more optimistic side, however, transportation's share of total energy consumption can be expected to decline as infrastructural development progresses. This development also entails a proportionately shrinking role for road transportation and a rapidly growing one for air transportation. Rail transportation does not appear to be making the contribution it could, or does in more developed regions. Nonetheless, the energy consumed by these five countries' transportation sectors is still growing at an annual

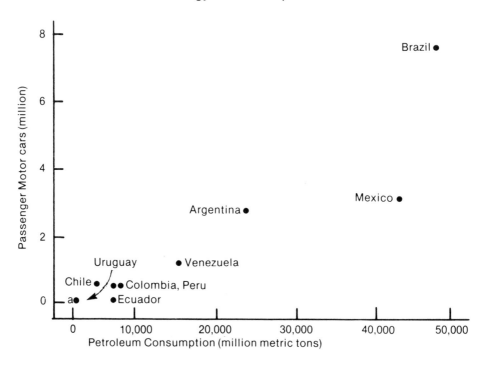

Source: U.N. Department of International Economic and Social Affairs, *1979 Yearbook of World Energy Statistics* (New York: United Nations, 1981); Business International Corporation, *Worldwide Economic Indicators, Comparative Summary for 131 Countries, 1981 Annual Edition* (New York: 1981).
[a]Bolivia, Costa Rica, El Salvador, Guatemala, Guyana, Honduras, Nicaragua, Panama, Paraguay.

Figure 5-9. Relationship between Energy Consumption and Passenger Motor car Usage in 1978

rate of 2.4 to 3 percent, a growth that will require careful consideration in the development plans of any Latin America nation. (Only Argentina has decreased its share of energy consumption in transportation. This range of growth rates is elaborated in chapter 4.

Issues for Transport Policy

The high utilization of energy in the transportation sector brings a convergence in problems of public policy—those of the transport sector with those of national energy constraints as they must inevitably affect overall developmental strategies and investments. There is already evidence of adjustment, new scarcities, and change. Some of the adjustment is obviously painful. For example, petroleum shortages in major metropolitan areas of Latin America such as Sao Paulo and Lima have produced bus and taxi strikes, along with the necessary general decrease in the use of private vehicles. Incidences of social unrest may be part of an overall adjustment. In Brazil, however, there is already evidence of change. A recent study by the Rio newspaper *O Globo* reports a 20 percent drop in the number of vehicles on city roads as a result of the increase in petroleum prices.[6]

The urban-based structure of transport networks in industrial economies has defined the nature of the policy problem for these countries, and the centrality of the fuel-economy issue. In developing countries investments in transportation assume a more holistic guise, since these often entail the simultaneous expansion of urban, rural, and regional networks, in addition to simultaneous investments in different modes of transport—rail, road, air, marine.

Even in the absence of an energy crisis the issues for public policy in the transportation sector would still be as critical, requiring focused attention to policy matters in terms of both the levels and figures of investments required. With escalating petroleum prices, the cost issues become even more salient. More important still are interventions to influence the demand for transportation and the policies designed to affect the future supply of transport facilities. The energy scarcities have precipitated a debate in the transportation sector that would have been inevitable sooner or later. Among the issues of concern are: determining the criteria for future investments in types of transportation modes, undertaking continued assessment of costs and benefits associated with alternative choices, and examining the factors that influence the conduct of public policy.

Energy-economy interactions, however, are not limited to energy uses in different sectors of the economy. Yet to be reviewed are the effects on the economy of changing prices of energy and of adjustments to these changes. The following chapter examines some macroeconomic effects of the new energy environment for Latin America, noting the region's overall adjustments and efforts to reduce the impacts and imbalances induced by higher oil prices.

Notes

1. See The World Bank, *World Tables*, 1980 (Washington, D.C., 1980). In 1977 seven countries in Latin America exceeded the United States in their share of transportation as a percentage of GDP. These are: Argentina, Bolivia, Colombia, Honduras, Panama, Uruguay, and Venezuela. The research assistance of Lily Ling is gratefully acknowledged.

2. Secretary of State for Transportation and Public Works, "Consumption and Costs of Energy in the Transportation Sector in the Republic of Argentina," prepared for the Seminario "Impacto del Costa de la Energia en el Sector Transporte," 1-3 December 1980, Bogota, Colombia. Translation available at the Department of Political Science, Massachusetts Institute of Technology, Cambridge, Mass.

3. Ibid.; and Secretary of State for Transport and Public Works, "Transportation Sector in Argentina," prepared for the Seminario "Impacto del Costa de la Energia en el Sector Transporte," 1-3 December 1980, Bogota, Colombia. Translation available at the Department of Political Science, Massachusetts Institute of Technology, Cambridge, Mass.

4. German Pulido Santana, "Considerations on the Transport Sector and Energy Consumption in Venezuela," prepared for the Seminario "Impacto del Costa de la Energia en el Sector Transporte," 1-3 December 1980, Bogota, Colombia. Translation available at the Department of Political Science, Massachusetts Institute of Technology, Cambridge, Mass.

5. Cloraldino Soares Severo, "The Energy Problem and Transport: The Brazilian Experience," prepared for the Seminario "Impacto del Costa de la Energia en el Sector Transporte," 1-3 December 1980, Bogota, Colombia. Translation available at the Department of Political Science, Massachusetts Institute of Technology, Cambridge, Mass.

6. *Latin America Weekly Report,* December 14, 1979, p. 78.

6 Macroeconomic Effects: Inflation, Balance of Payments, and External Debt

The more immediate effects of the oil price increases pertain to the economy and, in particular, aggravate persistent macroeconomic problems of inflation and balance of payments deficits.[1] For Latin American countries which already suffer some of the highest rates of inflation in the world periodic oil price hikes create added strains on payments positions. The inevitable response to these pressures is to cut investment programs. Yet external debts, created by earlier patterns of expenditures, increase, adding to the strain. Despite all these pressures Latin America has adjusted remarkably well to stresses and strains. The problems are legion, but the adjustments have been impressive, nonetheless. It is difficult to untangle the problems associated with growth from those created by chronic payments problems and structural distortions. Although most of the region's problems are not created by the changing price of oil, the adjustments of the 1970s were propelled by these changes.

Inflation

Inflation is Latin America's perennial economic problem. It has assumed new proportions with the oil price increases throughout the 1970s. The region's structural problems were exacerbated, worsening what appeared to be an already drastic situation. For oil-exporting countries the sudden inflow of oil revenue contributed to inflation pressure, although their inflation rates were moderate compared to the other industrializing countries of Latin America. For oil-poor countries expansion of public and private spending that far outstripped economic productivity, aggravated by higher fuel prices, contributed further to the structural problems endemic to inflation.

A comparison of inflationary levels in Latin American countries reported by the Inter-American Development Bank reveals the wide range of inflation levels in the region and changes over the period 1976-1979. This comparison is useful, although it cannot reveal much about the effects of the "oil shock." Of importance is the growing number of states that are classified as having "high inflation." Argentina, Uruguay, Brazil, Chile, and Peru stand out as experiencing very high inflation, although inflation for all of these countries except Brazil decreased slightly in 1980 (see table 6-1). The oil-exporting countries, Venezuela, Mexico, and Ecuador, have experienced more moderate inflation, but this inflation is not abating and shows signs of continued increases. Clearly, it cannot be claimed that the influx of oil revenues diminishes inflation; these three countries all exhibited stable inflation rates during 1976 to 1978, and it is possible that they were somewhat shielded from the dislocating effects of massive expenditures for energy imports.

According to estimates of consumer price increases provided by the U.N. Economic Commission for Latin America, the rate of inflation for many Latin American countries declined from 1977 to 1980. Even the average rate of inflation for the region as a whole has shown signs of improvement. These signs are fragile at best, but there is no evidence of overwhelming deterioration. Table 6-1 ranks the countries by the extent of their inflation. In some cases, however, the sheer magnitude of inflation makes direct comparisons difficult. If balance of payments effects are taken into account, it becomes more plausible to argue that Latin American nations have adjusted remarkably well to the oil price hikes.

Balance of Payments

The oil price increase of 1973 had the general effect of contributing to the balance of payments deficits of most Latin American countries in 1974 and 1975. The negative impact on the current account of the balance of payments of the net importing countries is demonstrated by the rise in the total deficit from $3.8 billion in 1973 to a peak of $12.1 billion in 1975.[2] This jump reflects higher oil prices as well as the deterioration of world trade following these increases. Since 1975, however, Latin America has made substantial adjustments. Higher prices for certain primary commodities in conjunction with a decline in the real price of oil contributed to the stabilization of current account deficits, if not the creation of surpluses, for most of the oil-importing countries of Latin America.[3]

In addition the economic burden of extensive development programs was being felt, and impacts of previous commitments were becoming apparent. However, as we note in a subsequent chapter, to some extent negative financial effects were being offset by increased availability of funds from oil-exporting countries that appeared on capital markets and also from the new assistance programs sponsored by both OPEC and individual oil-exporting countries.[4] Although extensive balance-of-payments deficits have been avoided, it has often been at the price of incurring further indebtedness.

Table 6-1
Inflation in Latin America

	1976[a]	1977[a]	1978[a]	1979[b]	1979[c]	1980[c]
Hyperinflation (over 200 percent)	Argentina 443.2					
	Chile 211.9					
High Inflation (15-200 percent)	Uruguay 50.7	Argentina 176.1	Argentina 175.5	Argentina 170.0+	Argentina 139.7	Argentina 88.9
	Brazil 41.9	Chile 92.0	Peru 57.8	Uruguay 80.0	Uruguay 83.1	Brazil 87.0
	Peru 33.5	Uruguay 58.1	Uruguay 44.6	Brazil 65.0+	Brazil 76.0	Peru 59.1
	Colombia 17.4	Brazil 43.7	Chile 40.1	Peru 60.0	Nicaragua 70.3	Bolivia 50.0
	Mexico 16.1	Peru 38.1	Brazil 38.7	Chile 40.0+	Peru 66.7	Uruguay 49.3
		Colombia 30.0	Jamaica 34.6	Colombia 25.0+	Bolivia 45.5	Chile 31.6
		Mexico 26.4	Mexico 17.5	Mexico 20.0+	Chile 38.9	Nicaragua 30.0
			Colombia 17.4	Venezuela 20.0	Paraguay 35.7	Mexico 28.2
			Guyana 15.3	Paraguay 20.0	Colombia 29.8	Colombia 27.0
				Bolivia 16.0+	Dominican Republic 26.2	Jamaica 26.4
				Ecuador 15.0+	Venezuela 20.7	Barbados 23.0
				Dominican Republic 15.0+	Mexico 20.0	Venezuela 22.2
				Costa Rica 15.0+	Jamaica 19.8	Honduras 20.7
				Panama 15.0+	Trinidad and Tobago 19.5	Costa Rica 18.2
					Guyana 19.4	El Salvador 17.2
					Honduras 18.9	Paraguay 16.6
					Barbados 16.8	Dominican Republic 15.7
					Haiti 15.4	Guyana 15.7
						Trinidad and Tobago 15.6
						Ecuador 15.1

Table 6-1 (continued)

	1976[a]		1977[a]		1978[a]		1979[b]		1979[c]		1980[c]	
Moderate Inflation (5-15 percent)	Guatemala	10.7	Ecuador	13.0	El Salvador	13.2	Trinidad and Tobago	na	El Salvador	14.8	Ecuador	15.1
	Trinidad and Tobago	10.5	Dominican Republic	12.9	Ecuador	11.7	Barbados	na	Guatemala	13.7	Panama	13.6
	Jamaica	9.6	Guatemala	12.6	Paraguay	10.8	Bahamas	na	Costa Rica	13.2	Guatemala	9.6
	Guyana	9.0	Trinidad and Tobago	11.9	Trinidad and Tobago	10.2	Haiti	na	Panama	10.0	Haiti	6.3
	Dominican Republic	7.7	El Salvador	11.9	Barbados	9.5			Ecuador	9.0		
	Venezuela	7.6	Nicaragua	11.4	Guatemala	8.0						
	El Salvador	7.0	Jamaica	11.4	Venezuela	7.2						
	Haiti	7.0	Paraguay	9.3	Honduras	6.2						
			Honduras	8.3	Costa Rica	6.0						
			Barbados	8.3	Bahamas	6.0						
			Guyana	8.2								
			Bolivia	8.1								
			Venezuela	7.7								
			Haiti	6.5								
Price Stability (less than 5 percent)	Barbados	5.0	Panama	4.5	Nicaragua	4.5						
	Honduras	4.9	Costa Rica	4.2	Panama	4.2						
	Paraguay	4.5	Bahamas	3.3	Dominican Republic	3.5						
	Bolivia	4.5			Haiti	3.4						
	Bahamas	4.3										
	Panama	4.0										
	Costa Rica	3.5										
	Nicaragua	2.8										

[a] Data from Inter-American Development Bank, cited in *Latin American Weekly Report*, November 2, 1979, pp. 9-10.
[b] Data from *Latin America Weekly Report*, November 2, 1979, pp. 9-10.
[c] Estimate of U.N. Commission for Latin America, as reported in *World Business Weekly*, August 24, 1981, p. 32.

Comparative trends in balance of payments and expenditures on oil imports are presented in figures 6-1 through 6-6. The purpose is to obtain a glimpse of the overall payments position. This view is partial at best, since it does not provide the entire context for financial assessment, nor the history underlying these trends, but only one set of indicators of the overall financial position. Of course any economy must be valued in terms of several objectives: inflation, payments position, debt management, and more socially oriented criteria such as employment and income distribution. Therefore comparisons such as these must be viewed with caution, given different national currencies, domestic inflation trends, and adjustment policies. Yet these trends do reveal payments positions for the past ten years and indicate both oil-related pressures and subsequent adjustment efforts.

In the case of Argentina, the third largest oil producer of Latin America, oil-price changes created an immediate and sharp increase in the country's deficit during 1974 and 1975. Argentina's ability to reach near self-sufficiency in petroleum production has almost totally negated the impact of oil prices on the balance of payments since then. Since 1975 oil-import expenditures have stabilized, permitting a rebound of the country's balance of payments position. Inflation has, nonetheless, continued at

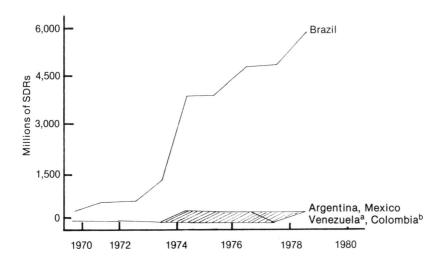

Source: International Monetary Fund, *International Financial Statistics, 1981* (Washington, D.C.: 1981); United Nations, *Yearbook of International Trade Statistics* (New York: United Nations, 1975-1979).

[a] Data available only through 1976.

[b] Data available only through 1977.

Figure 6-1. Oil Imports of the Five Giants

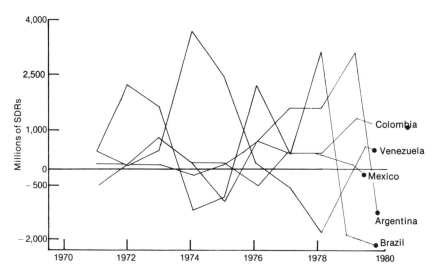

Source: International Monetary Fund, *1981 Balance of Payments Yearbook* (Washington, D.C.: 1981).

Figure 6-2. Balance of Payments of the Five Giants

exhorbitant levels. However, since the government is adopting a strategy of opening up the economy, attracting foreign capital, and encouraging competition with the international markets, it may open Argentina to new sources of international economic pressures. The surplus since 1976 is noteworthy, indicating the effectiveness of the government's capital outflow policies, but temporary due to crises of confidence.

The change in Bolivia's international position, from a net exporter of oil to a net importer, is not reflected in the country's balance of payments deficit, once again suggesting the lack of direct correlation between the two. Since the country's long-term oil position is not favorable, the government has been particularly concerned with expanding the natural gas found in association with light oil, thereby increasing use of existing resources. Bolivia relies disproportionately (over 80 percent) on hydrocarbons for energy, compared to 60 percent for Latin America as a whole.

The economy of Brazil has been among the most affected by the oil price increases of 1973 and then of 1979. Recovery in the payments position by 1976 was followed by a sharp deterioration and a dramatic deficit in 1979. With imports of almost a million barrels per day, not even the Brazilian economy can absorb such expenditures without negative effects. Trade liberalization measures announced in January 1979 were aimed at removing barriers to bilaterial and multilateral trade negotiations. These included an increase of 4.5 percent in the annual rate of depreciation of the

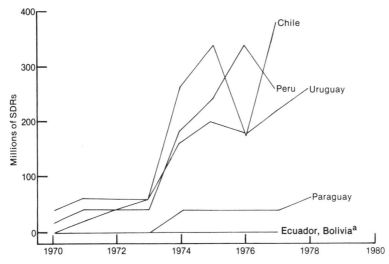

Source: International Monetary Fund, *International Financial Statistics, 1981* (Washington, D.C.: 1981); United Nations, *Yearbook of International Trade Statistics* (New York: United Nations, 1975-1979).

[a] Data available only through 1973.

Figure 6-3. Oil Imports of Other Latin American Countries

cruziero.[5] Early in the year the import bill for oil products for 1979 was expected to exceed $6.5 billion and create a current account deficit on the order of $10 billion. The government's pace of devaluation, designed to respond to this deterioration, raised the price of imports and hence oil in general. In the first six months of 1980 the overall deficit was $3.3 billion, or $100 million more than the deficit for all of 1979. By June 1980 estimates for the year ranged from $10.5 billion to $14 billion. The balance of trade was negative, due largely to increases in food imports. The combination of these factors led to a bleak picture indeed.[6] Imported oil cost $7 billion in 1979 and was expected to reach at least $10 billion in 1980.[7] Deterioration in the payments position of Brazil had reached legendary proportions, "levels known to other nations only in times of war."[8] Inflation appeared to be running at 75 percent, due largely to increases in costs of imported goods. At some point the government had considered allowing petroleum prices to rise sharply in line with international prices, but the attempt to reduce oil consumption and buttress the alcohol program is not overtly successful as yet.

For Chile an unfavorable import bill and attendant payments position has been offset to some extent by copper prices. The dramatic improvement in the country's balance of payments is due also to government efforts to encourage foreign capital.

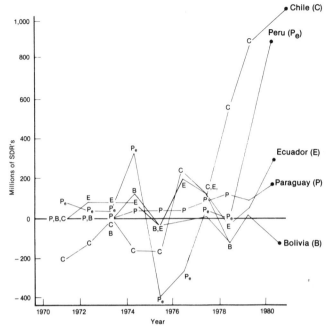

Source: International Monetary Fund, *1981 Balance of Payments Yearbook* (Washington, D.C.: 1981).

Figure 6-4. Balance of Payments of Other Latin American Countries

The distinctive feature of Colombia's payments position is its apparently favorable balance. Despite the fact that Colombia has become an importer since 1976, oil imports have not been a major strain on the balance of payments. Future effects will be determined by the volume of imports and the success of exploration activities designed to expand domestic uses of oil.

As net exporters of oil both Ecuador and Mexico show an improved balance of payments position. Since 1973 oil has been Ecuador's main foreign exchange earner and accounted for 51 percent of total exports in 1978. Although Ecuador's economy traditionally depended on agricultural exports, oil exports, which began in August 1972, contributed to a rise in GNP from $2.2 billion in 1971 to $5.9 billion by 1977. Government revenue quadrupled almost overnight.[9] Nonetheless, Ecuador's reserves and production levels have stagnated since government policies toward the companies discouraged exploration.

The change in Mexico's position from an importer to an exporter of petroleum, like that of Ecuador, has had little effect on the country's balance of payments. Oil revenues, however, rose from $3 billion to $14 billion in five years, with a growth rate of 36 percent. For the period 1980 to

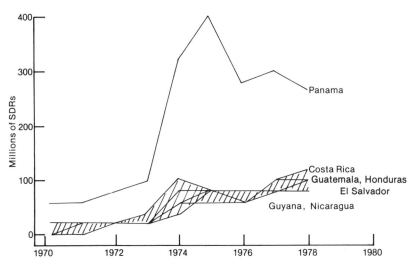

Source: International Monetary Fund, *International Financial Statistics, 1981* (Washington, D.C.: 1981); United Nations, *Yearbook of International Trade Statistics* (New York: United Nations, 1975-1979).

Figure 6-5. Oil Imports in Central America

1982 it was expected that Mexico would earn over $32 billion from oil sales (parenthetically, this figure is about the same as the estimated public external debt for 1980).[10]

Steady growth in the Mexican economy is creating strong internal demand. Growth of GNP was 8 percent; demand increased by 9.8 percent in real terms. The difference between GNP growth and overall demand is reflected in a 26.3 percent increase in imports of goods and services. Large and unexpected agricultural imports counteracted the effect of growing oil sales on the country's payments position, a situation that will persist as long as the Mexican industry cannot deliver investment goods at the rate necessary to offset the clear payments deficit. Figures for 1980 show a 56 percent jump in imports, due largely to food, particularly because the previous crop cycle exhibited the worst performance of the agricultural sector for this deterioration was that growth of oil exploration and production-while GDP growth was 7.5 percent.)[11]

In sum, despite a 113 percent increase in oil exports in 1979 (valued at $4 billion), the Mexican trade deficit was $1 billion worse than the previous year, according to the Mexican Foreign Trade Institute. A contributing factor for this deterioration was the growth of oil exploration and production required massive imports of machinery and equipment. Approximately $1 billion was spent by PEMEX in 1979 on purchase of equipment. Total

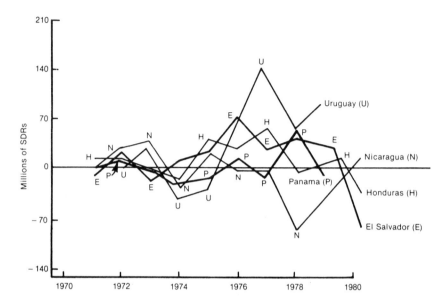

Source: International Monetary Fund, *1981 Balance of Payments Yearbook* (Washington, D.C.: 1981); International Monetary Fund, *International Financial Statistics, 1981* (Washington, D.C.: 1981).

Figure 6-6. Balance of Payments in Central America

imports for machinery for the oil sector rose 67 percent, and exports overall covered 71 percent of imports.[12]

In contrast to trends in other countries, Paraguay has shown impressive growth and an improving payments position. The country has no oil, no minerals, and no access to the ocean. But it has achieved a solid growth rate by using its other resources effectively and not pursuing wild expansionism.[13] Agricultural expansion and completion of hydroelectric power projects initiated in the 1970s are two significant cornerstones of development. Construction of planned hydroelectric projects jointly with Argentina could contribute to reduction of oil dependence. In addition sales of electric power to neighboring states were estimated in 1980 to bring $100 million to $150 million in direct revenues if present projects are completed.[14]

Peru's export boom during the later half of the 1970s accounts largely for the country's improved payments position. Higher prices for exports of silver and copper contributed to a trade surplus of over $1 billion in 1979, with still more improvements anticipated in the next two years. The current account showed an improvement and a marked surplus in 1979 relative to the previous year. Peru's recent transition from an importer to a net exporter of oil has enabled it to escape the balance of payments predicament of other countries in the region. As a result of strong export earnings, the country's international reserves have increased, allowing the government to cancel balance of payments refinancing agreements scheduled for 1980 with international banks. Peru is able to meet commitments on servicing debt payments and to save over $300 million in interest payments (over roughly a seven-year period, 1979-1986).[15]

Although Uruguay is totally dependent on external sources for petroleum, improved prices for its exports (meat and manufactures), growing tourist trade, and associated expanding construction activity together contribute to a burgeoning of economic activity. International reserves have risen sharply, and foreign investment is growing. Oil payments account for 30 percent of total imports in 1979, but the country is not expected to have substantial difficulties in meeting its import bill. The favorable payments position registered for the last several years reflects an economic boom.

As the major foreign exchange earner of Venezuela, oil accounts for over 90 percent of all exports. Today Venezuela boasts the highest per capita income in Latin America ($2,652).[16] With the oil price increases of 1973, the country's balance of payments surplus increased immediately to over $4 billion from $656 million in 1973. The effect of the OPEC price increases was to eliminate the current account deficit of $20 million in 1972 to a surplus of $787 million several years later. The country's GNP rose from $18 billion in 1972 to $35.8 billion in 1978. The oil boom brought with it massive imports for both consumer demand and investment programs, leading to an extensive import bill and a deteriorating balance of payments position for 1977 and 1978. In 1979 the country's balance of payments position improved with the rise of oil prices once again.[17] Compensatory payments to oil companies following nationalization of the oil industry appear against the country's payments position, contributing to the earlier deficit. The combination of increased oil exports and higher oil prices will lead to greater receipts from oil sales and is expected to improve the country's payments position. The recovery in 1978 to 1979 reflects import cuts as much as the new price hikes of December 1979. Foreign revenues at the end of the year were $7.7 billion, an increase of $1.3 billion over the previous year.[18]

In the early 1980s Venezuela was, once again, seeking to attract foreign investors. In the late 1960s and early 1970s foreign capital was entering the country at an approximate rate of $100 million to $200 million a year, primarily from the United States. The extensive impact of foreign oil companies on the Venezuelan economy had contributed to mistrust of all foreign investors. By the same token the impact of the government's nationalizations on foreign investors was profound: mistrust reigned there as well. Today foreign investment is strictly controlled, limiting profit remitted to 20 percent of capital and retained earnings.[19] The government has devised means of encouraging foreign investors without necessarily returning to the practices of the 1960s. The Superintendency of Foreign Investments will now attempt to approve projects within thirty days by means of accelerating the flow of capital. But the government acknowledges that "it is a great error to think that foreign investment can contribute to . . . equilibrium in the balance of payments."[20]

There is no single story to tell for all of Latin America. But as a region Latin America is not deteriorating financially because of oil imports. Colombia, Bolivia, and Argentina are all nearly self-sufficient. Peru, Mexico, Ecuador, and Venezuela are exporters. Chile has higher copper revenues to offset oil expenditures. Uruguay has an improving trade situation. Paraguay is developing hydroelectric power. Only Brazil seems to be chronically suffering on an impressive scale. But this situation may change, as Brazil recovered from the 1973 price hikes and the 1974-1975 recession to register balance of payments surpluses for 1976 to 1978. Although popular impression would lead one to think that all Latin America is ailing, the region is adjusting well.

The striking phenomenon is that oil exporters are not significantly better off than importers. Two forces are at work: first, oil wealth tends to stimulate consumer demand, and imports absorb any previous surplus; second, oil importers are successfully finding means of improving their payments position, a central theme of chapter 10. Thus there are pressures tending toward improvements in the balance of payments. But any improvements, by necessity, entail costs as well.

External Debt

Debt management has emerged as an important issue for economic development ever since increases in the price of oil first led most developing countries more heavily into debt. Middle-income countries are now faced with liquidity difficulties; low-income countries have stark problems of inadequate real resource transfers. The fear is that developing countries will fall victim to an international crisis of confidence if they seem unlikely to be able to repay foreign debts when they fall due. Should this occur, they will lose capital necessary to sustain further economic growth. Important economic concerns for the 1980s include the need to devise means of expanding financial flows and alternative methods of financing international debts.

External public debt as a percentage of GDP is presented in table 6-2 for twenty three Latin American countries.[21] The changes from 1970 to 1979 reveal the relative difficulties encountered by different countries in main-

Table 6-2
Outstanding and Disbursed External Public Debt

	Millions of Dollars		Percentage of GDP		Debt Service as Percentage of GNP	
	1970	1979	1970	1979	1970	1979
Argentina	1,878	8,716	7.6	8.6	1.9	1.5
Bolivia	477	1,835	46.4	38.7	2.2	5.4
Brazil	3,227	35,092	7.2	17.7	0.9	3.1
Chile	2,066	4,767	26.4	23.6	3.1	6.2
Colombia	1,249	3,426	18.1	12.6	1.7	2.4
Costa Rica	134	1,277	13.8	33.0	2.9	6.6
Ecuador	213	1,563	13.3	21.5	1.5	7.4
El Salvador	88	397	8.6	11.5	0.9	1.0
Guatemala	106	482	5.7	7.0	1.4	0.5
Guyana	na	na	na	na	na	na
Honduras	90	746	12.8	36.3	0.8	5.3
Mexico	3,206	28,805	9.7	24.5	2.1	8.8
Nicaragua	155	1,101	20.6	62.9	3.2	3.2
Panama	194	2,106	19.0	83.9	3.0	15.7
Paraguay	112	491	19.1	14.4	1.8	1.5
Peru	856	5,931	12.7	42.9	2.1	6.6
Uruguay	267	914	11.0	13.3	2.6	1.8
Venezuela	728	9,797	6.6	20.0	0.7	3.2

Source: The World Bank, *World Development Report, 1981* (Washington, D.C.: 1981).

Note: "External public debt outstanding" represents the amount of public and publicly guaranteed loans that has been disbursed, net of cancelled loan commitments and repayments of principal. The data refer to the end of the year indicated and are from the World Bank Debt Reporting System. In estimating external public debt as a percentage of GNP, GNP was converted from national currencies to dollars at the average official exchange rate for the year in question.

taining an independent external monetary policy. The greater the debt outstanding, the greater are the pressures placed upon national governments for policy change. The structure of public debt lies at the heart of national autonomy: the exercise of discretion in financial decisions is strongly delimited by the nature of the debt outstanding. Increases in debt outstanding during the 1970s are, in many cases, dramatic. Some are due to the extenuating effects of social and economic upheaval (such as Nicaragua which tripled its debt during this period); others to the convergence of slowing economic growth accentuated by rising oil prices. The trends in many countries, like Brazil and Mexico, reflect less economic performance than the accumulation of long-term impacts and multiplier effects generated by the changes in oil price. The effects are the same: new constraints on national autonomy. The most obvious constraints are apparent in the countries of Central America.

Relative to other countries of the region the direct impacts of oil price increases on Argentina have not been extensive. The country has one of the lowest levels of external debt as a percentage of GDP. The increased debt incurred by 1978 is, of course, due partly to oil prices. By contrast, Bolivia's external debt ranks among the highest in South America (38.7 percent of GDP by 1979). This debt structure is generated by the strong pattern of growth in the mid-1970s. Government policy of encouraging high rates of growth as a means of reducing social inequities and using high oil export taxes to raise revenue for financing projects contributed to a sharp increase in long-term foreign debt. The cost of debt service rose to 32 percent of export revenue in 1978 and is forecasted to use about 40 percent in the early 1980s. In this context the government's concern for expanding uses of alternative energy sources becomes critical.[22]

Brazil's external debt, modest by regional standards, is due largely to financing of balance of payments deficit—their deficit being legendary in both magnitude and duration. Debt service is expected to account for as much as 60 percent of export earnings. Brazil's debt performance over an eight-year period points to the economic difficulties at hand.

The anticipated rise in Ecuador's domestic oil consumption will eat into the country's exports. By 1984 Ecuador may even become a net importer.[23] The external public debt, which is already over 20 percent of GDP, is expected to rise despite the government's attempt to be more selective in contracting foreign debt. The U.S. arms deal for $1 billion adds substantially to this burden.

The near-tripling of Mexico's external debt (as a percentage of GDP) is roughly in proportion to the country's oil earnings. External borrowing is expected to increase, although steps are being taken to reduce debt-servicing costs and to obtain more favorable servicing conditions. The public debt budgeted for 1980 is commensurate with the 1979 deficit on the current account plus projected cumulative deficit on that account for 1979 to 1982. Debt service was expected to amount to 14 percent of goods and services produced, for this period, but, in fact, it was considerably lower, only 8.8 percent.[24]

Venezuela's external debt expanded over threefold as a percentage of GDP (1970 to 1979) and has not improved since. External borrowing to finance development projects, in conjunction with declining international reserves, contributed to an expanded external public debt. Heavy financing needs (and debt services) had drawn reserves down considerably, followed by an improvement in the early 1980s.

Thus once again oil wealth tends to be fully absorbed by accelerated development plans. Among the oil importers those with negative balance of payments also seem to have high debt service ratios. Debt management could become an even more important issue than either inflation or expenditures for oil imports.

Conclusion

While it may be difficult to be unduly optimistic about Latin America's adjustments to the oil price increases, or to economic pressures more broadly defined, there is evidence that the problems of the 1970s have been weathered rather well. Inflation, while high and endemic in the region, has not worsened unduly. For some countries there is even some improvement. Balance of payments deficits, though shared by almost all countries, have, nevertheless, also shown some improvement. In some cases strong capital inflows in conjunction with considerable borrowing may have created a temporary, yet notable, improvement. In others the deterioration in payments position is due as much to imports necessitated by massive investment programs as by a higher oil bill. The clear danger, however, lies in levels and rates of external borrowing. For almost all countries the external debt burden increases. But even this source of pressure may find some relief. As will be discussed in a subsequent chapter, there have been new sources of capital in financial markets and new financial opportunities.

This chapter ends our review of energy and economy in Latin America—the region's energy profile and direct economic implications of changing oil prices. The following chapters, on policy and political implications, look at development plans in the region, the new role of the state and state enterprises in managing a changing energy environment, and the emerging opportunities for the region internationally. Behind a gloomy front may lie some real prospects for improvement and change.

Notes

1. This chapter examines the effects of the oil price increases on Latin America only with respect to the most glaring consequences. Structural problems endemic to the economics of the region are not analyzed here, although reference is made whenever appropriate. For recent assessments of economic performance, see especially "Survey: Latin America, A Continent at Odds with Itself." *World Business Weekly*, August 24, 1981. For an earlier survey, see George W. Grayson, *The Politics of Mexican Oil* (Pittsburgh: The University of Pittsburgh Press, 1980); although the focus is on Mexico, other oil-exporting countries are also reviewed. Statistical reviews are presented in The World Bank, *World Development Report* (Washington, D.C., 1981); International Monetary Fund, *Balance of Payments Yearbook* (various issues) and *International Financial Statistics* (various issues, especially 1981). I am grateful to Peter Haas and Lily Ling for research assistance.

2. "Latin America: After the Oil Crises," *Bank of London & South America Review*, 13 (December 1979), p. 705.

3. Ibid.

4. See, for example, "Special Report: Latin America and Middle East Draw Closer," *Latin America Weekly Report*, December 7, 1979, pp. 68-69.

5. *Latin America Weekly Report*, September 19, 1980, p. 4, and November 23, 1979, p. 44.

6. Ibid.

7. Ibid.

8. Ibid.

9. George W. Grayson, *The Politics of Mexican Oil* (Pittsburgh: The University of Pittsburgh Press, 1980), p. 122.

10. "Latin America: After the Oil Crises," p. 715.

11. *Latin America Weekly Report*, February 22, 1981, p. 1.

12. Ibid., pp. 1, 6.

13. "Paraguay Achieves Impressive Growth Rate by Developing Agriculture, Electric Power," *IMF Survey*, 9 (January 21, 1980), pp. 18-20.

14. Ibid., p. 20.

15. "Latin America: After the Oil Crises," *Bank of London & South America Review*, pp. 717-718.

16. Grayson, *The Politics of Mexican Oil*, p. 118.

17. *Latin America Weekly Report*, March 21, 1980, pp. 4-5.

18. Ibid.

19. *New York Times*, July 15, 1980, p. D1.

20. *Wall Street Journal*, December 31, 1980, p. 10.

21. The World Bank, *World Development Report*, 1981.

22. "Latin America: After the Oil Crises," *Bank of London & South America Review*, pp. 707-708.

23. Ibid., pp. 713-714.

24. "Latin America: After the Oil Crises," *Bank of London & South America Review*, pp. 714-715.

Part III
Policy

7 Development Planning: Energy and Public Policy

At this point we turn to the evolution of planning perspectives in Latin America and the emerging effects of a changing energy environment on the overall priorities for development and in the transportation sector in particular. As mentioned earlier, interest in transportation is twofold: the transport sector is a large user of energy, particularly petroleum; investments in transportation reflect investments in infrastructure development and built-in commitments to certain patterns of energy use. Energy consumption patterns cannot be radically altered on short notice.

Development Plans

The major sources of information and evidence used in this chapter are development plans and documents pertaining to economic programs. The use of development plans is predicated on the view that government plans represent official statements of intent and include broad directives for investments and choice of priorities. No assumption is made regarding the effectiveness of planning, the implementation of strategies, or the realization of programs. Documents of economic programs constitute a *political* statement of priorities, a reflection of choices as governments wish to represent them formally, and a posture of *public policy* for purposes of political identification and broad orientation of national resources.

In drawing upon the record of formal development plans in Latin America, we begin with the 1960s and trace the evolution of public perspectives, stated in these plans, throughout the 1960s and 1970s. The review is comprehensive, and, with a few exceptions due to lack of availability, the entire record is examined. We ask the following questions:

1. What priorities seem to be identified as targets for public policy?
2. How are infrastructure issues defined, and what role do transport issues play?
3. When do energy-related issues emerge as central to government planning?
4. To what extent do countries differ in their approach to energy issues and transport policy?

To a large extent the development process reflects a reality perceived by decision makers, or a reality they would like to see. Development programs follow some predetermined parameters of reality. By building upon prior reality, they set forth objectives and strategies that shape the reality of the future.

Political power and power distribution are endemic to the process of reality definition and the nature and pace of the development process. Growth, equity, welfare, and distribution are conventionally regarded as the criteria upon which to evaluate a country's development record. The distribution of benefits and costs then becomes a central aspect of this evaluation. Underlying this distribution is the question of who makes the decisions and who gains or loses as a result. Since economic performance is essentially a question of outcomes that are a function of choices, choices inevitabily reflect the distribution of political power and the ability to exert political control.

In the 1960s most Latin American countries were engaged in infrastructure development, expansion of government, rural change and modernization, and the building of road networks and basic communication infrastructure. In the 1970s these concerns were overshadowed by a concentration on developing petroleum production, exploiting hydroelectric potentials, expanding both air and maritime transport networks to international routings, and establishing the basis for more diversification in economic structure. Different sectors of the population were affected by different thrusts of emphasis.

The Giants of Latin America

Argentina, Brazil, Colombia, Mexico, and Venezuela have extensive options for developing their energy base. Being large consumers of petroleum by regional and international standards, they, nevertheless, have the potential for diversification and the expansion of their commercially exploitable resources. Trends exhibited by the giants on public policy in the 1970s in both energy and transportation may well lead to similar policy responses elsewhere.

The energy profile of Argentina has especially good prospects for energy diversification, combining resources of natural gas, hydroelectric power, vegetable fuel, and oil. In addition the government has displayed policy concern for distortion in composition of supply and demand, by means of a set of priorities in the energy sector that focuses on expanding availability of different energy sources rather than reducing demand. There is, however, a notable absence of any direct connection between energy planning and investments in the transportation sector.

Within the twenty-year period 1960 to 1980 three areas of development were greatly accentuated by a series of government plans. The 1965-1969 plan, which was issued during a time of social turmoil, pledged to maintain growth rates, increase consumption to match expanded production, and improve the living standard. In stemming inflation left in the wake of the plan, heavy emphasis was given to the agricultural sector. The early 1970s saw a policy shift from these rudimentary development goals to increased institutional development which promised greater national autonomy. Finally, in the mid-1970s the pressures of rising oil import prices forced the government to show a greater concern for the energy sector, and it defined energy problems largely in terms of location of resources within the country rather than overall availability.[1]

The plan for 1974-1977 initiated to develop a largely autonomous energy sector argued that Argentina had energy resources in sufficient quantity to cover the country's short- and long-term needs. However, almost all resources are located at great distances from main centers of consumption (Gran Buenos Aires, El Litoral, and Cordoba), which account for only a quarter of the country's energy resources but for over 80 percent of total consumption. The plan also sought to rectify faulty government planning of earlier times which had distorted the energy supply and made insufficient uses of potentially important sources of energy, even though domestic production had increased more than five fold between 1960 and 1973.

The single most important aspect of the plan's proposed strategy for the energy sector was to increase the state's control and management of national resources. To this end state enterprises were declared to be the only legitimate and comprehensive mechanism for rationalizing uses and development of the country's energy resources, and the private sector was relegated to a clearly subordinate position. The strength of the state, always a pervasive element in Argentinian politics, surfaced unchallenged in policy making for the energy sector. Expansion of investments in nuclear energy and the desire to make Argentina a nuclear giant in the region emerged from this plan.[2]

By the beginning of the 1980s Argentinian planners made a sustained attempt to incorporate energy *cost* parameters in transport planning. This recognition of energy-economy interactions is reflected in part in periodic statements reviewing the sector as a whole. But insofar as investment strategy is concerned, the connections between energy policy and transport planning have not yet been made.

Like Argentina, Brazil's development planning orientation shifted dramatically from the promotion of economic growth and improved socioeconomic distribution to, as the 1972-1974 plan states, "placing Brazil, within one generation, in the category of developed nations."[3] This new approach to modernization included increased emphasis on the nation's nuclear power potential.

Despite the evolution of development policy, however, the basic structure of the transportation sector remained relatively static until the mid-1970s, even as the sector itself expanded rapidly. The middle of the decade, which witnessed a clear shift toward reducing dependence on external energy sources, also saw a renewed focus on the transportation sector in order to accommodate this reduction. Energy conservation and balance of payments stabilization were also major foci of development policy during this time.

With the advent of the 1980s Brazil's primary focus has been on mitigating its own energy crisis—followed by earlier established priorities of maintaining a more favorable balance of payments, minimizing foreign debt, controlling inflation, and increasing the economic growth rate. The overall theme embracing these goals is largely national economic growth, viewed as essential in its own right, with income and resource distribution placed in a subordinate position.

Brazil's changing policy perspectives are documented in numerous developmental plans and related public policy statements. While basic themes have remained constant, emphases have shifted. In the mid-1970s the primary goal of public policy was expressed as "meeting the energy crisis without sacrificing accelerated growth."[4] Central to growth was the necessity of expanding the supply of energy. The country's long-term objectives provided for self-sufficiency in that sector. These energy policy objectives were defined as (1) reducing dependence on external sources of energy, which requires expansion of domestic oil supplies by massive exploration programs in the continental shelf, the development of the shale program, and diversification of internal sources of energy uses; (2) expanding energy uses from hydroelectric sources, given the country's endowments; (3) developing a coal program aimed at expansion and modernization of production methods; (4) expanding development research in nonconventional energy sources; and (5) expanding research in different aspects of mineral uses for nuclear reactors. Petrobras was given primary responsibility for developing and operating the energy sector, beyond oil-related issues.[5]

By the middle of the 1970s, in the plan for 1975-1979, Brazil had designed a set of policies to reduce dependence on petroleum, bearing directly on the transportation sector. These included a program for electrifying railways and the establishing of new rail networks; a policy of gradually increasing transport loads of railways and waterway networks, and modification of bus services and installation of new and express bus services to replace private automobiles. The plan stipulated the further determination of special funds for these purposes. Investments in alternative energy sources played an important role in the new efforts and advanced the development of alcohol as a gasoline additive and substitute as well as increased uses of coal for broader industrial purposes.[6]

The plan for 1980-1985 again marks energy as the first priority, with the nation's more conventional problems being subsequently addressed. The plan is primarily concerned with the fact that 40 percent of energy consumed in Brazil comes from foreign sources. As a result it deems essential the development of alternatives to these sources as well as the development of alternatives to petroleum.[7]

In its specific attention to the transport sector as a major user of energy, Brazil's plan for 1980-1985 comes closest to integrating energy and transport policy. The plan specifies the importance of maximizing integration of the national transportation system and increasing incentives for more rational uses of combustibles, particularly petroleum derivatives. Operationally, the plan argues the importance of maintaining transportation systems in line with principles of energy conservation and rationalizing transport uses in economically efficient terms.[8]

Energy substitution in the transport sector is the most distinctive feature of the Brazilian case. In 1980 government estimates placed expected savings in gas use due to alcohol substitution at 40 percent of all gas consumed. Expansion of urban mass transit is anticipated as well as the establishment of a series of specific conservation measures. These include limits of speed, increases in weekend tolls, new regulations for parking in cities, schedule changes for industry, banks, and commerce, among other measures. Brazil's comprehensive approach to transport planning utilizes both economic instruments (prices, tariffs) and administrative instruments, encouraging decentralization of industrial activities through urban planning under the present circumstances of severe energy constraints.[9]

Brazil's importance in the context of Latin American energy policy lies not only in the sheer size of the country and the magnitude of resources consumed but in the availability of options. Brazil's policy of energy diversification provides a model for other developing countries—not in terms of similarities of endowments but in the effective implementation of research and investment programs.

The symbolic effects of Brazilian policies for energy diversification may be more important than their actual success. Brazil's leadership in policy identification and attempts for implementation has reinforced the country's leadership role in Latin America. The Brazilian posture is increasingly viewed as a model for regional autonomy and self-reliance. The fact that Brazil is far from self-reliant in energy resources does not invalidate the image projected both regionally and internationally. It is an image made possible by the sheer possibilities of choice. And the Brazilians are making as much mileage politically by fostering the image.

Among the giants of the region, Colombia shares with Brazil an emerging expression of concern for energy issues in development planning, primarily the production of coal, oil, natural gas, hydroelectric power, and vegetable fuels, which have export potential in almost every case, and a new interest in the connection between energy and transportation. Colombian planners, however, are more hesitant in the formation of their related policies.

The nation's history of development planning is among the longest in Latin America. The plan issued in 1962 addressed itself directly to the population dimensions of future transport needs, declaring the necessity for facilities to be established in energy, transportation, and communication to facilitate the development process.[10] Transportation planning was assigned a similarly high priority in the following development plan for 1969-1972.[11] The focus on transportation continued to be strong, with a new emphasis placed primarily on the more efficient use of existing networks rather than expansion of facilities. With the 1974 plan came a shift of emphasis from transportation to electricity. Rural electrification was viewed as an important element in improving income distribution, as an indirect source of employment and an indirect means of contributing to social and economic integration.[12] The concern for integration is a theme that persists throughout Colombia's development plans.

In its failure to give special emphasis to energy issues, the plan for 1975-1978 made apparent that the importance of new energy constraints for development was not yet fully appreciated.[13] Colombia does not have the same magnitude of energy dependence that plagues Brazil, thereby making the issue of energy policy less urgent. Yet Colombia's cosponsorship of the conference on energy and transportation with the Inter-American Development Bank in December 1980 is an indication of the government's concern and willingness to go on record as supporting the need for new policies in the energy and transportation sectors. Beyond that, however, there is little evidence that the government is actually pursuing new directions in energy policy.

On paper, the government's broader development objectives include exploiting domestic resources (coal, hydroelectric power, petroleum), maintaining high export levels of goods, stabilizing import prices within the petroleum sector, and regulating consumption, especially with respect to identifying and implementing conservation measures. Nonetheless, unlike Brazil and Argentina, Colombia's energy-related policies are not regarded as being exclusively in the domain of state enterprises. This difference is partially due to the structure of politics in Colombia and the role of the bureaucracy in the political process. Colombian planners are technicians with a certain concern for maintaining a consensual basis for decision making and implementation. In Brazil and Argentina they reflect more closely the power structure and the objectives of the leadership.

Mexico and Venezuela—the new oil exporter and the traditional exporter—bring to Latin America's energy issues the realization of a diverse set of problems and postures. The one characterization that may have evolved in common is a dominant role for state enterprises amid a growing importance of the national oil companies. This importance goes beyond oil-related issues and may possibly transform the countries' traditional political structure. In this respect development planning for both countries serves as much to reflect reality as to determine it. Planning documents reveal the gradual emergence of the state enterprises; and the content of public policy as it has evolved over the past two decades reflects the effects of this new dominance. Beyond that, however, Mexico and Venezuela share little in the development planning experience for the issues at hand.

By the end of the 1970s Mexico's development planning placed emphasis on expansion of oil production and export potential and expansion of natural gas utilization. A gradual articulation of energy policy was in the making, with the state oil enterprise determining and implementing policies in the petroleum sector.

The 1979-1982 plan, Mexico's most recent officially available planning document, emphasized the need for a broad energy policy while retaining the earlier focus on the country's automobile industry. The government's industrialization strategy was designed to expand Mexico's industrial export potential, decentralize new industrial locations to expand coastal and other populated areas, and create a more balanced market structure for domestic industries. The plan's frequent reference to the importance of abolishing "oligopolistic concentration" is a statement that runs contrary to the new dominance of state enterprises. The many facets of such concentrations in the Mexican polity are not, of course, an issue that can be deemed appropriate in government documents presenting official intents, but the references belie a sense of discomfort which is mirrored by social strains emerging in Mexican politics. These strains, somewhat due to the new dominance of PEMEX as well as to the effects of growing oil revenues, may provide a new idiom for expressing Mexican development policies.[14]

The most recent national energy program released by the Ministry of Natural Resources and Industrial Development called for the following production levels: 2.7 million barrels per day of crude in 1982, 3.5 million b/d in 1985, and 4.1 million b/d in 1990. The intent is to limit exports so that oil earnings do not account for more than 50 percent of the country's foreign exchange earnings.[15] This target has been widely debated in policy circles and pressures for expansion of production persist. Linkages between transportation and energy policy are emerging. PEMEX officials complain that infrastructural problems impede oil production and expansion of production capacity. Most critical is the "failure of Mexico's transportation system to keep pace with rapid development of the oil production sector."[16] Port facilities are considered inadequate and impede deliveries of equipment.

An official report on Mexico's industrialization and the role of the petroleum sector notes the government's strategy of using surplus oil revenues to restructure the economy and contribute to expansion of employment opportunities. The report clearly stresses the government's direct interest in expanding the role of the state specifically in the petroleum sector in its overall economic development. A policy of maintaining energy prices below world prices as a means of giving impetus to exploration and development is articulated, as is the government's goal of self-sufficiency in refined products and obtaining maximum value added in the use of oil. PEMEX's jurisdiction in the planned basic and secondary petrochemical industries is stressed, yielding the clear implication that in all areas of oil and energy PEMEX makes policy. The role of the state has always been dominant in Mexican politics, determining the distribution of power and economic benefits. Indeed, state dominance is endemic to the nature of the political process. But the evolution of a particular state enterprise tied to the generation of the country's wealth is a new element in Mexican politics. Debates over oil production targets have become debates over energy policy, economic policy, and political power—all at once. Any changes in oil production therefore will reflect changes in the power of PEMEX. Oil policy becomes economic policy, and economic power becomes political power.

Venezuela has a unique position in Latin America because it is one of the giants of the region, a major oil exporter, a rapidly industrializing country—and it is also a member of OPEC. Each of these factors influences the leadership's perceptions of priorities, and each has had an impact on the evolution of the country's development plans. The country's history of formal planning is extensive, with at least seven development plans along with numerous other documents for policy directives. During the mid-1960s expansion of the energy sector was of paramount importance. Also of high priority were improving the nation's transportation infrastructure and modernizing air transport facilities.[17]

Within the energy sector petroleum and mineral policy appeared again as high priorities in an economic assessment issued in 1973 by the Central Office of Coordination and Planning. The report was essentially a survey of the country's economic status. Petroleum and mineral policy headed the list of national priorities. A major feature of the 1973 planning report was an assessment of Venezuela's oil exports to the United States. The statement was made that, in recent years, oil exports had declined as a result of U.S. import policy. Concern for relations with the United States dominated in this policy document.[18] But new foreign elements intervened later on; the plan for the period 1976-1980 replaced this singular concern with explicit recognition of Venezuela's role in OPEC and possibilities of using oil and oil policy as a leverage in international relations.[19]

The 1976-1980 plan maintained the emphasis on energy, with a detailed strategy for electricity and hydrocarbons. The government envisaged expansion of the role of the public sector for management of electricity and a decline in the contribution of the private sector. The proposed strategy for implementing plans for the electricity sector included reorganizing state electrieal enterprises, expanding the role of public enterprises, and nationalizing foreign firms operating in this sector.

A similar type of strategy for implementing plans for hydrocarbons was outlined in the 1976-1980 document. The strategy included mobilization of the administrative capacities of the Venezuelan Petroleum Society and the Ministry of Hydrocarbons, regulating product supply by means of periodical adjustment of value of exports within the guidelines of OPEC, raising the level of hydrocarbon use as an instrument of international negotiations, and achieving the maximum yield for export. Among the tactics espoused were maintenance of traditional markets, diversification of markets, growth of new exports for Venezuelan products, and insurance of self-sufficiency of equipment.[20]

For Venezuela therefore the plan clearly stipulated the political use of petroleum as an instrument of international negotiation with the explicit intent of increasing the value of the product. While the logic and rationale of linking decisions about oil to foreign policy, and to international relations, was not fully anticipated in the plan, the formal intent is to tie the country's export policies and production targets to OPEC directives. At a minimum one could argue that Venezuelan officials perceived oil as a potential instrument for the pursuit of a multiplicity of international objectives. Recorded in a clause of the plan is explicit support for OPEC, consolidation of the Organizacion Latinoamericana de Energia (OLADE), and stimulation of initiatives that permit greater regional communication for better utilization of the area's natural resources.[21]

Yet the connection between energy policy and internal sectoral policies was not articulated. Transport investments and energy-related policies remained far apart. The plan's priorities for transportation were defined in terms of improving and modernizing the existing system and coordinating different modes of transportation. Underlying these goals was the concern for encouraging economic decentralization. In short, priorities for the transportation sector were defined in conventional terms, within the context of developmental requirements rather than adjustments due to changes in energy prices and availability. In this sense the plan is singularly devoid of appreciation of new constraints on economic development and growth. It is somewhat paradoxical that Venezuela's first official planning document following the initial oil price increases of 1973 omits reference to the new situation created by changes in the world oil market.

Comparing Venezuela to other countries of the region, several features stand out. While, like Mexico, the country's petroleum sector is strong, it does not dwarf other sectors. In fact, the country's actual production is steadily declining, and there is a concern for expanding investments in the exploration of new reserves as well as in production capacity and capacity utilization. Even with this decline, Venezuela's formal rhetoric argues for expansion, whereas, by contrast, the other OPEC member in Latin America, Ecuador, is working toward reducing the rate of expansion of petroleum facilities. Because the country's extensive transport network, set in place by the early 1970s, creates strong claims on domestic uses of energy (as is true for the other giants, perhaps with the exception of Colombia), it reduces the options for developing new infrastructure facilities tied to the new energy constraints. In this respect the less-developed countries of the region have a major advantage.

Other Countries in South America

Of the other countries in South America, Ecuador is the only major oil exporter. Its membership in OPEC places it among the few states where oil plays a predominant role in the economy. Indeed, Ecuador is the only country in Latin America where the oil sector assumes almost total preponderance—as an agent of development, as the sole generator of revenue, and as the major employer. Ecuador's resource policy is geared almost exclusively toward petroleum. While there is expansion of domestic uses of vegetable fuels, the focus is obviously on oil. Planning documents in Ecuador consider rationalization of petroleum production, given known reserves, undertaking programs of exploration and development, and increasing the country's international involvement for purposes of improving its own bargaining position with buyers and international oil companies. Ecuador is the smallest producer in OPEC, in fact smaller than many non-OPEC oil producers. Being a marginal producer, it carries little influence within OPEC. Thus the government's concern with expanding its influence represents a realistic assessment of reality. The government's expressed emphasis on policy and planning for the petroleum sector is at the expense of the country's overall energy endowments or future investments in alternatives to petroleum. Even transport planning is geared toward the demand generated by the petroleum sector.

Ecuador's first plan, after the initial oil-price increases of October 1973, for the period from 1973-1977, focused on national integration as the basic goal. Among the priorities assigned to the energy sector were improving the distribution of income derived from petroleum sales and increasing the nation's proven reserve position. With respect to hydrocarbons the plan stipulated the need for aligning the country's reserve constraint and attaining a position of overall self-sufficiency. Perhaps expressing a sentiment common among small countries, the plan reiterated support of, and solidarity with, other oil-exporting countries.[22]

The trend toward a larger role for the state, revealed in other Latin American countries, is evident in the case of Ecuador. Responsibility for executing policy in the petroleum sector is clearly given to CEPE (Corporacion Estatal Petrolera Ecuadoriana), the oil company. CEPE's responsibilities, outlined in the plan, are extensive, including establishing programs for exploration of areas where mineral beds might exist for purposes of increasing known resources, intensively exploring resources in order to sustain an adequate balance between reserves and production, building state refineries to meet domestic petroleum needs and ultimately to export finished products, contracting for studies evaluating the state's reserves, determining the future role of particular refineries, studying markets for Ecuadorian crude petroleum, and establishing a system of auditing investments by foreign companies in Ecuador.[23]

Of the many policies pertaining to the petroleum sector enumerated in the plan, the stipulation that the state oil company establish its own transportation facilities and networks bears noting. Coordination between CEPE's transport networks and those of Ecuador's petroleum fleet (Flota Petrolera Ecuadoriana) appears to have been included as an afterthought.[24] The point here is that transport planning is subsumed under the jurisdiction of the state's petroleum company. With sectoral policy subsumed under petroleum policy, the policy approach is not one of coordination but of co-optation: oil policy becomes overall economic policy.

Among the countries of South America Ecuador is unique in tying economic policy to oil policy. Energy policy is therefore primarily oil policy. Yet even in this context the connections between energy and other sectors of the economy are barely appreciated.

Bolivia's energy profile is distinctive for the high use of vegetable fuels in final consumption, in conjunction with considerable use of hydroelectric power and large-scale production, but only marginal usage, of natural gas. Nonetheless, the country maintains a separate energy policy from transport planning. This makes Bolivia somewhat similar to Brazil, once adjustments are made for differences in scale, but considerably more self-sufficient, in that the policy approach to energy issues stresses self-sufficiency.

The country's twenty-year Socio-Economic Strategy of National Development (1971-1991) has the longest single time horizon for a development program in Latin America. The basic objectives of the plan include accelerating development, maximizing benefits from economies of scale, and encouraging foreign participation in national production. The goals and strategies enumerated for energy include a commitment to export gas to Argentina and nationalizing the petroleum industry. Its socioeconomic strategy argues for liberalizing measures governing investments in exploration and development of energy resources.[25]

Regional cooperation is a theme clearly articulated by the Bolivian plan. This cooperation is rendered as a cornerstone for the country's transport policies, particularly expanding the rail network. Planning conferences with Brazil and Argentina are underway for the establishment of a railroad and roadway infrastructure to assist in the region's development, in effect connecting Bolivia with states to the south and east.[26]

The plan for 1976-1980, designed as a program of investment rather than a general strategy, addressed itself to energy issues but did not list the energy sector in the set of broad objectives at the onset of the plan. In the body of the document clear reference is made to hydrocarbon policy in terms of investments in exploration and development. The government argued that among the obstacles preventing the expansion of the country's domestic resources was a restricted exploration policy. The General Law of Hydrocarbons was a step toward liberalizing exploration activities. According to the law, promulgated in March 1972, the Yacimientos Petroliferos Fiscales Bolivianos (YPFB) contracts for the services of private petroleum enterprises to carry out operations of exploration in an area of 14 million hectares, and reserved explicitly for this purpose. But, as government planners argued, continued difficulties persist in the exploration phase, due largely to insufficient subsidies. Planners attributed declines in petroleum reserves witnessed for the period 1969-1974 to inadequate investments in exploration.[27]

The Bolivian plan for 1976-1980 proposed no dramatic departures for policy in the energy field, however. It did not fully articulate connections between the energy and other sectors, but it did express cogently the planners' own assessments of difficulties in expanding petroleum production.[28] Since national integration is a theme that runs continuous throughout official documents, it is not surprising that in the 1976-1980 plan, as with the longer strategy document for 1971-1991, transport policy was regarded as a means of improving the country's infrastructure facilities and, by extension, facilitating cohesion, mobility, and national integration.

Chile has a long history of development plans. Underlying this is a central interest in national autonomy. In the mid-1970s alone three economic development plans were prepared. The first, covering the years 1976-1981, upheld self-sufficiency as the paramount goal within the energy sector. The transportation sector generally was considered adequate for the country's needs.[29] While the following plan for 1979-1983 did not discuss energy in such specific terms, it noted Chile's fundamental energy problem, that the country imported 45 percent of total petroleum consumed (for 1978).[30] In view of the cost incurred, these imports provide a serious economic drain. The plan for 1979-1984 maintained an emphasis on the dependence problem.[31]

This last document set forth critical policy positions: energy prices must reflect real production costs, generation, transmission, and distribution, and the state would not intervene in price formation. In addition an energy-related tax system was to be established to provide for the elimination of exemptions and to reduce price distortions in the sector. Nonetheless, the plan reserved for the state the right of intervention, levying taxes whenever required as incentives or disincentives to control energy consumption.[32]

Chile has considerable potential for expanding its usable resource endowments. Dependence on imported oil, though significant, is regarded in plan documents as a manageable phenomenon if appropriate price policies are adopted to reflect real scarcities, reduce distortions, and encourage investments in petroleum and coal mining. Essential to the country's approach to its energy problems is expansion of electricity-generation capacity. The plan for 1979-1983 reviewed the performance of the state electrical company, CHILETRA, noting expansion of its own investments.[33]

The National Energy Commission—Comision Nacional de Energia (CNE)—recently created, assumes the following functions: proposing objectives, plans, and energy policies; undertaking feasibility studies for individual projects; dictating technical norms for development; and analyzing technically the structure and level of energy prices. But Chile's energy posture, as presented in this plan, stipulates that the development of each energy source be done separately. There is no overall approach to planning for coal resources, hydroelectricity, and petroleum. This situation, pervasive in almost all other countries, makes it difficult to rationalize investments and prices and to identify structural inconsistencies.

An unusual feature of Chile's transport policies is its international orientation with relation to meeting the country's international transport needs. Yet, although maritime transportation is given special attention, no connection between energy and transportation policies has been made. There is no clear statement about the constraints imposed by energy prices on transportation and the effects of these constraints on the country's transport policy. Another important feature is a strong emphasis on the private sector in implementing transport programs and managing transport facilities.

For Peru the focus continues to be on the public sector. Peruvian policymakers displayed a noted concern for the role of public sector enterprises in resource management. Yet, despite the emphasis given to both the energy and transportation sectors, there is relatively no appreciation shown for the effects of energy constraints on transport policy. Peru's development-planning orientation for the 1970s stressed expanding the country's overall resources, with particular attention to electricity, petroleum, and attendant investments required, and plans were also set forth for enlarging the transportation sector according to the needs of the population and areas of production.

The planning document issued in 1977 was based on developing the country's interior zones and encouraging the growth of public enterprises associated with rural areas.[34] Earlier plans of the 1970s spoke of developing the hydrocarbon sector in order to attain "national self-sufficiency" and the use of growing exports and resources, and expanding refinery capacity was noted as a major goal, as was the development of national petroleum technology.[35]

In the 1970s a notable shift occurred. In the earlier part of the decade the document issued emphasized the role of state enterprises in developing and managing the country's energy resources. The government argued that the concentration of production in relatively few enterprises facilitated the development of natural resources. Toward the end of the decade planners argued for a growing role for both the private sector and foreign concerns in investments in hydroelectric projects. However, the public sector continued to predominate despite expression of increases in private investments for energy development.

Two parallel trends persisted: the appreciation of need for an energy policy and concern for rationalizing energy use and, by the same token, concern for expanding and consolidating the country's transportation network. But no connection was made between energy policy and transport or other sectoral policies.

Uruguay has continually made self-sufficiency its national goal. Since the 1965-1974 development plan, which opened with the statement that the nation was endowed with a variety of energy resources, the level of total energy consumption per capita has risen significantly. The strategy then for self-sufficiency in energy included (1) a broad economic objective that took into account the availability of natural resources, import demand, and financial responsibilities to insure an adequate energy supply to satisfy all forms of demand from industry, public works, and individual consumption alike; (2) a program of investment for the electricity sector, covering generation, transmission, and distribution as well as an electrical network; and (3) the allocation of investments for combustible fuels, including refining and storage, in order to expand the nation's derivatives and its capacity for distribution.[36]

Self-sufficiency was projected for sectoral priorities as well. Objectives for the transportation sector included meeting the domestic demand generated by the economic and social development to date, expanding international networks to achieve a substantial substitution of imports for services and encourage exports of such services, and attaining a degree of efficiency within the existing system at minimum economic costs. The theme of self-sufficiency so pervasive in Uruguay's plans represents a recurrent theme in Latin America. This theme was rhetorically strong for many countries prior to the oil price increases of 1973-1974. By the end of the decade newer policy perspectives emerged in the effort to adapt to new conditions. The rhetoric of self-sufficiency gradually gave way to that of interdependence.[37]

Paraguay, a country that despite a lack of extensive natural resources has achieved a remarkable degree of economic progress in recent years, has issued only one development plan in the past decade, which sets forth priorities and projections for the years from 1971 to 1975.

The plan focuses on the growth of income and employment and economic integration at all levels.[38] The improved, diversified use of disposable resources and the consolidation of external financial equilibrium for substantial export growth is also stressed.

The establishment of the hydroelectric plant of Acaray in 1968 initiated a new phase in the nation's electricity production. Government policy became oriented toward improving hydraulic resources both in the capital city of Asuncion and in the more populated zones of the interior. The installed capacity of ANDE and future enlargements will permit meeting the nation's energy demand for several years. The use of the hydroelectric resources of the Parana River in conjunction with Brazil and Argentina is contemplated to serve these countries' energy needs.[39]

The program for the transportation sector, outlined jointly with that of the communication sector, specifies a number of goals for the country's land, water, and air transport systems. The greatest emphasis is on highways and road construction. Development planners hope to coordinate the organizations responsible for road construction and maintenance and to conduct an intense, systematic study of automotive traffic, both passenger and cargo.

Plans for the nation's waterways call for the construction of vessels that can function well on the nation's river routes, the development of adequate and convenient ports that are located near productive zones and land transport routes, the expansion and improvement of port installations in order to decrease costly delays, and the encouraged revitalization of the private merchant fleet. For the railroad system, on the other hand, a comprehensive and systematic investigation of the sector itself is envisaged. The main goals for air transport are the expansion and modernization of the airport facilities in Asuncion and other major cities, the improvement of services, and the expansion of the sector's operative capacity, at both the domestic and the international levels.[40] In sum, Paraguay's main policy concerns show remarkable foresight in taking account of cooperation possibilities with Brazil and Argentina and focusing on expanding routes, integrating networks, and consolidating institutional mechanisms.

Central America

In sharp contrast with the rest of Latin America are the socioeconomic development, the infrastructure facilities, the energy profile, and the demographic characteristics of Central America in conjunction with the question of size. The contrasts are apparent in official planning documents as the preponderant issues of economic development and public policy entail building infrastructure facilities and expanding access roads and transport networks. The following observations are selective, highlighting some distinctive features for countries in the region.

Belize is representative of the initial, or early, development focus on infrastructure facilities. Investments in the transportation sector and other energy projects are part of a broader concern for infrastructure development. The most recent development plan of 1964-1970 focused on electrification, the development of a transportation network to facilitate access to productive areas and rural-urban integration of materials, and institutionalization of governmental services.[41]

The development history of Costa Rica over the past two decades reveals a similar concern for basic facilities. The transportation sector was given highest specific priority during the mid-1960s; by the 1970s, on the other hand, a more comprehensive approach to the economic development strategy emerged, with little explicit attention given to transportation other than the expansion of road networks.[42] Similarly, the energy sector received minimal specific emphasis. While the implications of meeting plan growth targets for energy use were not examined, Costa Rica had made the transition from a focus on infrastructure development, so characteristic of least-developed regions, to broader, more middle-range concerns.[43]

El Salvador in the mid-1970s approached energy largely in terms of developing hydroelectric power potential and implementing existing programs of electrification. For the transportation sector priorities include obtaining better statistics on consumption by transport mode, reforming the mass transit system, placing greater reliance on diesel oil for the rail system, and encouraging bicycle use. But even by the end of the decade the transportation sector's use of petroleum did not emerge as a high priority for the government's development agenda. El Salvador is far from unique in this respect, of course. Yet there appears to be a singular lack of appreciation for energy-economy interactions.[44]

The same cannot be said of Guatemala. In the most recent development plan, issued for 1979-1982, the government proposed as a major objective the conservation of its natural resources. Among the broad goals of the plan were the expansion of transportation and construction facilities to rural areas as a means of creating employment opportunities and of improving income distribution. The plan assigned a high priority to the development of hydroelectric power and placed major stress on possible integration with the electrical systems of El Salvador and Honduras, as well as prospective collaboration in building a joint refinery and alcohol and fertilizer plants. Guatemala is distinctive, however, for its sustained search for oil. Thus

anticipated investments in exploration and development, building of pipelines, and establishing oil-related facilities have led to recommendation for
the creation of a state enterprise for petroleum called PETROGUAT.[45]

Regional integration appeared high on the priorities in Honduras during
the mid-1960s. The development of land transportation networks was
regarded as a significant step toward accelerating the integration of domestic markets and contributing to the integration of the Central American
Common Market. Throughout the 1970s Honduras's development priorities
have remained fairly constant, with basic priority assigned to increasing the
annual growth rate of the GDP by 6.5 percent, improving the living standard,
and regulating the use of natural resources. In recent assessments the Agency
for International Development (AID) has viewed energy as a problem in the
development process due to the impact of oil on the balance of payments
and extensive deforestation. Further, the increasing cost of energy impairs
the integration of rural areas into the market system and reduces incentives
to increase the value added through processing and manufacturing. AID's
assessment is that the El Cajon Hydroelectric project, jointly sponsored by
the IBRD and the IDB and scheduled for operation in 1985, will alleviate
immediate energy problems.[46]

Nicaragua is one of the least-developed countries of Latin America.
Although it has the largest area of any country in Central America, its land
transportation system in 1965 accounted for only 13 percent of total roads
in the region, all of which were concentrated in the Pacific zone where density
was greatest. With this in mind, the 1965-1969 plan allocated 12.7 percent
of total public investments to the transportation sector, with 82.5 percent of
this amount being channeled toward road construction. The plan laid stress
on renewable sources of energy due to exceedingly high electricity costs and
argued for expanding considerably the uses of wood, coal, and kerosene as
basic fuels in rural areas.[47]

In Panama, by contrast, the plan of 1970-1980 placed major emphasis
on electrification and exploring hydroelectric production. Although there
was some concern for the importance of coordinating programs of electrification with those of transportation and urbanization, there were no concrete policy directives for implementation purposes.[48]

Conclusion

For Latin America attention to energy issues is increasingly critical, and in
only the most recent development plans is the connection between energy
and the economy clearly noted. It yet remains to be fully recognized.

Given the region's economic development and policies for expanding infrastructure facilities, the following trends emerge from analysis of economic trends and development planning:

With respect to planning in the transport sector, these are as follows:

Investments in the transport sector are usually oriented toward specific projects rather than toward buttressing the transportation share of economic activity or GDP.

The highly urban nature of Latin America is not reflected in its overall transportation policies. However, more highly urbanized nations tend to focus on incorporating rural areas into the industrialized infrastructure.

Among the more modestly industrialized countries with international interests, expansions of international surface networks usually take priority over development of international air and water transportation (for example, Bolivia's focus on expanding highways to link with its bordering nations).

More highly industrialized countries, with a greater transportation infrastructure in place, tend to place greater emphasis on expanding international networks. Such countries, notably Argentina and Brazil, devote more attention to air and maritime transportation than do the less industrial countries.

Most development plans in Latin America—as in many other regions—focus on road construction. Yet with few exceptions the automobile is seldom mentioned. (The exceptions, of course, pertain to Mexico and Brazil, which emphasize the use of cars and the development of a national auto industry.)

With respect to energy and development planning:

There yet remains for fully developed energy policies to emerge. Only in the major exporters—Mexico, Ecuador, and Venezuela—is the petroleum sector a target for policies, and only in the giants—Brazil, Chile, and Argentina—is the energy sector in its entirety considered.

In general energy conservation is not a priority in transportation policy; however, a few development plans call for limiting automobile production as a means of saving energy.

The public sector usually sets forth energy as well as transportation policies, but there appears to be a trend toward greater participation of the private sector in the implementation of policies and management of investments.

For some countries there is a renewed interest in regional cooperation and a revival of earlier concerns for coordinating transport policies. This is gradually being manifested in the energy sector.

In all states, however, the public sector is assuming a greater role in energy policy planning and execution. The creation of potentially strong state enterprises is central to planning in the energy sector.

In retrospect two central themes appear to have dominated the Latin American planning scenes over the past two decades. First was the emphasis on investments in infrastructure facilities. The scarce factors were capital and technology. Energy constraints were nonexistent. Low oil prices were, there as elsewhere, taken for granted. Second came a greater concern for building social facilities and social services. Again, capital and technology—knowledge and skills—constituted the main constraints in these efforts. Of course in many cases financial constraints often masked lukewarm political commitment to development.

The petroleum costs have become so high that the potential economic disruption, balance of payments problems, and increasing national indebtedness have pre-empted other aspects of development. Even the traditional attention given to the two thrusts of development could no longer be continued. A developing country could not meet normal development objectives if it ignored the new framework that drastically changed energy prices and placed new pressures on policy choices. Yet, while new constraints emerged, in Latin America, as elsewhere, recognition of these constraints was slow.

This convergence of circumstances created the conditions favoring the pre-eminence of the public sector and expansion of the government's role. The public sector is assuming responsibility for guiding adjustments to new conditions, according this sector new legitimacy. In many Latin American countries the strong voice of the public sector is affecting the entire political structure. The full effects remain yet unknown, but the trend is clearly discernible. For in the developing countries the role of the state, always strong in defining priorities, is rendered stronger still by the new energy situation, with governments becoming the sole arbiters of development planning.

Notes

1. Consejo Nacional de Desarrollo, *Plan nacional de desarrollo, 1965-1969* (Buenos Aires, 1965). The research assistance of Nancy Wright is gratefully acknowledged.

2. Consejo Nacional de Desarrollo, *Plan nacional de desarrollo y seguridad, 1971-1975* (Buenos Aires, 1971).

3. *Primeiro plano nacional de desenvolvimento—PND, 1972-1974; Lei n. 5.727-de-4-11-1971-referenciada* (Sao Paulo, 1971).

4. Ibid.

5. Ibid.

6. *II Plano nacional de desenvolvimento, 1975-1979* (Brasilia, 1976).

7. *III Plano nacional de desenvolvimento, 1980-1985* (Brasilia, 1976).

8. Ibid.

9. Ibid.

10. Consejo Nacional de Politica Economica y Planeacion, *Plan general de desarrollo economico y social, Primera parte; el programa general* (Bogota: Departamento Administrativo de Planeacion y Servicios Tecnicos, 1962).

11. Departamento Nacional de Planeacion, *Planes y programas de desarrollo, 1969-1972: documento DNP-417*, 1969.

12. Antioquia Departamento Administrativo de Planeacion, *Sintesis de los planteamientos* (Medellin, 1974).

13. Departamento Nacional de Planeacion, *To Close the Gap: Social, Economic, and Regional Development Plan, 1975-1978* (Bogota, 1977).

14. Secretaria de Patrimonio y Fomento Industrial, *Plan nacional de desarrollo industrial, 1979-1982* (Mexico, 1979).

15. Ibid.

16. Ibid.

17. Oficina Central de Coordinacion y Planificacion, *Plan de la nacion, 1965-1968* (Caracas, 1967).

18. Luis Enrique Oberto and Antonio Casas Gonzalez, *Venezuela y el CIAP* (Caracas: Oficina de Coordinacion y Planificacion de la Presidencia de la Republica, 1973).

19. *V (Cinco) Plan de la nacion, 1976-1980*, Decreto 1.454, "Gaceta Oficial de la Republica de Venezuela" (Caracas, 1976).

20. Ibid.

21. Ibid.

22. Junta Nacional de Planificacion y Coordinacion Economica, *Plan integral de transformacion y desarrollo, 1973-1977: resumen general* (Quito, 1972).

23. Ibid.

24. Ibid.

25. Ministerio de Planificacion y Coordinacion, *Estrategia socioeconomica del desarrollo nacional, 1971-1991* (La Paz, 1970).

26. Ibid.

27. Ibid.

28. Ministerio de Planeamiento y Coordinacion, *Plan nacional de desarrollo economico y social, 1976-1980* (La Paz, 1976).

29. Oficina de Planificacion Nacional, *Plan nacional indicativo de desarrollo, 1978-1983* (Santiago, no date).

30. Ibid.

31. Oficina de Planificacion Nacional, *Plan nacional indicativo de desarrollo, 1979-1984* (Santiago, no date).

32. Ibid.

33. *Plan nacional indicativo de desarrollo, 1978-1983* (Santiago).

34. Instituto Nacional de Planificacion, *Plan global de desarrollo, 1977-1978* (Lima, 1977).

35. Ibid.; and Instituto Nacional de Planificacion, *Plan nacional de desarrollo, 1975-1978* (Lima, 1975).

36. Comision de Inversiones y Desarrollo Economico, *Plan nacional de desarrollo economico y social, 1965-1974* (Montevideo, 1965).

37. Ibid.

38. Presidencia de la Republica, *Plan nacional de desarrollo economico 1971-1975* (Paraguay, 1970).

39. Ibid.

40. Ibid.

41. *Belizian Seven-Year Development Plan, 1964-1970* (Belize?, 1964).

42. Comite de los Nueve Alianza para el Progreso, *Evaluacion del plan de desarrollo economico y social de Costa Rica, 1965-1968* (Washington, D.C.: Union Panamericana, 1966); and Oficina de Planificacion, *Plan nacional de desarrollo, 1974-1978: estrategia y plan global*, Version Preliminar (San Jose, 1974).

43. Oficina de Planificacion, *Plan nacional de desarrollo, 1974-1978*.

44. Consejo Nacional de Planificacion y Coordinacion Economica, *Plan de desarrollo economica y social, 1973-1977* (San Salvador, 1972).

45. Consejo Nacional de Planificacion Economica, *Plan nacional de desarrollo, 1979-1982* (Guatemala, 1978).

46. Consejo Superior de Planificacion Economica, *Resumen del plan nacional de desarrollo economico y social, 1965-1969* (Tegucigalpa, 1966).

47. *Evaluation of the National Economic and Social Development Plan of Nicaragua*, 1965-1969 (Washington, D.C.: Alliance for Progress, 1966).

48. Departamento de Planificacion, *Estrategia para el desarrollo nacional, 1979-1980* (1970).

8 Role of Government: State Petroleum Enterprises

Although the history of state petroleum enterprises in Latin America is a long one, dating from 1922 in Argentina, only in recent years has their potential as public instruments in the process of industrialization been realized. In 1970 there were at least 10 state petroleum enterprises in Latin American countries, some simply registration offices, others diversified corporations with full control over a country's energy sector. During the 1970s it became apparent that energy is so pivotal to a country's economy that several state petroleum enterprises began to permeate almost every aspect of domestic policy, from creation of employment, to inflation management, to the selection of key public officials. Foreign policy was similarly affected, and the director of the state enterprise frequently became the chief negotiator of loans, terms of trade, and networks of collaboration with other countries.

Most state petroleum enterprises in Latin America take the legal form of public corporations created by the state, which owns their entire financial capital.[1] The corporate form gives them a measure of financial and administrative independence necessary for the flexibility to adjust rapidly to changes in the industry. Their basis of finance is permanent revenue-earning assets, but, being instruments of public policy, they are not always profit oriented. Sometimes decisions are taken on noncommercial grounds, and government subsidies are frequently necessary. Control is exercised by the minister of petroleum or mines, who may be included on the management board. Some state petroleum enterprises require approval of decisions by the council of ministers. With the exception of areas already committed to foreign operators, they have exclusive jurisdiction over all national energy-producing territory. They are also the primary instrument for state takeovers. Guidelines are given in their statutes, and they must conform to all relevant legislation, such as injunctions against concessions or, as in the case of Mexico, against using foreign operators for technology or finance.

Evolution of State Enterprises

All over Latin America state petroleum enterprises originated in self-defense against the power of the transnational oil companies. From the

This chapter was written by Diane Beth Hyman with the research assistance of Elizabeth Leeds.

141

Latin American perspective international companies maximized profits without regard for welfare in host countries; they looked for oil where it was most accessible, refined and marketed it in consuming countries, and priced it far below its competitive levels. Natural gas was flared and wasted. Clearly, this view has some basis in reality. Far-reaching concession privileges existed, sometimes covering the entire territory of a country for sixty to ninety-nine years, with no mandatory relinquishment of areas unexplored or deemed noncommercial and very modest royalties. Host countries could not manage local production because of lack of technology, finance, and trained personnel. Inevitably, the government's role was limited to regulation of customs tariffs, import and export licenses, and fiscal regimes. Initial exploration risks were borne by the transnationals; subsequently, states attempted to gather more information about the workings of the industry; gradually the concept of national optimization took on more urgency.

Significant oil production began in Mexico in 1910 and in Venezuela in 1914. Mexico took the first step by reserving rights to the subsoil in its constitution of 1917. Argentina formed the first state company in the region (1922), followed by Chile (1926), Uruguay (1931), Peru (1934), and Bolivia (1936). Mexico once again acted dramatically in 1938 by nationalizing its entire petroleum industry. Production plummeted, but a precedent had been set. Further state petroleum enterprises were created in Colombia (1951), Brazil (1954), and Ecuador (1973). Finally, Venezuela nationalized its petroleum industry in 1976.

The barriers to entry of the public sector were formidable, given the vertical integration of the industry, the enormous capital requirements, economies of scale, and the high risk in upstream operations.[2] The first state-controlled activity was domestic marketing, then some refining. With the proliferation of foreign oil companies, technology became more accessible and bargaining terms improved. Gradually state enterprises entered into exploration, development, production, and conservation of discovered reserves. Significant exploration remained dependent on collaboration with transnationals.

Today state petroleum enterprises in Latin America operate in all phases of the industry. They remain the primary advisor to national governments in the development of petroleum resources, as well as the supervisor of foreign operators within national boundaries. Internally, their activities include exploration, production, refining, and marketing of petroleum and its products. Sometimes they enter into joint ventures, service contracts and production-sharing agreements with foreign organizations, control transportation and storage, and acquire tanker fleets for international distribution. Some have undertaken exploration outside the home country. Downstream activities have expanded into petrochemicals, fertilizers, iron and steel, and some construction.

State petroleum enterprises in Latin America are now serving as a critical link in technology transfer against a background of technological control by transnational companies in the region. They form a pool of scientific knowledge and skilled people who are "given the opportunity to borrow, adapt, and, above all, experiment with ideas until these become part of an economically usable technology."[3] A number of them have set up specialized research institutes: Argentina (1942), Mexico (1964), Brazil (1957), and Venezuela (1973). In addition to disseminating imported technology, some have developed, and even exported, indigenous technologies. Extensive work has been done in secondary and tertiary recovery methods.

As their status has changed from "marginal suppliers in a buyers' market to significant suppliers in a sellers' market," national oil companies have developed more bargaining power in the international market.[4] There is a trend toward an increase in the number of buyers and a diversification in marketing methods.[5] State oil companies have entered into contracts with the majors, independents, and nationals. They have made bilateral deals with governments, concessional deals with developing nations, and have operated on the spot market. In some cases, most notably Mexico, there have been domestic pressures to restrain production demands on the part of consuming nations in the long-term interests of the national economy. Ecuador and Venezuela are members of OPEC, and there is much debate in Mexico about future membership in the organization. The price of oil exports from Latin American countries is generally kept at or above OPEC levels.

Since 1975 regular meetings of Latin American state enterprise leaders have been held in the forum of ARPEL (Asistencia Reciproca Petrolera Estatal Latinoamericana, 1964). ARPEL is an attempt at regional integration of the petroleum industry through exchange of information and promotion of commercial transactions between members.[6] The Latin American energy association, OLADE, includes sources of energy other than petroleum in its scope. Its charter is to meet real development needs of the region and to promote rational use of resources both inside and outside Latin America.[7]

State Companies of Major Oil Producers

Mexico

Petroleos Mexicanos (PEMEX) was established in 1940 to centralize the administration of properties which had been expropriated from the international oil companies in 1938.[8] For more than a decade following the loss of foreign technological expertise and capital, production stagnated. The world price of oil was low as Venezuelan and Middle Eastern fields began to produce in abundance. Domestic prices for energy were subsidized in the interests of the industralization process, and PEMEX was chronically short of investment capital. Pressures of increasing domestic demand brought about a reevaluation of policy and a commitment to increasing production. Domestic prices were allowed to rise in 1959; from 1959 to 1972 more than 2,500 exploratory wells were sunk. But by 1971 Mexico had become a net importer of crude, with imports rising in 1973 to average 65,000 barrels a day. PEMEX was subject to the continuous rise in operational costs and rising international fuel prices. In 1974 President Luis Echeverria set top priority on exploration of deposits, providing PEMEX with a share of self-generating resources by allowing prices for natural gas to rise 110 percent and oil prices to rise by 85 percent. Another price hike of 33 percent was authorized in late 1976. As PEMEX's international credit rating improved, it began to borrow substantial sums from abroad. Intensified exploration was rewarded by vast increases in reserves (1980 proven reserves—60.1 billion barrels; potential reserves—250 billion barrels).[9] Oil euphoria took hold in the country. PEMEX has become the center of expectations and controversy.

President Jose Lopez-Portillo was widely regarded as the nation's first oil man.[10] In fact oil expertise has become a new qualification for the presidential candidate of 1982. The second most important figure in the country was PEMEX Director General Diaz Serrano. In the 1970s he "traveled hither and yon like the Foreign Relations Minister, he negotiated loans like the Treasury Minister, and he worked out trade agreements like the Commerce Minister."[11] Over the past five years PEMEX's staff has risen from 80,000 to 120,000, making the company the largest single employer.[12] The only way for manual workers to get a coveted job with PEMEX is through the Union of Petroleum Workers (STPRM). The union controls about U.S. $88 million in assets, invested in land, social services, agricultural cooperatives, retail outlets, and small industries.[13]

There is considerable controversy between conservationists and expansionists in setting production levels. Opponents of PEMEX charge that the company has concealed the extent of new discoveries and is increasing production above government set limits.[14] The president has stressed that the initial target of 2.25 million to 2.5 million b/d for 1982—which was reached this year—is not a ceiling.[15] Export commitments are similarly over the 1.1 billion b/d target. Critics oppose proposed expansions in capacity, arguing that raising production levels will exacerbate inflation (the rate was estimated at over 25 percent for 1980) and will waste a nonrenewable resource.[16] Nevertheless, Mexico's ambitious industrialization has set domestic demand at a growth rate of 8 percent/year, with projections for

1982 reaching 1.2 million b/d. PEMEX's share of total exports rose by the middle of 1980 to 64.5 percent (almost U.S. $13 billion) from 45 percent in 1979 (U.S. $4 billion), vital in reducing the balance of payments deficit and foreign indebtedness.[17]

Although the company received a subsidy to keep domestic prices at one-sixth the price of exported gas and one-fifth the price of exported fuel oil, it continued as a net contributor to the government. Its contribution through taxes to public sector savings went from $665 million in 1975 to nearly $900 million in 1977, although devaluation of the peso in the interim halved its dollar value.[18] Its claim on all federal monies budgeted for investment was 20 percent in 1979 (about U.S. $9.5 million),[19] U.S. $17.7 billion (400 billion pesos) in 1980.[20] To put that figure into perspective, the budget for the federal government itself was 549 billion pesos in 1980.[21] Within the context of other public agencies and enterprises PEMEX's 1975 revenue was 75 percent higher than the second largest agency, the social security institute, and three times higher than the third and fourth largest enterprises, the basic commodities agency and the state-owned electric company.[22]

About 71 percent of PEMEX's 1979 income (259,026 million pesos) was generated from sales. The rest came from credits and bond issues in Mexico and abroad. Some of the credits were tied to purchases of foreign equipment and technology, which amounted to U.S. $1 billion in that year, or over half of Mexico's total expenditures. Critics worry about such purchases eroding the positive effect on the balance of payments. About U.S. $9 billion, or half of the current investment program, is being raised in foreign capital markets.[23] The Bank of America announced in July of 1981 a record-breaking U.S. $4 billion loan for PEMEX.[24] The domestic role is increasing, however. Recently, forty-five Mexican institutions provided a loan of 1,300 million pesos. Led by a Mexican institution, an international group of ten banks provided a credit of U.S. $240 million.

According to Diaz Serrano, 93 percent of the engineering work is done with domestic resources, and 75 percent of the technology and 100 percent of the manpower and equipment are national.[25] Foreign firms are hired on a service-contract consulting basis to a limited extent. Exchange agreements of oil for technology have been concluded with Canada, Spain, Sweden, Brazil, and Japan. Mexico is justifiably proud of its petroleum technology, having exported its methods to other countries, including the United States. The Mexican Institute of Petroleum (IMP) has developed widely used methods of secondary recovery and serves as the training base for PEMEX personnel. There has been intense anti-Yankee opposition to selling to the U.S. the bulk of Mexico's oil exports. The United States now takes about 77 percent of the total.[26] A gas deal for 2 billion cubic feet/day fell through, but the United States still receives 300 million cubic feet/day.[27] Rather than increasing gas sales to the United States, Mexico has undertaken conversion of industry from oil to gas. Construction of a gas line to Central America has been proposed. It is still uncertain how much gas domestic conversion will consume and what the exportable surplus will be. Mexico is determined not to sell any one country more than 50 percent of its exports or supply any one country with more than 20 percent of its oil imports.[28] President Echeverria's commitment to become oil supplier to the Third World never really materialized, as Mexico needed the foreign exchange from the highest bidders. Contracts have been concluded with Japan, Brazil, France, Italy, and Sweden, among others.

PEMEX is the nation's single largest industrial investor. The exploration and investment program totals U.S. $18 billion for 1972 to 1982, with large sums being spent to increase refining and petrochemical capacities.[29] PEMEX has a monopoly over basic petrochemicals. Mexico became self-sufficient in refining in 1979 and projects self-sufficiency in petrochemical production (2 million tons/year) by 1982.[30] Much has been spent to remove transportation bottlenecks: expansion of pipelines, work on ports and roads, construction of sea and rail tankers. PEMEX has invested in the manufacture of seamless pipe and has signed a contract with the government steel agency to explore for iron ore and coal as well as hydrocarbons.[31]

Perhaps the biggest challenge facing PEMEX is coping with the social turmoil created by its expansion into the southern states of Campeche, Chiapas, and Tabasco. These have been among the poorest areas of the country and are now experiencing rapid change through massive infusions of capital and demographic growth. Migrants seeking work have set up shanty towns beside the limited housing provided for PEMEX workers. Infrastructure is sorely pressed; inflation has soared. Peasants have reacted violently to the expropriations of their properties. "Mayors, city councils, peasant leagues, agricultural organizations, and other economic and community groups issued formal protests and, at times, impeded the oil monopoly's work by blockades and other forms of opposition."[32]

In sum, PEMEX is the most powerful force in Mexico today. Its backing by the government is unequivocable, though its economic, social, and political impact is regarded with caution by some. Its activities have provoked more outspoken opposition to the government than at any time in recent Mexican history. Its role as a catalyst for profound political change remains to be seen.

Ecuador

Corporacion Estatal Petrolera Ecuadoriana (CEPE) was created in 1973 in a wave of oil nationalism. This nationalism is belied by the fact that Texaco operates 98 percent of the country's production and holds 37.5 percent of a joint venture with CEPE.[33] The technical price of exploration and development requires foreign investment, according to the civilian president, Jaime Roldos Aguilera. CEPE has concluded an agreement for exploration with Yacimientos Petroliferos Fiscales Argentinos (YPF) of Argentina.[34]

CEPE has been deprived of funds for investment throughout its history, recently warning that it could face bankruptcy by 1982 unless assigned more funds. Its share in revenue from oil exports (which totaled U.S. $1 billion for 128,000 b/d last year) was reduced to 7 from 28 percent in 1974. To calculate CEPE's share, the price of a barrel was frozen to $23.50.[35] The government's policy of maintaining domestic prices among the lowest in the world is at the center of controversy with industry: this policy is largely responsible for the drain on CEPE's self-generating resources. Gasoline sells for $.18 to $.19/gallon. Predictably, however, attempts at even slight increases have been met by violent protest. The inevitable outcome has been a sharp rise in domestic consumption of products, 33,700 b/d in 1973 to 76,000 b/d in 1980.[36] There is also evidence of lively smuggling of oil to neighboring countries. Texaco has been discouraged from proceeding on proposed investment projects by government production controls, the decline in exportable surplus, and low domestic prices. In recent years its share of production has been 75,000 b/d, but its net exports have totaled only 15,000 to 17,000 b/d.[37] In 1979 CEPE asked Texaco to pay its royalties of 18.5 percent in crude oil instead of cash to take advantage of higher world oil prices.

Despite the government's plan to raise oil production by 35,000 b/d,[38] it seems unlikely that CEPE will be able to provide the 12 percent of investment capital envisioned in the 1980-1984 development plan. Its deficit for 1981 is expected to be U.S. $316 million.[39] The company will spend U.S. $404 million this year on developing new oil reserves (estimated proven reserves in 1980—1.55 billion barrels)[40] and will invest U.S. $160 million in oil production, up from U.S. $44 million in 1980.[41] Other projects include a U.S. $300 million fertilizer plant[42] and an increase in the capacity of the Esmeraldas refinery from 5,600 to 90,000 b/d.[43] The Mexican Institute of Petroleum is to provide technical assistance for that expansion. CEPE has taken direct control of the Amistad gas field and has signed contracts with foreign companies for development of it.[44] Texaco has held off of an extensive program of secondary recovery by water flood in Ecuador's largest field, Shushufini, which contains an estimated 300 million barrels of crude oil.[45] It has also shelved plans for creation of a joint venture company with CEPE, Petro-Amazonas, which would have been responsible for drilling and production.

Ecuador's major markets are Caribbean refiners, Chile, and the United States.[46] In March of 1981 CEPE agreed to supply South Korea with 15,000 b/d of crude oil over two years.[47] As a member of OPEC Ecuador formally follows its pricing policies. Over three years ago there was a policy of "new pragmatism'': market-oriented pricing, attempts to reach agreement with Texaco, expansion in drilling with incentives to the private sector.[48] But in 1979 the current civilian government took over from the military, and there has been a record of dispute between the government and the private sector. CEPE has been caught in the fray, kept short of substantive government support.

Venezuela

Petroleos de Venezuela (PDVSA or Petroven) was set up in 1976 to implement the nationalization of the country's oil industry. In the 1960s Venezuela declared that there would be no more concessions, only service contracts, which would have to be approved by the long-established state oil company, CVP. Since nationalization, Petroven has acted through fourteen subsidiaries, including CVP. (These are: Amoven, Bariven, Boscanven, CVP, Deltaven, Guariven, Lagoven, Llanoven, Maraven, Meneven, Palmaven, Roqueven, Taloven, and Vistaven.) Ten are successors to former foreign companies, and three were private Venezuelan companies. Although CVP has been given preferential treatment in allocation of operating acreage, its production has remained low. The principal producers have been Lagoven (ex-Creole), Maraven (ex-Shell/Conoco), and Meneven (ex-Gulf). Together they accounted for 85 percent of total production of crude oil in 1976.[49] The subsidiaries have retained the services of the previous owners for a fee corresponding to the $.20/barrel production margin which is allowed in the Middle East for ex-concessionaires. A recent amalgamation has resulted in a new configuration of subsidiaries: Lagoven, Maraven, Meneven, and Corpoven (operations); Inteven (research and development); Bariven (equipment purchasing); and Pequiven (petrochemicals).[50] Major decisions, including the annual budgets, must be submitted to the National Executive (council of ministers) for approval or modifications, according to a 1966 article in the statute of CVP.

Petroven is one of the largest companies in Latin America. It is seventeen times larger than the second largest in the country, the National Institute of Public Works. The public sector is extremely powerful in Venezuela; six of the ten largest companies are state owned. There has been a decline in the oil industry's workforce as well as in production since nationalization. In 1979 the workforce was 32,000 with an output of 2.4 million b/d, compared with 1957 when 46,000 workers produced 2.8 million b/d. It is estimated that by 1984 another 11,000 workers will be necessary, about 2,400 of whom will be skilled engineers.[51]

The net profit of Petroven in 1980 totaled U.S. $3.3 billion, up U.S. $400 million from the year before. Sales were U.S. $18 billion, up by $4 billion.[52] The 1979 production average was 2.36 million b/d (up 8.8 percent from 1978).[53] These exports have accounted for 72 percent of government revenues and 95 percent of foreign exchange earnings.[54] Here, as in Mexico, the government is trying to maintain production at an eventual average level of 2.22 million b/d for 1980 to 1985.[55] Profits are expected to rise to U.S. $4.9 billion by 1985, based on a 17.5 percent annual cost increase, 11.4 percent for depreciation, $230 million for technology assistance agreements, and 10 percent from increased royalties.[56] Proven reserves now total approximately 19.5 billion barrels.[57] As in Mexico and Ecuador, domestic prices have been kept very low. Premium gasoline costs about $.34/gallon.[58] Efforts to raise prices have been complicated by political and inflationary pressures.

Petroven's budget for 1981 is U.S. $4 billion, increasing from the U.S. $2.9 billion allocated for 1980 and the U.S. $1.5 for 1979.[59] Planned spending for 1979 to 1988 is slightly over U.S. $25 billion, allocated as follows: production, U.S. $11 billion; exploration, U.S. $5 billion; refining, U.S. $4.8 billion; domestic marketing, U.S. $1.6 billion; development of the Orinoco heavy oil belt, U.S. $2.5 billion; tankers, U.S. $450 million.[60] Most of the capital is to be generated internally. Besides projects for secondary and tertiary recovery, the exploration program has scheduled drilling of 343 exploratory wells in 1981.[61] Most of the oil is 25 degree API or less and contains much sulphur and other metals.[62] Refinery upgrading is essential, since most of the refineries acquired after nationalization were built to produce heavy fuels to meet demands of East Coast markets in the United States. Both domestic and foreign demands now require lighter yields. A U.S. $2.2 billion refinery upgrading program should be completed by 1983, increasing the run of heavy crude to 362,000 b/d 1979 from 1976 levels of 123,000 b/d.[63]

Lagoven has started the tendering process for the first production complex in the Orinoco heavy oil belt. Venezuelan firms will be given preference for the 700 contracts to be awarded, but the general contractors will be foreign. At a total cost of U.S. $8 billion, it will be one of Latin America's largest construction projects.[64] There are plans for drilling, building a plant to remove carbon molecules from the crude oil, building a new oil town for 30,000 people, and laying down 300 kilometers of pipelines. Development of the Orinoco Belt is assigned high priority, given record world oil prices and estimates of extracting and upgrading Orinoco oil at only U.S. $13-15 billion.[65]

Venezuela is becoming less dependent on foreign technology. This fact is reflected in the new terms negotiated in 1980 on expired three-year contracts.[66] The new contracts will run for a maximum of two years. The per barrel fee (average $.25/bbl) has been replaced by payment for services rendered. The confidentiality clause, under which information could not be shared among Petroven's subsidiaries, has been eliminated. Five new sales contracts, to run for a maximum of two years, have also been negotiated between Petroven and Exxon, Shell, Gulf, BP, and Phillips (in petro-chemicals).[67] The sales period has been reduced to twelve months, and the 10 percent margin clause, according to which the buyer could unilaterally change the quantities purchased, has been eliminated. Also to be included is a certificate of destination to avoid diversion to the spot market.

Venezuela is actively pursuing a policy of export diversification, particularly in light of Mideast tensions. The majors are taking less: 80 percent of exports in 1976, 65 percent in 1979, an estimated 50 percent in 1980.[68] There has been an increase in direct sales to final clients. In 1980 Venezuela's direct customers included Colombia, Costa Rica, Brazil, and Italy. Light and medium oils are tied to the purchases of heavier oil. Generous financing of Caribbean and Central American oil bills has had political overtones. Efforts to contribute to democracy and stability in the region led to the beginning of a foreign aid program in 1975. Since then the government has authorized spending of U.S. $5.8 billion and disbursed U.S. $3.94 billion.[69]

The country's foreign policy is overwhelmingly dependent on oil. After President Luis Herrera Campins took office in 1979, he put petroleum counselors in Venezuelan embassies in OPEC and other major petroleum importing and exporting countries. Interministerial collaboration has been strained because of lack of clear guidelines and conflicts over authority.[70] The intent of the policy, however, does indicate the government's view of the role of Petroven not only in the economy but in politics as well.

Brazil

Petroleo Brasileiro (Petrobras) was formed in 1950, giving the company monopoly rights over exploration, production, and all new refineries. Previous legislation in 1938 declared the petroleum industry a public utility under the direction of a National Petroleum Council. Until recently there was an absolute injunction against the use of foreign technology and resources. Realizing Brazil's vulnerability to interruptions in foreign supply as well as the drain of oil imports on the trade balance, Petrobras is now depending on private and foreign resources for exploration.

Petrobras is one of the forty largest corporations in the world. Its 1978 sales amounted to U.S. $6.6 billion, with profits of U.S. $1 billion from refining, distributing, and transporting activities. It employs about 40,000 people.[71] The problem is that it cannot find oil. Over the past few years the company's production of domestic oil has fallen to 169,000 b/d.[72] Criticized for not finding oil at home, as opposed to its exploration success in such countries as Iraq, it has mounted a public relations campaign. Domestic consumption rose 6.7 percent in 1979 despite high prices.[73] Artificially high prices for gasoline (just under $3/gallon) are used to subsidize lower prices for diesel and fuel oil used in industrial production. Notwithstanding advances in alcohol fuel and hydroelectric power, Petrobras has emergency plans ready to ration petroleum. Currently, 85 percent of its oil requirements are imported.[74]

The company's budget for 1980 was U.S. $2 billion, with 64 percent going for exploration, development, and production (an increase of 27 percent over 1979).[75] For 1981 to 1985 exploration outlays are projected at U.S. $3.6 billion.[76] At the end of 1980 estimated proven reserves stood at 1.33 billion barrels, up from 1.264 billion barrels the previous year.[77] The objective of the five-year plan ending in 1985 is to drill 1,750 wells and to produce 500,000 b/d.[78] Imports would then account for 67 percent of the market.[79]

Risk contracts have existed since 1975, but their terms have been substantially relaxed to attract private and foreign capital. Contractors have been given increased decision-making powers in determining whether fields are commercial and in taking oil in payment once a field is producing. Under the contracts the companies pay exploration expenses, and any oil produced remains in the country to be purchased by Petrobras at agreed levels. By August of 1980 fifty-one contracts had been signed,[80] the largest number held by BP, Esso, and Shell. Vast tracts of 4 to 5 million square kilometers have been opened to the private sector for exploration.[81]

Braspetro, the foreign arm of Petrobras, has been exploring in such countries as Egypt, Chile, and Iraq. In 1980 it relinquished rights to develop giant discoveries in southern Iraq in exchange for a guarantee of oil shipments. Iraq normally supplied 400,000 to 500,000 b/d of Brazil's import requirements of 900,000 b/d,[82] but disruptions there have led to attempts to diversify away from the Gulf. Petrobras was authorized in October 1980 to make up for Iraq's shortfall by buying 200,000 b/d from various sources, including the Soviet Union, Mexico, and Venezuela. It is cooperating with the latter country in heavy oil technology, energy conservation, and petrochemicals.

Petrobras is also giving up its oil import monopoly. It is asking private foreign companies which have marketing networks in the country, principally Esso, Texaco, Shell, Mobil, and Arco, to import crude oil.[83]

Circumstances have weakened Petrobras as a state monopoly, but the government's commitment to it remains firm. Significantly, Petrobras was excluded from a recent 10 percent cut in spending by Brazil's other state companies.[84]

Comparisons of Major Producers

Autonomy of operations for the state petroleum enterprises in Mexico, Ecuador, Brazil, and Venezuela varies according to statutory limitations, the degree of reliance on foreign know-how, and financial resources. All were created in a wave of nationalism, but Ecuador and Brazil have had limited success in achieving independence from private and foreign capital and expertise.

PEMEX is emerging as the most significant in terms of its impact on the domestic policymaking process. Constrained by wide-ranging injunctions against foreign companies, it has had to grow independently until it has become what some have called a "state within a state." The president works closely with the Director General, who operates independently of the ministries, is constitutionally empowered to expropriate lands, and is the country's largest single employer. Public criticism of the company's investment priorities, occasional inefficiency, and corruption have provided one check to its power. Another is the influence of the petroleum workers' union. Venezuela's Petroven is decentralized, with major decisions still subject to the approval of the council of ministers. It seems, however, that the Energy Minister is the primus inter pares, given the predominance of oil in the domestic economy. Having retained the services of ex-concessionaires, Petroven has been slow to acquire necessary technology, but progress is being made. CEPE of Ecuador has been in the middle of a tug-of-war between successive governments and Texaco. The terms of CEPE's relationship with Texaco have been largely outside the control of the state enterprise. Dissatisfaction on both sides and lagging production and investment are evident. Brazil has been forced away from its extreme oil nationalism, but Petrobras is still the chief negotiator and supervisor of outside operators. With its own highly developed technology, it has had various successful ventures outside its own borders.

All the countries except Brazil have limited the self-generating resources of the state petroleum enterprises by keeping domestic prices low. This policy is a result of attempts to subsidize the industrialization process (Mexico), to control inflation (Mexico and Venezuela), and to avoid civil strife (Ecuador). Attendant increases in domestic demand have cut into the exportable surpluses. The most extreme victim is CEPE, which is almost bankrupt. Mexico's prices have been allowed to rise somewhat, and PEMEX is now sufficiently credit-worthy to issue bonds and raise loans both domestically and abroad. Venezuela and Mexico have also been grappling with the problem of setting production limits.

Mexico has made the most concerted effort to use the petroleum bonanza to maximize the value added of its exports and diversify the economy. It is self-sufficient in refining, and the petrochemicals industry has been given top priority status. Venezuela has been somewhat less successful in diversification, having to invest large sums in upgrading its refineries to process heavy crude yields. It has made some progress in petrochemicals and in its tanker fleet.

All the companies except CEPE have been trying to diversify their petroleum trading partners. Nevertheless, Brazil still depends on the Middle

East for 85 percent of its requirements, Mexico sells 77 percent of its exports to the U.S. (in spite of itself), and Venezuela sells 50 percent to the majors. Direct deals with foreign governments are becoming more common, as are oil-for-technology agreements. Mexico and particularly Venezuela have been using their resources to gain political leverage in the region. Concessionary terms have been extended to a number of countries in the Caribbean and Central America.

State Enterprises in Other Countries

Argentina

Yacimientos Petroliferos Fiscales Argentinos (YPF) was the first state petroleum enterprise in Latin America, founded in 1922. The government began to restrict foreign operators in the mid-1930s, and by 1958 YPF was given a formal monopoly. It was authorized to enter into what are now known as production-sharing agreements with foreign private companies. During the Peron regime the industry was essentially closed to private capital. After the military takeover in 1976, the government of General Jorge Videla opened options for exploration, development, and production to foreign and domestic private companies. According to the terms set then, the state would own all oil discovered or produced, with contractors being paid in cash according to negotiated agreements. In 1978 a risk contract law was passed, providing incentives for exploring with YPF 1,230,000 square kilometers of onshore sedimentary basins and 1,323,000 square kilometers offshore.[85] Two new contracts were signed with the Royal Dutch/Shell group for areas previously reserved for YPF.[86] Other contracts include those with Amoco, Cities Service, Shell, and private Argentine companies.

Argentina is 92 percent self-sufficient in oil, but secondary recovery from older wells accounts for about 54 percent of output.[87] If the country is to achieve self-sufficiency by 1985 and maintain it to 2000, nearly 7 billion barrels of proven reserves will have to be recovered.[88] In 1979 oil production peaked at 471,233 b/d.[89] End-1980 proven reserves stood at 2.456 billion b/d.[90] YPF said that a total of 900 wells would be drilled in 1980 (330 by the private sector), up from 700 the previous year.[91] The government has appropriated U.S. $24.4 billion for a 1977-1985 program of restructuring Brazil's energy base.[92] Besides finding new oil deposits, the plan depends on maximum utilization of natural gas, hydroelectric projects, and nuclear power potential. Gas is controlled by a separate state company, Gas Del Estado. Finally, YPF is empowered to contract foreign loans. For example, in 1980 it was granted a loan from a consortium headed by Deutsche Genossenschaftbank and Lloyd's Bank International for U.S. $300 million.[93] It is planning to upgrade its two largest refineries at a cost of U.S. $500 million.[94]

Colombia

Ecopetrol was formed in 1951 as Colombia's state oil enterprise. It operates alone and in association contracts with foreign companies, usually taking a 50 percent share of joint ventures.

Colombia too has persisted in maintaining low domestic prices. High fuel imports at current world prices finally prompted the government to authorize Ecopetrol to raise its prices a relatively modest 30 percent in 1980. With crude selling at $1.70/bbl in 1979,[95] the company reported losses of U.S. $222 million in 1979.[96] Estimates for 1980 fuel imports were put at U.S. $1 billion.[97]

Recent discoveries in the Arauca 1 deposit have encouraged optimism that the country could achieve self-sufficiency by 1985.[98] Exploratory drilling has been stepped up: 48 wildcats were scheduled for 1979, an increase from 23 in 1978 and 27 in 1977. In 1979, 18 were drilled by Ecopetrol and the rest by fifteen foreign operators.[99] Production was forecasted at 126,000 b/d in 1980, rising from 122,550 b/d in 1979.[100]

There is active foreign interest in Colombia's potential, despite Texaco's selling off of its 50 percent share in the Putumayo region and its stake in the Trans-Andean pipeline. Besides objecting to the low prices paid for domestic oil production, Texaco did not feel that the region held long-term commercial potential. Ecopetrol will take a 50 percent working interest in the discovery by a group led by Elf Aquitaine.[101] It has concluded an agreement with Occidental, whereby the latter will pay for all exploration costs, but, if there is a commercial find, Ecopetrol would then become a fifty-fifty partner, sharing development costs. A 20 percent royalty would be paid in kind before the production split. Ecopetrol would buy Occidental's share of production at world prices.[102]

A 20,000 b/d expansion of Ecopetrol's refinery at Cartegena is scheduled for completion in 1982. This project is being financed in part by a U.S. $4.3 million loan from the U.S. Export-Import Bank.[103] Other projects under study include plans to sell liquefied natural gas to the United States, a plant for making methanol to blend with motor gasoline, and a fertilizer plant with capacity to produce 247,000 tons/year of urea and ammonia.[104]

Peru

Petroperu was set up in 1934 during the government of the leftist and nationalistic General Juan Velasco. International companies were offered up to half of the oil they found in their own exploration. Peru is Latin America's fifth oil-exporting country (after Venezuela, Mexico, Ecuador, and Trinidad). In the last three years production has nearly tripled to reach 200,000 b/d.[105] Proven reserves are estimated to be between 600 and 750 million barrels.[106] Oil exports were more valuable than copper exports for the first time in 1979 (U.S. $797 million), averaging 60,822 b/d. Although they declined the following year to 53,973 b/d, earnings were estimated at U.S. $820.5 million.[107] Petroperu finally made a profit, from a debt position of U.S. $388 million in 1979. The debt was refinanced by a consortium of international banks led by Banco de la Nacion (Peru) and Chase Manhattan.[108]

In the early 1970s Peru began an extensive and costly exploration program. Of the sixteen companies awarded contracts, only Occidental and Petroperu were successful in finding viable deposits. The others relinquished their areas. Esso's concession was expropriated in 1969.[109] Petroperu signed a thirty-five-year contract with Occidental in 1971, agreeing to pay the latter's taxes. Under a contract revision in 1980, Occidental will receive 9 percent of production after all costs are met, a reduction from the previous 30 percent. Belco (the second main investor) and Occidental must now pay taxes of 68.5 percent from their own shares of oil and also provide supplies for the domestic market.[110] New contract provisions require all foreign companies to pay taxes. The desired profit split is 60-40 in favor of Petroperu.

The most recent legislation (1981) is designed to increase foreign investment. To maintain self-sufficiency, U.S. $900 million in private capital for exploration is needed by 1985.[111] A key incentive is a tax credit against income which is reinvested in Peru's oil industry. The 90 percent reinvestment allowance for state petroleum enterprises will remain in effect. Under a revision of the law passed the year before, Petroperu can now contract with other companies for advanced recovery operations. Previously, these had been reserved for the state company, with the exception of the Occidental/Bridas agreement for the Talara fields.[112] The company itself will spend $40 million for exploration this year.[113]

A number of private companies are forming joint ventures to rehabilitate the old Talara fields on the northwest coast of Peru. Some of these fields were discovered as far back as 1863, and, although they are declining in production, they are still desirable because the grade is light and the sulphur content is low. An additional production of 100 million barrels is expected. As of 1979 the state company was expecting a loan from the World Bank of U.S. $10 million for these projects.[114] The Japanese have first claim on Petroperu's oil exports as repayment for a loan of U.S. $330 million in 1974 used to help finance the Trans-Andean pipeline and other petroleum projects.[115]

Energy Management in Latin America

Throughout the last decade there has been an intensification of efforts to find and produce oil in Latin America. The sense of urgency has somewhat mitigated the spirit of nationalism under which the state petroleum enterprises were created. Foreign capital and expertise are once again welcomed by countries unable to exploit their potential on their own. Negotiations with outside contractors, nevertheless, remain constrained by protective legislation favoring the state companies. Latin American producers have increasingly demanded a higher share of profits from explorations by foreign companies.

Generally, low prices for petroleum and products prevail. Subsidies for domestic consumption—which is increasing—are depriving the state oil enterprises of needed funds for investment. Besides domestic pricing policies, financial autonomy is dependent upon the following factors: authorized and paid-up capital, disposal of income and formation of reserves, budgeting and investment planning, and the ability to secure loans.[116] A strong equity base and a reasonable debt/equity ratio are characteristics of corporate strength which apply to public corporations as well as private. Financial autonomy is particularly important in being able to withstand shocks to the rest of a country's economy.

There is a dynamic interaction between the state oil companies' domestic investments and the realization of national plans. Sometimes decisions are taken that cannot be justified from a strictly monetary point of view, such as PEMEX's laying down of pipelines in remote areas to promote balanced national development. The companies face competing claims for investment both upstream and downstream. Their downstream involvement abroad increases their access to the industrialization process, as they develop technical skills and secure relationships with foreign companies and governments.

Since the companies are the principal negotiators of oil trade and loans for development of their countries' petroleum industries, they are key players in the foreign policy decision-making process. Direct government-to-government sales increase in times of shortage. The countries are attempting to diversify their trading partners, but, as we have seen, their success has been limited. Sometimes credits are extended in exchange for claims against future oil exports, such as Japan's claims on Petroperu's export surplus. A number of companies have received loans from development agencies, such as the World Bank and the Export-Import Bank.

A number of Latin American countries have in operation programs for alternative energy sources. Brazil has been most aggressive in its production of alcohol from sugar cane. Maximum utilization of natural gas is the policy in several countries, including Bolivia, Mexico, and Argentina. According to a 1979 government order, conversion to natural gas of commercial heating systems in Buenos Aires must be completed within six years.[117] Important hydroelectric projects are underway in Brazil and Argentina.

Prospects for Cooperation

Cooperation among the Latin American state petroleum enterprises can take place within the regional energy associations, OLADE and ARPEL.

OLADE is plagued by bureaucratic complexity, but ARPEL has been quite successful in establishing linkages between the oil importing and exporting state enterprises. Its two objectives have been increasing trade and raising the level of technical know-how among its members. It sponsors mutual technical assistance, training courses, research, expert meetings, and various publications. It also acquaints local manufacturers with the requirements of the petroleum and petrochemicals industry. Partly as a result of these activities, heavy capital goods and services industries have been established in Argentina, Brazil, and Mexico, supplying much of the requirements of member countries. ARPEL undertook the task of training technicians in Ecuador when CEPE joined the organization shortly after its formation in 1973.[118]

Technical research centers also exchange information on a regular basis. The countries involved are: Argentina—YPF's Department of Research and Development; Mexico—The Mexican Oil Institute; Brazil—Petrobras' Investigation Center (CENPES); Bolivia—the YPFB Oil Technology Center; Venezuela—the Oil Technology Institute (INTEVEP). Some have developed new technologies which have been exported internationally.

Bilateral deals have been particularly important in recent years. For example, between Mexico and other Latin American countries these agreements include the following: for Jamaica, technical assistance for a refinery; coordinated research on basic and secondary petrochemicals for Venezuela and a shared commitment to supply Central America and the Caribbean with 160,000 b/d (which Venezuela had previously supplied alone);[119] for Costa Rica, a feasibility study for a refinery and petrochemical complex; and for Brazil, assistance for refining and marketing Mexican crude oil. Finally, there is talk in Mexico about the formation of a Latin American oil-exporting organization with Venezuela, Bolivia, Guatemala, Peru, and possibly Colombia. Together these trends point to new directions for regional cooperation and a new effort to expand utility of these countries' capabilities. The role of state enterprises in developing and managing energy resources is paramount, as are their efforts in fostering cooperation. State enterprises thus assume a dual role: managers of national resources and initiators of regional cooperation.

Notes

1. Hasan S. Zakariya, "State Petroleum Enterprises: Some Aspects of Their Rationale, Legal Structure, Management, and Jurisdiction," in U.N. Center for Natural Resources, Energy, and Transport, *State Petroleum Enterprises in Developing Countries* (New York: Pergamon Press, 1980), pp. 33-41.

2. C.A. Heller, "The Birth and Growth of the Public Sector and State Enterprises in the Petroleum Industry," *State Petroleum Enterprises*, pp. 8-16.

3. D.H.N. Alleyne, "The State Petroleum Enterprise and the Transfer of Technology," *State Petroleum Enterprises,* p. 112.

4. Abdulhady Hassan Taher, "The Future Role of National Oil Companies," in Public Information Department of OPEC, *OPEC Future and World Energy Markets* (London: MacMillan, 1980), p. 84.

5. Gustavo Rodriguez Elizarras, "Latin American Energy Panorama," *OPEC Future and World Energy Markets,* pp. 37-42.

6. C. Varrell Pastor, "Latin American State Petroleum Enterprises and Their Association in ARPEL," *State Petroleum Enterprises,* p. 84.

7. Rodriguez Elizarras, "Latin American Energy Panorama," p. 39.

8. See Edward J. Williams, *The Rebirth of the Mexican Petroleum Industry* (Lexington, Mass.: Lexington Books, D.C. Heath, 1979), pp. 5-7.

9. *Petroleum Economist,* 42 (November 1980), p. 498.

10. Edward J. Williams, "Petroleum and Political Change in Mexico," unpublished paper available from the author.

11. Williams, *The Rebirth of the Mexican Petroleum Industry,* p. 125.

12. *New York Times Magazine,* January 11, 1981, pp. 22-25, 56, 58, 59.

13. *Petroleum and Development,* June 20, 1980, pp. 9-10.

14. Ibid.

15. *Platt's Oilgram News,* May 1, 1980, p. 1.

16. *Wall Street Journal,* July 21, 1980, p. 17.

17. *New York Times,* August 22, 1980, p. A6.

18. Williams, *The Rebirth of the Mexican Petroleum Industry,* p. 100.

19. Ibid.

20. *Latin America Weekly Report,* June 20, 1980, pp. 9-10.

21. Ibid.

22. Williams, *The Rebirth of the Mexican Petroleum Industry,* p. 99.

23. *Petroleum and Development,* June 20, 1980, pp. 9-10.

24. *World Business Weekly,* July 6, 1981.

25. *Platt's Oilgram News,* May 1, 1980, p. 3.

26. *Latin America Weekly Report,* November 28, 1980, p. 1.

27. *Petroleum Economist,* 47 (February 1980), p. 86.

28. *New York Times,* February 19, 1981, p. D6.

29. *Petroleum and Development,* June 20, 1980, p. 9.

30. Ibid.

31. *Latin America Weekly Report,* August 1, 1980, pp. 8-9.

32. Williams, *The Rebirth of the Mexican Petroleum Industry,* p. 154.

33. Frank E. Niering, Jr., "Ecuador: Continued Obstacles to Development," *Petroleum Economist,* 48 (February 1981), p. 53.

34. *Platt's Oilgram News,* August 7, 1980, pp. 2-3.

35. *Latin America Weekly Report,* July 11, 1980, p. 5.

36. Niering, "Ecuador," p. 54.

37. Ibid.

38. *New York Times,* March 12, 1981, p. D8.

39. *Latin America Weekly Report,* July 11, 1980, p. 5.

40. *Petroleum Economist,* 47 (July 1980), p. 319.

41. *New York Times,* February 12, 1981, p. D13.

42. *Petroleum Economist,* 48 (February 1981), p. 83.

43. *Latin America Weekly Report,* August 15, 1980, p. 6.

44. *Latin America Weekly Report,* January 4, 1980, p. 4.

45. Niering, "Ecuador," p. 54.

46. *Platt's Oilgram News,* August 7, 1980, p. 3.

47. *Petroleum Economist,* 48 (March 1980), p. 126.

48. Niering, "Ecuador," p. 54.

49. Donald O. Croll, "Search for New Oil Reserves," *Petroleum Economist,* 44 (September 1977), p. 349.

50. *World Business Weekly,* August 3, 1981, p. 39.

51. *Latin America Weekly Report,* December 14, 1979, p. 79.

52. *World Business Weekly,* August 3, 1981, p. 39.

53. Ibid., p. 36.

54. Ibid., p. 29.

55. *Platt's Oilgram News,* August 13, 1980, p. 1.

56. Ibid.

57. *Platt's Oilgram News,* January 9, 1981, p. 2.

58. Frank E. Niering, Jr., "Venezuela: On Course for the 21st Century," *Petroleum Economist,* 47 (May 1980), p. 193.

59. *Petroleum Economist,* 48 (February 1981), p. 83.

60. *Petroleum Economist,* 46 (August 1979), p. 343.

61. *Petroleum Economist,* 48 (February 1981), p. 83.

62. Niering, "Venezuela," p. 193.

63. Ibid.

64. *Petroleum Economist,* 47 (December 1980), p. 543.

65. Niering, "Venezuela," p. 194.

66. *Petroleum Economist,* 47 (March 1980), p. 134.

67. Ibid.

68. Niering, "Venezuela," p. 192.

69. *New York Times,* November 23, 1980, p. 10.

70. *Platt's Oilgram News,* November 3, 1980, p. 3.

71. *New York Times,* September 21, 1979, p. D1.

72. Ibid.

73. *Petroleum Economist,* 47 (October 1980), pp. 454-455.

74. *Petroleum Economist,* 47 (January 1980), p. 38.

75. Frank E. Niering, Jr., "Brazil: Open-Door Policy to Oil Search," *Petroleum Economist,* 47 (November 1980), p. 491.

76. *Petroleum Economist,* 48 (March 1980), p. 126.

77. Ibid.

78. *Petroleum Economist,* 47 (September 1980), p. 406.
79. Niering, "Brazil," p. 489.
80. *Petroleum Economist,* 47 (September 1980), p. 406.
81. Niering, "Brazil," pp. 489-490.
82. Niering, "Brazil," p. 488.
83. *Petroleum Economist,* 46 (September 1979), p. 383.
84. Niering, "Brazil," p. 488.
85. Frank E. Niering, Jr., "Argentina: Private Capital Aids Oil Drive," *Petroleum Economist,* 46 (October 1979), p. 410.
86. *Petroleum Economist,* 46 (May 1979), p. 209.
87. *Petroleum Economist,* 48 (January 1981), p. 38.
88. *Petroleum Economist,* 46 (June 1979), p. 259.
89. *Petroleum Economist,* 47 (March 1980), p. 134.
90. *Petroleum Economist,* 48 (March 1981), p. 126.
91. *Petroleum Economist,* 47 (February 1980), p. 86.
92. Niering, "Argentina," p. 409.
93. *Latin America Weekly Report,* October 3, 1980, p. 3.
94. *Petroleum Economist,* 47 (December 1980), p. 543.
95. *Petroleum Economist,* 46 (December 1979), p. 250.
96. *Latin America Weekly Report,* May 16, 1980, p. 5.
97. Ibid.
98. *Latin America Weekly Report,* May 23, 1980, p. 5.
99. *Petroleum Economist,* 46 (April 1979), p. 175.
100. *Petroleum Economist,* 47 (February 1980), p. 86.
101. *Petroleum Economist,* 47 (January 1980), p. 319.
102. *Petroleum Economist,* 47 (July 1980), p. 319.
103. *Petroleum Economist,* 48 (March 1981), p. 126.
104. *Petroleum Economist,* 47 (October 1980), p. 455.
105. *New York Times,* January 1, 1980.
106. Frank Niering, Jr., "Peru: Latin America's New Oil Exporter," *Petroleum Economist,* 46 (July 1979), p. 283.
107. *Petroleum Economist,* 48 (March 1981), p. 126.
108. *Petroleum Economist,* 46 (August 1979), p. 343.
109. Niering, "Peru," p. 285.
110. *Petroleum Economist,* 47 (June 1980), p. 267.
111. Niering, "Peru," p. 283.
112. *Petroleum Economist,* 48 (February 1981), p. 79.
113. Ibid., p. 83.
114. Niering, "Peru," p. 286.
115. *Petroleum Economist,* 48 (February 1981), p. 83.
116. See D.H.N. Alleyne, "Financial Provisions of State Petroleum Enterprises in Developing Countries," in *State Petroleum Enterprises,* pp. 152-153.

117. Niering, "Argentina," p. 412.

118. Pastor, "Latin American State Petroleum Enterprises and Their Association in ARPEL," pp. 82-91.

119. *Petroleum Economist,* 47 (October 1980), p. 450.

9

Political Change and Social Adjustments

The changing energy environment has created new social strains in most countries of Latin America.[a] Social costs are mounting for everyone. For the oil-rich countries, those exporting petroleum and potential exporters, the social costs have been more in the nature of distributional effects and associated political dislocations. The combination of new wealth and new constraints creates new social tensions. For oil-importing countries, the oil-poor states, social strains have resulted from political attempts to adjust to new scarcities. Persistent fear of supply interruption and changing oil prices threaten to create new economic stresses. For everyone, however, there is evidence of strain and efforts to adjust to new situations. On balance, at least three types of political costs are becoming apparent:

1. costs generated by government attempts to respond to new constraints through new policies, regulations, and so forth;
2. costs created by new investment patterns and allocations for growth, such as those due to oil investments, or infrastructure projects related to availability of finance;
3. costs due to political adjustments to rapid economic change—new wealth or impending poverty, as the case may be.

The convergence of these factors contributed to changing the political environment for many of the countries of the region. For Venezuela and Ecuador, the traditional exporters, changes in the nature of policy itself are contributing to new social and political strains. For Mexico, the new exporter, oil riches are already producing social stress. For all states of the region, the one uniform effect of these converging strains is the growing importance of state and government regulation.

[a]The most pervasive surveys of social and economic costs associated with oil price increases do not untangle those costs due to the events of 1973 from those due to the structural and societal characteristics of Latin American countries. This distinction highlights traditional distortions and the way they can be aggravated by sudden infusions of wealth or by the successful exploitation of a country's raw materials. For general survey, see, for example, E.V.K. Fitzgerald, "Some Aspects of the Political Economy of the Latin American State," *Development and Change*, 7 (1976), pp. 119-133; Douglas Bennett and Kenneth Sharpe, "The State as Banker and Entrepreneur: The Last Resort Character of the Mexican State's Economic Intervention, 1917-1976," *Comparative Politics* 10 (January 1980), pp. 165-189; E.V.K. Fitzgerald, "The State and Capital Accumulation in Mexico," *Journal of Latin American Studies* 10 (1978), pp. 263-282; and George W. Grayson, *The Politics of Mexican Oil*, (Pittsburgh: The University of Pittsburgh Press, 1980), especially chapter 5 which includes comparisons with Venezuela and Ecuador.

Government Policies and Social Unrest

The experience of countries with direct policy intervention in the energy or transportation sectors is still fairly new. Several examples in Latin America stand out as specific efforts to reduce oil consumption. It is still too recent to observe their impacts. But there is evidence of the public's reactions to new policy. Energy-related policies are becoming intensely political.

In January 1977 Brazil announced a set of policy measures which included a mandatory deposit of 2 cruzieros a liter on gasoline and of CR$250 a metric ton on fuel oil, the amounts to be paid by the consumer and to be returned after two years without interest or indexation. Brazil also sought to institute a 50 percent increase in road tolls on weekends for passenger automobiles. Regulations limited access of cars to certain city centers and instituted a new system of staggering working hours and systematic increase in the price of diesel fuel and fuel oils. These measures were designed to save about $120 million in the oil import bill.[1] Such policy interventions were not without their immediate social costs. Strikes and riots broke out in Brazil, Peru, and Santo Domingo specifically over increases in petroleum prices and shortages of supplies. In Ecuador, for example, the government has devised a variable petrol-pricing structure in the effort to ward off riots. The municipal transport system, there as elsewhere, is under pressure, increasing prospects of large-scale disturbances. In short, direct interventions in the petroleum sector created considerable unease.

The same may be said of government efforts to develop remedial policies for the inflation-ridden economic environment in most countries of the region. While problematic in their own right, in a worldwide context inflation rates in many countries in Latin America are not dramatic. Inflation-fighting measures such as tighter credit contributed to decreasing buying power and have had a negative impact on economic growth. By some assessments it is believed that the rate of employment has also been adversely affected.

There is yet another source of social strain evidenced most clearly by the case of Mexico. The government tried to abandon plans to limiting oil production in order to help curb inflation. Some officials regarded any proposal to expand oil production to the limit as inflation producing and likely to create further destabilization. Hence efforts to curb production were made. The complex economic process of reconciling a set of seemingly irreconcilable objectives—maximizing economic growth, reducing unemployment, curbing inflation, and so forth—were all built around predicted levels of export earnings. However, irreconcilable objectives remain irreconcilable and hence aggravate social strains. Continued production at current rates may contribute to the inflation-stress-conflict process that appeared to Mexicans to be so clearly demonstrated by Venezuela. The perennial problem of unemployment which plagues most Latin American countries emerged at the forefront once again in oil-rich countries. The requirements of rapid industrialization tied to a strong energy sector almost invariably impose strong preferences for capital-intensive investments. Mexico has been no exception. Together the state company, PEMEX, and the electricity industry absorb the bulk of public investments. Job creation is allegedly suffering. There appears to be no impending or realistic approach to the high rate of under- and unemployment, estimated in 1979 at 10 million individuals. Changes in oil production policies may change this situation; nonetheless, social disruption, whatever its source, cannot be easily averted.

These problems are not new. For example, in Mexico government incentives for the growth of capital-intensive industries in the 1960s, especially the petrochemical, oil, and steel industries, had grave effects on labor and employment generation. Industry, broadly defined, hired 258,000 workers in 1965 to 1970 but only 104,000 in 1970 to 1975.[2] The figures indicate that the continuing shift from labor to capital-intensive production explains the declining demand for workers. "If creation of employment continues to lag behind economic growth, Mexico will have to find jobs for about thirty-eight million people by the year 2000. . . . Employment would have to grow at an annual rate of 4.1 percent simply to maintain the 1977 level."[3] At that time, one-half of the economically active population was without year-round work. Presently an additional 800,000 men and women enter the labor force each year. Predictions for the future are dire, since 45 percent of the Mexican population is under fifteen years of age.

These broad trends bear largely on general macroeconomic conditions, but they are not directly created by Mexico's new wealth. Untangling the causes of social strain is almost impossible to do given the scanty information available. However, despite protests and social unrest, there is some evidence of adjustment to new scarcities. For example, in Brazil there has been a decline in the use of private vehicles. The situation in many countries is transitional: the stress evidenced is a by-product of adjustments to new energy constraints, and these adjustments are, by necessity, propelled by government policies and interventions.

Social Consequences of New Investment Patterns

For oil-rich states sudden increases in oil revenue unleashed a new pattern of domestic investments. In Mexico, for example, within five years the country's oil income had risen from $3 billion to $14 billion. Patterns of investment appear to be distorting the process of economic growth and aggravating structural dislocations. In the first two years two-thirds of all export earnings came from oil; non-oil exports stagnated. Agricultural production specifically was low, partly out of neglect. In 1979 about $2 billion were spent on grain imports. Imported luxury goods were readily available. Oil wealth is being used in larger shares of the federal budget. Infrastructure investments are suffering. Specifically, the transportation sector is being neglected. Railroads are over fifty years old. Highway construction and maintenance are being neglected.

The social and economic impact of oil exploration and development has contributed to the disruption of agricultural development plans through erratic and unplanned economic changes. The "pull" of labor has accentuated "squatter settlements" and contributed further to migrant flows from rural areas. At the same time PEMEX and other large enterprises suffer from labor shortages of both skilled and semiskilled labor.

In Venezuela oil-related industrial programs had already contributed to labor shifts and unemployment. Between 1950 and 1976 the percentage of people living in the countryside declined from 45 to 17.4 percent of the total population. While the official unemployment rate is only 6 percent, the underemployment rate (earning less than the legally mandated minimum wage) is 20 percent.

The agricultural sector has been considerably weakened due to the migration of small-scale farmers to the cities. Demand for food has risen in response to the high birth rates, and expanding purchasing power due to increased petroleum revenues. In 1973 to 1974 these, combined with crop failures in 1975, resulted in the rapid rise in the importation of agricultural products. For example, in 1976 Venezuela imported $814 million of processed foods. This was equal to 9 percent of the total export earnings. Food imports contributed to a $2.053 billion balance of payments deficit in 1978, an increase of $156 million over the year before. The financing of deficits and large invesment projects resulted in a $7,740 million foreign debt. On a per capita basis the foreign debt is bigger than Mexico's.[4]

The government declared it would place half of its total oil income in the Venezuelan Investment Fund as a means to reduce inflationary pressures and control the developmental process. The fund is designed to finance a new petrochemical industry and infrastructural projects such as shipbuilding, a massive steel complex, and a long-range agricultural program designed to attain self-sufficiency.[5]

Political Dislocations and Power Relations

For the oil-rich states changes in oil prices and massive oil income resulted in transformations in internal power relations as well. Four trends stand out: the rapid expansion of the bureaucracy and government agencies, the growing importance of the military as one of the strongest and most coherent political forces, the importance of the banks, and, last, the clear growth and predominance of public enterprises related to petroleum and energy.

In Venezuela revenue from oil sales allowed the government's income to grow from $3.8 billion in 1973 to $11.8 billion in 1978.[6] As has happened in Mexico, the public payroll has swelled—from 300,000 to 800,000 or more. Capital equipment has increased ninefold in as many years. Industry has been highly capital intensive, without an adequate pool of specialized labor.[7] One of the main beneficiaries of the new wealth was the military, whose official budget rose from $494 million in 1975 to $615 million in 1978, which is about 5.9 percent of public expenditures. Expansion of banking facilities also emerged, as did their new political power. There is some speculation that income distribution deteriorated, but resulting estimates are simply that.[8]

Among observers of Latin American politics, Venezuela has emerged as the classic case of the "petroleum syndrome." The relationship between growth, equity, and social change has been seriously disturbed, and the traditional patterns of social and political relations have changed. The emerging importance of technocrats and entrepreneurs in the political system changed more traditional patterns of power and wealth. The basis of the new power is depletable resources, and not productive capacity. Hence the implications of investment patterns go beyond merely economic concerns and bear directly upon the country's political arrangements and future structure. The role of the private sector in economic development now assumes strong political dimensions.

Distribution of benefits tied to key economic decisions is rendering oil-related decisions synonomous with decisions bearing on the viability of the polity itself. Oil income has become the major lubricant of political stability in Venezuela. Oil-related decisions have become the most important arena for public policy—second only to the current distribution of oil income. The conjunction of an oil boom and an electoral majority may be short-lived if serious economic dislocations are created by patterns of investments that are not readily translated into productive capacity. Essential political decisions in Venezuela, as in other oil-exporting countries, pertain to production policies, production ceilings, and investments in oil and other sectors. In Venezuela politics once again have become the process for overt distribution of economic benefits, and the political system the arena for conflicts over distribution.

In Mexico the historical fact that the country has already undergone its social revolution (of 1910) and by 1938 had nationalized the oil industry obscured the political implications of the new power of the oil sector. The state petroleum enterprise is clearly a new and dominant actor in Mexican politics, with its role not yet formally defined and not clearly incorporated into the body politic. Shades of technocratic domination emerge, and the party system has yet to accommodate the state enterprises formally.

PEMEX, the state oil company, is itself under considerable pressure. Its foreign customers pressed for lower prices. The government protested PEMEX's intentions to lower prices. The company has been searching for means of accommodating divergent interests and pressures. The company's move to cut prices an average of $4 a barrel on June 1, 1981, led to a storm of protests and a chain of reactions culminating in the resignation of its director general. Buyers appear less eager for Mexican oil and losses from foregone sales were already considerable by early July 1981.[9]

In Ecuador, while one-fourth of the 1975 budget has been earmarked for social services and infrastructure facilities, in reality the military has been a major beneficiary. The military received half of the government's 16 percent of royalties from oil. It has reserved for itself control of activities such as cement production, metal works, petroleum tankers, and construction of state refineries. As a dominant agent in economic activity, the military in Ecuador has clearly gained from the new wealth. There, too, evidence of deterioration of income distribution emerges. In 1969 the poorest 20 percent earned 4 percent of the national income. By 1975, two years after the major oil price increases, the poorest 20 percent earned 2.5 percent of the national income.[10] In addition to changes in control and distribution of economic benefits, it is apparent that in Ecuador implementation of the most recent five-year development plan is running into serious problems, largely because of the lack of political support—in addition to more conventional problems of inadequate planning and financial management difficulties.

In Brazil the apparent lack of success of Petrobras to make any significant strikes borders on becoming a political issue. "Why wouldn't God have conceded this present to us?" lamented the company's first president.[11] Large sectors of the country's public are angry at Petrobras' apparent inactivity domestically, especially in view of its success in Iraq. "If we can discover oil abroad, why can't we do so in our own country?"[12]

These reactions are all symptomatic of increasing expectations, far in excess of actual performance. Political systems in Latin America are all, to some extent, cognizant of the pressures created by a changing energy environment. The nature of the pressures differs, as do the political responses. The positive side, though underestimated here, appears more clearly in the international arena. The evidence so far points to one unsettling conclusion: the energy situation has created destablizing tendencies on the domestic scene, with attendant social and political costs. This instability may be the inevitable correlate of adjustments and change. It does not necessarily reflect social pathology or massive political dislocation. It may be too premature to pass judgment on the overall effects of a changing energy environment. The costs reviewed in this chapter are illustrative of the type of visible social problems.[13] However, the severity of these problems remains unclear. Although observers of the Latin American scene tend to stress the dislocating effects of the new energy environment, caution and a modicum of optimism may well be in order. The most favorable adjustments have occurred in the region's position internationally, where the evidence is less ambiguous, and despite the overall costs, some tangible benefits are becoming apparent as well.

Notes

1. See *IMF Survey*, February 1977, and Cloraldino Soares Severo, "The Energy Problem and Transport: The Brazilian Experience," December 1980. Prepared for the Seminario "Imacto del Costa de la Energia en el Sector Transporte," 1-3 December 1980, Bogota, Colombia. Translation available at the Department of Political Science, Massachusetts Institute of Technology, Cambridge, Mass.

2. *Latin America Economic Report*, August 17, 1978, p. A-19, as reported in George W. Grayson, *The Politics of Mexican Oil* (Pittsburgh: The University of Pittsburgh Press, 1980), p. 107.

3. *Latin America Economic Report*, May 13, 1977, p. 72, as cited in Grayson, *The Politics of Mexican Oil*, p. 108. Today the estimates may differ to some extent.

4. Ibid., pp. 117-125. Their estimates are for the late 1970s and thus out of date.

5. Grayson, *The Politics of Mexican Oil*, p. 118.

6. Ibid., p. 119.

7. *Wall Street Journal*, February 13, 1981, pp. 1 and 22. The numbers for Mexico, however, are different. See also *Wall Street Journal*, February 3, 1981, pp. 1, 22.

8. Grayson, *The Politics of Mexican Oil*, p. 119.

9. *Petroleum Economist*, 48 (July 1981), p. 307.

10. See Grayson, *The Politics of Mexican Oil*, pp. 122-125, for estimates.

11. *New York Times*, September 21, 1979, pp. D1, 12.

12. Ibid.

13. For a discussion of the economic and political consequences of expanding oil revenues in Venezuela and the problems associated with cuts in oil production, see Terry Karl, "The Political Economy of Petro-Dollars: Oil and Democracy in Venezuela," December 1981. Ph.D. dissertation, Department of Political Science, Stanford University.

**Part IV
New Perspectives**

10 International Politics: Problems and Opportunities

Latin America's response to the changing energy environment and attendant constraints has created new opportunities for the region internationally: new relationships with other developing countries signalling prospects of cooperation and a new, more assertive role vis-à-vis international institutions, signalling a new posture globally. Neither of these trends is entirely new, but the decade of the 1970s witnessed the consolidation of a more active Latin American role in international politics. In the 1980s an international transformation may be in the making in relations among developing countries and with international institutions. Important developments in new sources of finance available to Latin America, cooperation in the energy field, and the attendant influence in international politics are not conclusive by any means, yet they highlight the evolution of trends that are becoming characteristic of Latin America politics in the world today.

New Sources of Finance: Regional and International Assistance

By the mid-1970s the oil crisis had stimulated the development of new funding organizations and opportunities for collaboration in the energy field. In addition to direct balance of payments assistance reorientation in the approach of international agencies toward Latin America appeared. The following examples illustrate a broader trend.

In 1977 the World Bank, cooperating with the International Monetary Fund, the Inter-American Development Bank, and the Caribbean Development Bank, established the Caribbean Group for Economic Cooperation. It was hoped that the new group would provide important sources of cooperation for member countries. More recently, the World Bank has proposed the expansion of its current $13 billion lending program planned for the next five years. Priorities for this program are exploration for and production of oil, gas, and coal, as well as the development of renewable energy systems. The bank estimated that its programs could generate the equivalent of 2.9 million barrels per day of oil equivalent, which amounts to about 9.5 percent of projected Third World energy consumption estimated for 1990.[1]

The Inter-American Development Bank (IDB), the major regional banking agency, has programmed over 50 percent of its lending for energy and transportation. The specific projects and priorities continue to be debated, but investments in road networks and in related facilities have been made. Since the IDB reflects consensus for the region, this investment thrust is significant, particularly given the industrial countries' comparatively lower appreciation of the comprehensive effects of the new energy environment. In some ways the IDB's move is a precursor of investment trends for development in the region.

Increased liquidity in international capital markets created by the greater amount of oil revenues in circulation also provided new opportunities for financial flows. Since the oil-exporting countries themselves have contributed financial assistance to the region, a new basis for cooperation is emerging. Part of that assistance is in the form of loans, generally for specific projects. This assistance, however, is in addition to the more conventional balance of payments support that is extended by OPEC countries.

In 1977 the OPEC Fund for International Development (OFID, formerly the OPEC Special Fund) began supporting a wide range of projects in Latin America. It has as well begun funding other development programs, such as the International Fund for Agricultural Development established in Rome in 1977 as an additional channel for Mideast and other oil-based funds seeking to stimulate agricultural development in the poorest countries. OFID pledged $100 million to the UNCTAD Special Fund in 1979.

Although Latin America has generally received only a small percentage (less than 16 percent) of the total Special Fund, expectations in the region have been for greater assistance in the future. Venezuela, one of OPEC's founding members, has been pressing for a reorientation of the Fund to provide a fairer distribution of OPEC resources. Venezuela's Energy Minister protested to his fellow OPEC members that, of the $1.6 billion provided by OPEC since the fund was set up, only $60 million had gone to Latin America as of January 1980. One of the reasons cited for the poor distribution was that most Arab nations have their own bilateral aid programs with Africa and Asia, thereby bypassing OPEC facilities. Thus, in effect, lending by Arabs is greater than appears in OFID commitments.

This type of support represents a new development in Latin American and Arab relations. The full extent of commitments by producer states may not be readily known, but at least several examples stand out:

The Saudi Development Fund committed $56 million to Brazil for electrification on December 10, 1977. This commitment amounted to 3.4 percent of the fund's loans for 1977 by value.

Iran committed $100 million to Peru in the first quarter of 1975 for the Peruvian national oil company.

Iraq pledged $10 million to Cuba on October 15, 1979, for hurricane relief.[2]

These commitments are illustrative at best, and their actual disbursement remains to be verified, but they do represent a new trend of assistance among nonindustrial countries. The record of the OPEC Fund for International Development for 1976 to October, 1981, in terms of millions of dollars committed, is presented in table 10-1. The overwhelming proportion of that assistance is for balance of payments support; however, there are some major commitments for power development and for public utilities and the social service infrastructure. Only one large commitment has been made in transportation and roads, to Costa Rica, which represents 2.6 percent of all OPEC Special Fund support to Latin America. Over 55 percent of that support has gone to balance of payments assistance and 9.7 percent to energy and power development. For the period 1976 to 1979 loans to Latin America constituted 10 percent of the OPEC Special Fund commitments. While this represents only a small proportion of the states in the hemisphere, it affected thirteen of the Latin American countries, signaling an emerging type of relationship among developing countries themselves.

OPEC Special Fund loans are generally at a 0.75 percent rate of interest, with 0.5 percent rates extended to the most seriously affected countries and balance of payments loans. States generally have a grace period of four to five years, and the loan reaches maturity at ten to twenty years from its issuance. The entire sum is frequently not disbursed in one sum. Balance of payments loans require the recipient country to generate amounts matching the loan.

In 1980 $25 million was committed to Latin America for balance of payments support, including $1.5 million to Barbados, $.5 million to Dominica, $1 million to Grenada, $5 million to Guyana, and $7 million to Jamaica. These loans are to be repaid over ten years, following a three-year grace period. The loans carry an interest rate of 4 percent plus a service charge of 0.5 percent.[3] OFID appeared to extend more stringent rates during 1980. In addition, OFID extended $3.5 million interest-free to Haiti for agricultural support for small farmers,[4] as well as unconfirmed loans of $5 million to Honduras for hydroelectric power and $10 million to Nicaragua for agricultural and industrial production.[6]

The increased role of OPEC in giving assistance to other developing countries is encouraging. It has provided the basis for an expanding dialogue among developing countries, which can improve their mutual understanding and cooperation. This trend reflects the first large-scale evidence that a strategy of self-reliance among the developing countries is emerging. This strategy is at the heart of the proposed new international economic order. Lending practices among developing countries may well be

Table 10-1
OPEC Commitments to Latin America in 1976-1981
(in millions of dollars committed)

Recipient	Balance of Payments	Power	Public Utilities, Social Services, Urban Development	Agriculture	Transport and Roads	Total
Barbados	6.5					6.5
Bolivia			5.0			5.0
Costa Rica			13.4		3.0	16.4
Dominica	1.0					1.0
Dominican Republic		1.0		1.9		2.9
El Salvador	1.75					1.75
Grenada	3.35					3.35
Guatemala	1.75					1.75
Guyana	23.6			4.0		27.6
Haiti	3.2		4.0	3.5		10.7
Honduras	1.75	10.2				11.95
Jamaica	21.0			3.0		24.0
Paraguay			2.9			2.9
Totals	63.9	11.2	25.3	12.4	3.0	115.8
Percentage of loans to Latin America	55.2	9.7	21.8	10.7	2.6	100

Note: Data for 1976-1981 come from OPEC Special Fund loans, extracted from annual reports, and compared with individually reported loans in the Financial and Monetary News section of *Middle East Economic Survey* up to October 12, 1981. (Figures include OPEC Fund for International Development loans).

the first concrete steps toward implementing new economic relations. How practical, effective, or viable they may be remains to be seen, but it would be a mistake to ignore these efforts.

Cooperation for Energy Development

New patterns of cooperation have also developed, involving not only financial flows but also exchanges of skills for technical and financial aid to the poorer Latin American countries by the richer powers in the region. These patterns point to a new economic and political power of countries that had not previously enjoyed such positions.

In 1976 members of the Andean Subregional Integration Agreement (Cartagena Agreement) agreed in principle to establish a fund of $400 million to assist in financing their balance of payments deficits. This is an important step toward regional integration, departing from previous cooperation, which was limited to financing projects by the Andean Development Corporation.

In 1978 representatives of Bolivia, Brazil, Colombia, Ecuador, Guyana, Peru, Surinam, and Venezuela signed the Treaty of Amazonia Cooperation, otherwise known as the Amazon Pact, finalizing an agreement after a long history of deliberations. By stressing mutual cooperation and integration of administrative facilities along border regions, the intent of the pact is to contribute to the integration of the metropolitan areas of countries in the Amazon basin. This would revive the long-neglected Amazon waterways as a means of transportation and exploit the agricultural potential of the region. River transport may, in fact, assume greater importance in the development strategies of the Amazon region than it has in the past.

The establishment of OLADE further reflects new prospects for regional integration. OLADE's mission is to create more balanced production and consumption of petroleum for the countries of the region, in the sense of helping Latin American countries produce energy. For instance, Venezuela announced during the September meeting of eight energy ministers in Caracas that it was increasing sales to Brazil (the region's largest importer) to 60,000 barrels per day with a final target of 100,000 barrels per day. In 1980 Mexico raised its exports to Brazil from 20,000 to 50,000 barrels per day.[7] So, too, in a three-week session of the Sistema Economico Latinoamerica (SELA), convened to evaluate the progress of the U.N. Special Sessions on Development, one of the first priorities to emerge was an expansion of the Mexican-Venezuelan energy plan for Central America and the Caribbean.[8] Mexico and Venezuela are clearly emerging as leaders in the area of energy.

Brazil and Venezuela have begun discussions not only of increasing oil sales but of exchanging heavy oil technology, energy conservation, and petrochemical technology. Brazil is interested in Venezuela's oil, and Venezuela in acquiring Brazil's developing alcohol fuel technology.[9] At the political level both countries stress the need for "full freedoms and human rights," which some observers regard as having the potential of acquiring momentum in Latin America.[10] The state oil companies of Brazil and Chile are considering possibilities of joint oil exploration. One aspect of this venture is the commitment that Brazil buy 10 percent of Chile's total copper production.[11]

Cooperation in the development of nuclear energy is also emerging. In 1980 Latin America's two nuclear powers, Argentina and Brazil, began discussing the possibility of creating a regional organization for regulating nuclear development, as noted earlier. Argentina's superiority in that area appears to provide some leadership in the talks. Both countries are taking a pragmatic posture: Argentina seeks access to information on Brazil's experience in detecting uranium deposits, in exchange for access to Argentina's skills in uranium processing and related engineering technology.[12]

Prospects for cooperation in pricing and marketing natural gas are emerging as well. Argentina invited Bolivia to develop joint pricing and marketing strategies for exploiting their deposits of natural gas. Given the size of these deposits, between them they are the major suppliers of Latin America. Brazil, a potential customer, had an agreement with Bolivia since 1974 to obtain supplies, but political difficulties between the two countries have rendered the agreement practically void. Brazil has now signed an agreement with Argentina, which encouraged Bolivia to take Argentina's joint strategy proposal seriously. Among the potential buyers for gas from Bolivia and Argentina are Uruguay, Paraguay, Chile, and Peru, and, of course, Brazil which is the largest potential importer.[13]

The formation of OLADE has started a trend toward regional cooperation and coordination of internal development programs of individual countries. At the Caracas meeting of September 1980, the energy ministers of eight countries (Brazil, Colombia, Dominican Republic, Costa Rica, Ecuador, Mexico, Nicaragua, and Venezuela) agreed to form a regional energy plan for the OLADE meeting in Bogota in November of that year. The plan was devised to provide more balanced production and consumption flows. In the main it noted that, while Mexico and Venezuela export most of their production outside the region—the regional production of crude being 5.52 million b/d (based on 1979 estimates) and consumption within the region only 4.40 million b/d—deficit countries have to import oil from outside. Therefore the plan proposed: (1) the development of indigenous energy sources aimed at regional self-sufficiency, (2) rationalizing energy production, marketing, and consumption to reduce dependence on hydrocarbons, (3) increasing financial resources from international institutions and industrialized countries and thus sources of revenue for developing energy projects.[14] An unwritten presumption underlying OLADE's efforts is that the diversity in energy resources, in level of economic development, in distribution of skills and technology, and in demographic structure now enables the countries of Latin America to consolidate a new basis for regional integration.

The energy sector, specifically, has provided the basis for new forms of broader international cooperation. Mexico emerges as a particularly strong nation in this context. The current leadership's general strategy has been diversity in exports to reduce dependence on the U.S. market, which currently accounts for 80 percent of all Mexican exports. France, West Germany, Sweden, Canada, and Japan seek Mexican oil. These countries offer nuclear technology and agricultural products in exchange for oil.[15] Mexico, however, has maintained an independent stand particularly with regard to Japan's pledge to increase Mexican oil development. Joint Japanese-Mexican economic committees have discussed the exchange of Mexican oil for Japanese investments and technical assistance in the auto, steel, and petrochemical sectors. One specific example is important: Japan has proposed to expand the Las Truchas steel complex in a package with the establishment of Japanese oil refineries.[16] However, Mexico's concern for curbing inflation places some constraints on meeting Japanese requirements. It has been argued that increased oil exports would be possible only if countered by increased Japanese investments.[17] But the exercise of choice can go both ways: Mexico offered to Japan oil supplies at lower prices in mid-1981, and the Japanese refused the offer. Conditions in the world market had changed, and a glut was in view. Japan's stockpiles were full. Mexican oil was no longer desirable—even at prices lower than had been offered by Mexico earlier.[18] A less controversial example is the new agreement between Mexico and Portugal involving industry, tourism, and technology. Mexico will provide Portugal with oil, and Portugal will provide expertise in heavy industry, petrochemicals, and tourism.[19]

Brazil has tried to reduce its own energy problems by establishing contracts with Iran and Iraq for oil exploration through its foreign subsidiary Braspetro.[20] This case is distinctive because it involves a non-oil exporter contracting for petroleum exploration outside its own boundaries. Since the Iran-Iraq war Brazil's position as a recipient of Iraqi oil has been favored somewhat by its role as a supplier of light armored trucks and other weaponry.[21] Parenthetically, however, since Brazil obtains half its imports from Iraq, the war has had a clear impact. Brazil is getting only part of the contracted quantity despite hopes for a preferential treatment.

New Influence in International Policies

With the discovery or increased production of oil in Latin America comes new political influence for these countries internationally and a new role for Latin America as a regional power. Some oil-rich countries of the region can now provide aid and technical assistance to their poorer neighbors. Oil wealth can also wield influence and pressure where none was possible earlier. Considerable evidence is available in the cases of Mexico and Venezuela. Mexico under President Lopez Portillo used its newfound economic power to create a regional sphere of influence, a change from Mexico's traditionally defensive position to a clearly more assertive one. Mexico has been actively seeking informal alliances in Central America, notably with Nicaragua and Jamaica. Mexico has been willing to provide oil at concessionary prices to Nicaragua and technical aid for exploring indigenous energy resources and related aid. Jamaica and Mexico have agreed to begin cooperating in an aluminum project.

In December 1980 Mexico unilaterally terminated fishing agreements with the United States, an act that was widely interpreted as a sign of new petroleum-based power.[22] Furthermore Mexico is beginning to compete with the United States and Cuba for political leadership of the region. The frequently cited example is Mexico's support of leftist groups in Nicaragua and El Salvador, Mexican politics toward Cuba, and Mexico's clear attempt to challenge Cuba's monopoly over revolutionary causes.

Venezuela too has been willing to use its oil to promote regional political interests. Christian Democrat objectives in the area are regarded as legitimate claimants on the country's resources. Venezuela's oil assistance program is expected to total $1 billion in the next five years. The action of Venezuelan president Luis Herrera Campins is seen as a means of building an anti-Marxist front in Central America.[23] The policy is to "help steer the troubled nations of Central America and the Caribbean toward democracy."[24]

Mexico and Venezuela are cooperating in a scheme to provide cheap oil to nine small nations of the region. Mexico in particular has rejected the idea, promoted by the United States, of a North American Common Market. The rejection is based on Mexico's concern that the idea is designed to provide the United States with greater supplies of Mexican oil.[25]

The new position has created trade relations and economic opportunities that would have been politically infeasible earlier. The Soviet Union made advances in the Latin American energy sector by providing technical assistance and equipment. These gains are viewed as a counteroffensive to the U.S. State Departent and international companies. In particular the Soviet Union has been active in hydroelectric projects in the River Plata Basin in Argentina, in Brazil, Colombia, and Peru. The United States is now viewing these moves as effective instruments of Soviet policy and penetration.[26] In addition the Soviet Union has made attractive trade offers to Brazil, despite opposition from Brazilian companies, to buy Brazilian agricultural products worth $2.5 billion and to supply equipment for about $1 billion. Such an arrangement would improve the Brazilian trade account vis-à-vis the United States. The Soviet Union has also agreed to sell crude oil in exchange for Brazil's wheat.[27]

Having new choices and new possibilities for exercising choice, Mexico has decided, however, not to send more than 50 percent of its exports to any single country nor supply more than 20 percent of any one country's oil imports. These decisions are clearly an attempt to reduce vulnerability and dependence inherent in close trade relations. The policy was adopted, not so much because of the risk of dependence on the United States from excessive share of sales, but of "greater danger that the United States would become excessively dependent on Mexican oil."[28] But these probes should not be overemphasized. Mexico has not considered seriously joining OPEC for fear of losing benefits associated with a close relationship with the United States. At the same time Mexico has not been averse to setting up a regional oil market.

In a recent agreement with Canada Mexico has agreed to sell about half the oil that Canada had requested. Canada is one of the five countries with which Mexico had expressed interest in making exchange agreements involving oil and technology. Canadian expertise is to be extended in certain industries—mining, aluminum, telecommunications, transport, oil and gas equipment, urban planning, and port development. A clear incentive in developing closer relations is the fact that both Mexico and Canada are interested in reducing trade dependence on the United States.[29]

Venezuela has been using its newfound economic influence in its relationship with the international oil companies to renegotiate successfully sales and technology contracts. New contracts significantly loosen ties between Petroleos de Venezuela and the oil majors. The objective is to allow PDVSA to push ahead with its own investment programs and, as a result of the new technology contracts, no longer be so dependent on foreign technology. Although Venezuela has recently opened up to foreign investors, the official long-term strategy is for greater self-reliance.

Peru too has successfully renegotiated foreign oil contracts. Newly developed petroleum production has for the first time allowed it to establish more favorable terms with the international oil companies.

The principle goals of developing countries—to obtain greater access to foreign technology and to establish more favorable terms of exchange—are clearly evident in Latin America. As a recent UNCTAD report observed, of developing countries those in Latin America have become more experienced in control over transfer of technology.[30] By imposing formal institutional controls on imports of, and access to, technology, Latin American countries have dramatically cut expenditures and increased their access to foreign "know-how."[31]

The availability of new sources of international lending, while an important development in its own right, obscures other issues that point to conflicting priorities between developed and developing countries. The three-week long U.N. Special Session on Development in August and September of 1980, called to assess the New International Economic Order, was beset with disagreements between the Group of 77 led by Brazil and the established international financial bodies, the World Bank and the International Monetary Fund. The Group of 77 argued for restructuring the present system of international trade and finance to give greater voice to the developing world. Industrial countries, on the other hand, pressed for discussion of the recycling of petrodollars and ensuring international financial stability. Officials of industrial countries argued that a greater Third World voice could be counterproductive, as it would lead to a loss of confidence in established institutions.[32]

Officials of the Sistema Economico Latinoamericano (SELA), by contrast, had more faith that negotiations between developing countries would bring the kind of results that would be more helpful than global negotiations that involved industrial nations.[33] The basic argument was that satisfactory negotiations might not take place and that direct negotiations among the developing countries themselves were called for.

The World Bank's recent offer to Brazil of U.S. $1 billion for the alcohol program was on the condition that contracts for equipment be open to international competition. This stipulation was a source of conflict. The program presently requires no imports and therefore is not a drain on Brazil's foreign reserves. The bank's condition would create new claims on the country's balance of payments.[34] While bank officials might argue that this stipulation is simply part of the bank's routine lending arrangements, the fact remains that such routine generates sources of conflict and emerges as a strong bone of contention.

Additional examples of Latin American countries' concern for retaining a degree of independence in emerging international arrangements is the decision by Mexico in March 1980 not to join the General Agreement on Trade and Tarrifs (GATT). This decision is a reversal of earlier expectations. Three factors were critical in the reversal; fear of devaluation, fear of a collapse in agricultural production which would lead to necessary imports, and the fact that Mexico was looking for flexibility in its control of oil production. Membership in GATT would create new constraints. It would prohibit government subsidies to domestic industry and to agriculture. Thus policies to increase agricultural production, to cut food imports, or to expand subsidies to agriculture would clash with GATT directives. By the same token membership in GATT would create new constraints in the oil sector. Mexico could not reduce oil exports unilaterally, a consideration that was interpreted by the Mexican Minister of Industry as a "dangerous tendency within GATT to seek guaranteed supplies of strategic resources."[35]

These trends indicate of course that there is room for conflict. In some cases the priorities of international agencies are not consistent with those of Latin American governments. For the most part, however, new forms of international cooperation established in the latter part of the 1970s will provide the basis for international cooperation of the 1980s.

All this points to one important conclusion: the most significant development is the growing role of regional organizations and the emerging prominence of agencies based in developing countries. The new organizations are becoming potential competitors with the traditional establishment of international organizations, the World Bank and the International Monetary Fund. This competition is not manifested in terms of dollar commitments but of differences in priorities and definition of objectives. With the availability of new financial resources these differences in priorities may become the basis for implementing alternative investment strategies and increasing the scope of bargaining and leverage vis-à-vis the traditional international organizations. The established agencies have defined priorities and strategies for over forty years. The new institutions based in developing countries are emerging as potential competition for defining the direction of development in the 1980s and beyond.

Notes

1. *Latin America Weekly Report*, September 12, 1980, p. 809, reporting on the World Bank, *Energy in Developing Nations* (Washington, D.C., August 1980). The research assistance of Elizabeth Leeds is gratefully acknowledged.

2. All sources in *Middle East Economic Survey,* December 28, 1977; October 15, 1977; April 4, 1975.

3. *Middle East Economic Survey,* May 12, 1980.

4. *Middle East Economic Survey,* December 29, 1980.

5. "MEED Special Report on Latin America," *Middle East Economic Digest* (September 1981), p. 28.

6. Ibid.

7. *Latin America Weekly Report,* September 26, 1980, p. 3.

8. Ibid., pp. 9-10.

9. Ibid., November 16, 1979, pp. 29-30. For a broader review of Brazil's current energy posture, see also R.F. Colson, "Brazil: The

Proalcool Programme—A Response to the Energy Crisis,'' *Bank of London & South America* (BOLSA), 15 (May 1981), pp. 60-70.

10. *Latin America Weekly Report,* November 16, 1979, pp. 29-30.

11. *Latin America Weekly Report,* March 21, 1980.

12. *Latin America Weekly Report,* January 25, 1980, pp. 3-4.

13. *Latin America Weekly Report,* February 15, 1980, pp. 5-6.

14. *Latin America Weekly Report,* September 19, 1980, p. 3.

15. *Latin America Weekly Report,* May 16, 1980, p. 6.

16. *Latin America Weekly Report,* April 4, 1980, p. 9.

17. *Latin America Weekly Report,* May 9, 1980, and May 16, 1980, p. 6.

18. *Petroleum Intelligence Weekly,* July 27, 1981, p. 11.

19. *Petroleum Intelligence Weekly,* May 9, 1980.

20. *Petroleum Intelligence Weekly,* February 1, 1980, p. 4.

21. *Petroleum Intelligence Weekly,* October 3, 1980, p. 7.

22. *New York Times,* January 11, 1981.

23. *Latin America Weekly Report,* August 1, 1980, pp. 5-6.

24. *New York Times,* November 23, 1980, p. 10.

25. *New York Times,* January 11, 1981, pp. 58-59.

26. *Latin America Weekly Report,* October 31, 1980, p. 8.

27. Ibid., p. 9.

28. *New York Times,* January 11, 1981.

29. *New York Times,* May 28, 1980, p. D5.

30. *Latin America Weekly Report,* November 28, 1980, p. 8.

31. Ibid.

32. This is a typical debate, characteristic of trends toward a new international economic order.

33. Discussion *among* developing countries is a new thrust in international strains due to demands of the Third and Fourth Worlds.

34. *Latin America Weekly Report,* October 10, 1980, p. 10.

35. Ibid., March 28, 1980; also *New York Times,* March 19, 1980.

11 Conclusion: New Issues for Public Policy

Some basic conclusions about energy, economy, and policy in Latin America provide a comprehensive perspective on the region's energy-related predicaments and insights into the new policy imperatives.

Energy: Adjustment and Innovation

The changing availability and price of energy has had decisive effects on the Latin American region. This summary reflects the basic trends:

Although the region's energy consumption continues to outpace crude oil production, overall imports of crude into the region declined somewhat. Further decline cannot be achieved in the immediate future, but there is clear evidence of effective reorientation of consumption patterns and of production possibilities. Alternatives to petroleum are explored in many countries, becoming a realistic solution to the energy problem worldwide. On balance, Latin America's energy profile holds favorable and optimistic possibilities. The diversification options are clearly available, and the region's capacity to adjust to changing energy conditions has been impressive.

Rising petroleum prices encouraged major reappraisal of petroleum development programs since 1973, particularly in those countries that are nearly self-sufficient. Argentina and Ecuador have passed legislation to increase private participation in petroleum development through risk contracts. Mexico, confronted with an increasing import bill and general deterioration of balance of payments, has increased the exploitation of newly discovered fields, becoming a net exporter in 1975. (Current debates regarding the appropriate rate of exploitation persist.) Furthermore, Mexico appears to be abandoning the low price policies that led to wasteful use of petroleum in the past.[1]

Development of indigenous energy sources in selected Latin American countries themselves became a reality. This includes increased oil production but, more important, the exploration and investment in alternative forms of energy, notably hydrolectric power, ethyl alcohol (such as gasohol in Brazil), methane (biogas), and geothermal energy (such as the hot springs in the Andean ranges). While none of these alternative energy sources is commercially viable on a large scale, the Latin American response to new opportunities has been considerable, marking new and ambitious trends in the industrializing world.

The nationalism that characterized Latin American oil policy for so long is being buttressed by pragmatic policies for the exploitation of oil resources and the consolidation of national policies. Energy policy as such has not yet evolved, but energy inputs into policy discussions and investment decisions are growing. The sense of pragmatism is now pervading almost every country's energy investment process, and a more rational view of issues and problems is emerging.

New and strong trends in regional cooperation, signaled especially by the formation of OLADE, represent not only the basis for institutional cooperation but the context for sharing technological information and eventual coordination of planning for energy development. For instance, OLADE has carried out a major study of nonconventional energy sources in Latin America, developed a strategy plan for development, and piloted a project for small-scale methane production in Ecuador. Technological cooperation, an essential component for increased self-reliance among countries of the region, is becoming more apparent in the relations between them.

The dominance of one Latin American country as an established exporter (Venezuela) and the rise to pre-eminence of another significant producer (Mexico), in conjunction with smaller suppliers (Ecuador and to some extent Peru), are providing this region with strong claims to future world oil supplies and with it greater influence on evolving institutional and financial arrangements. The cooperation within Latin America appears to be leading toward a stronger, more cohesive stance in the broader international energy environment.

With greater regional cooperation the convergence of economic power will translate into greater political influence. This influence can and will be exerted to affect the structure of transactions in energy within the region and to influence patterns of utilization. This means that greater political leverage regionally can be translated into more effective impacts on energy-relations transactions internationally.

Economy: Macroeconomic Problems and Adjustments

During 1979 Latin America's gross domestic product increased by nearly 6.3 percent. This growth was a substantial improvement over the 4.3 percent between 1975 and 1978. It is also greater than during the 1960s, when rates of growth averaged about 5 percent. The overall growth in the 1970s compared favorably with those of the industrial countries and those of the developing states. The growth was uneven, however, with the largest countries growing faster. But everyone in the region appeared to be experiencing gains despite the apparent declines for 1980 when overall growth was 5.3 percent.[2] The 1970s can be regarded as notable for their achievements, particularly for the recovery in 1979, despite the persistence of severe structural problems.

Latin American countries continue to suffer high inflation rates. In 1980 twenty countries exhibited inflation rates greater than 15 percent. Even countries that traditionally had greater price stability seemed to follow the pattern of the advanced industrial states. Rates of inflation are high, and inflation-related problems extensive, but overall there does not appear to be a deterioration due exclusively to oil.

The balance of payments burden for the net importing countries in Latin America increased dramatically. The total deficit rose from $3.8 billion in 1973 to $12.1 billion in 1975.[3] It was estimated that current account deficits reached $20 billion in 1979, and the prospects for the early years of the present decade are not dramatically better. This increase reflects changing oil prices as well as deteriorating terms of trade. In general balance of payments problems have been less severe than anticipated in the early 1970s, and most countries are adjusting well. If anything, payments problems appear increasingly related to investment programs and import requirements. The implementation of extensive development programs already in progress is reflected in greater borrowing and increased external debt for almost all countries of the region.

Balance of payments strains have been partially offset by the supply of capital made available to developing countries by oil-producing countries which began to appear on international financial markets. International monetary reserves improved considerably. Gross reserves more than doubled between 1974 and 1979. Contributions of direct foreign investments were substantial. Availability of new liquidity on international markets also contributed to new opportunities for countries of the region.

Development programs became strongly affected by changes in oil prices, leading by necessity to a reappraisal of investment strategies. This reappraisal is now becoming manifest in a concern for energy issues in development programs for the 1980s, reflecting a realization of new constraints on growth, distribution, and implementing programs for social equity.

Review and evaluation of energy use in economic activity, particularly transportation, are becoming the issue in public policy. Although energy-related constraints are not effectively introduced in planning or in the bureaucratic apparatus, decision makers in the transportation sector are becoming especially sensitive to energy issues.

Policy: New Context for Development Policy

The Latin American region is not a developing one in the conventional sense. Combined changes in energy and economy have exerted far-reaching influences on industrialization and urbanization. The developmental issues for the future will involve addressing problems of urban concentration and economic diversification. Already the extent of urbanization of the region presents distinct challenges for investments in transportation.

Governments of net importing countries, invariably taking drastic measures as a result of the energy "crisis" impinging on development planning, concentrated on investments, administration, implementation, and regulation in the transport sector.

The choices of the future for all sectors of the economy pertain to combined pressures of technology and priorities for investment. Public policy and political objectives will provide the criteria for technological choice. The critical issue for public policy is that the energy situation in all sectors requires a reassessment of national economic objectives and of production possibilities. Investments decisions are embedded in the structure of decision making.

The interjection of policy preferences in debates regarding technological choices must be predicated on analyses and information emanating from the profile of the region itself. In the last analysis, it is the nature and the type of information available that will guide public policy; today's information provides the context for tomorrow's policies. It is essential then that knowledge for public policy be both relevant and accurate.

The energy crisis has persuaded Latin American governments to make trade-offs among developmental objectives. Nevertheless, generic social objectives in development impose constraints on policy innovation for all governments. These objectives prohibit:

1. generating or increasing social inequities,
2. taxing or imposing additional costs on disadvantaged groups,
3. increasing communication obstacles among social, regional, or income differentials,
4. mobilizing or consolidating social and political opposition.

The bounds of permissible behavior, to be practical and pragmatic, will inevitably be shaped by these concerns.[4]

Policies designed to control energy consumption create a new role for national governments. Changes in budgeting allocations may place government agencies in a serious dilemma. Mexico, for example, now allocates over one-third of its total budget to the capital-intensive energy sector, with PEMEX and the electricity industry absorbing the bulk of these allocations.

The allocation of resources to labor-intensive industries is relatively small, and job creation is suffering accordingly. The priorities designed to reduce the macroeconomic impacts of energy situations may well generate broad social costs. There is no immediate solution to the high unemployment rate (estimated at roughly 10 million).[5] The complex processes of reconciling the requirements of different economic sectors, the urgent need to generate new jobs, and the control of inflation are predicated on export earnings from oil sales. Policies to limit the expansion of oil production will require new sets of calculations and assumptions.

The criticality of the energy sector in both oil-producing and oil-importing countries is giving government greater regulatory power. In Venezuela the nationalization of the petroleum industry in 1976 led to the creation of one of the largest companies in Latin America. This occurred in conjunction with the rapid expansion of the public sector. Of the ten largest companies in Venezuela, six are state owned. In the oil-importing countries government regulation of consumption patterns is necessary. Some of this regulation is explicit; in other cases it is still evolving. Governments in Latin America are experiencing the dual pressures of being regulators of public policy as well as innovators and managers of resources.

The changing energy environment has yet another set of implications for public policy, placing in focus an inevitable dilemma in investment planning and choice of priorities. The dilemma is this: even in the absence of energy constraints governments are unable to meet all development objectives simultaneously. The goals of growth, equity, welfare—in conjunction with concern for regional self-sufficiency, reducing balance of payments problems, maximizing income or income per capita, increasing consumption, assuring political stability—are by their nature complex and difficult to achieve even singly, let alone simultaneously. Trade-offs among goals, the necessity of selecting priorities, are the inevitable conflicts that arise among these objectives, however, and constitute the policy context for national governments.

While generally in the transportation sector discrete, less pervasive decisions can be made without direct concern for the broader development context, large-scale investments in that sector are by necessity embedded in the fabric of public policy. For the more developed countries of the region government planning has taken explicit account of investments in the transportation sector. For others investment in transportation is still in an early phase. Several countries stand out in their clear recognition of the role of transportation. The degree of emphasis differs, as do the financial allocations to that sector. Nevertheless, there is a dominant trend for more explicit recognition of the importance of this sector and greater concern for long-range decision making, rather than incremental, short-term responses to immediate crises.

In the main the transport sector is treated almost uniformly in development plans in terms of building networks or completing existing projects. The focus is on expansion rather than on efficient use of existing facilities and is due in large part to the lack of information regarding the efficiency or means of increasing the effectiveness of the existing infrastructure.

Given the choice of developmental objectives, and assuming it is made explicitly, at least three types of criteria have been identified for policy in transportation:[6]

1. criteria that seriously call into question the availability of the existing transport system, performance, and network concerning energy consumption, environmental considerations, equity issues, congestion, cost, or load;
2. criteria that under normal conditions do not cause serious problems but may be aggravated under conditions of economic strain, affecting public expenditures, revenue constraints, or economic disruption, and the like;
3. criteria internal to transportation facilities that are used conventionally for evaluation of performance, such as reliability, speed, flexibility, efficiency, or convenience.

These *criteria* of course do not refer to the specific options themselves, and the *mechanisms* for these options are varied. The mechanisms in this case are the policy instruments utilized in making choices and the attendant sanctions and means of enforcement. At least six generic mechanisms have been identified:

price controls and regulation,

activity control and regulation,

network control and regulation,

mode utilization control and regulation,

taxes on users or classes of users,

taxes on routes.

Several countries in Latin America are beginning to use these mechanisms, or variants of them. Speculations aside, there is one trend to which some degree of certainty can be attributed, namely, the growing strength of the state in regulating, managing, and controlling national resources. State enterprises in Latin America are becoming agents and managers of future development. The agenda for the state is more comprehensive than ever before, and as a result public policy in Latin America is being shaped in ways for which there are no solid precedents. Domestic and international processes are being linked in new ways for which policy directives are yet to be delineated.

New Influence and New Opportunities

The changing energy situation has created a new international and domestic environment for Latin America. The immediate economic and policy problems have been extensive, but the region's ability to adapt has been impressive. The gains made, in the long run, outweigh the costs incurred. Almost without exception the whole of Latin America has demonstrated a capacity to adapt, identify new policy options, and initiate public debates for policy development and implementation. Political costs are always engendered, and there are always costs for change: political strain, instability, and pressures are not new in Latin America. What is new is an apparent demonstrated capacity for adaptation and change, a capacity that is often not given adequate attention in conventional assessments of the region.

There have been substantial gains for Latin America in the international arena. In addition to new patterns of trade, aid, and cooperation for energy development, there are also .new opportunities for exercising greater leverage on international issues. The region's giants are assuming a position of leadership among the developing countries and even providing a bridge to understanding with the industrialized countries. But there may be new cause for concern: for the oil-rich countries new wealth can create new patterns of dependency. The economies of Mexico, Venezuela, and Ecuador—and to a lesser extent other countries of the region—are now being linked to the international economy in new ways. New patterns of trade are emerging, with new sources of finance and new opportunities for access to modern technology. How these opportunities are utilized in the 1980s will determine the region's political and economic autonomy. Despite speculations that Latin America may today be entering into a new form of dependence, shaped by new ties and opportunities, the new realities point more toward greater global interdependence and greater regional integration.

Notes

1. *Latin America Weekly Report,* January 25, 1980, p. 1.
2. A recent assessment of the region's economic performance highlights some of the difficulties. See "Survey: Latin America: A Continent at Odds with Itself," *World Business Weekly,* August 24, 1981, pp.

29-37; see also World Bank, *World Development Report* (Washington, D.C., 1980).

3. For a review and an assessment until 1979, see "Latin America: After the Oil Crises," *Bank of London & South America* (BOLSA), 13 (December 1979), pp. 704-720. Figures for 1973 and 1975 are from p. 705.

4. Adapted from Alan Altshuler with James P. Womack and John R. Pucher, *The Urban Transportation System: Politics and Policy Innovation* (Cambridge, Mass.: The MIT Press, 1979).

5. See George W. Grayson, *The Politics of Mexican Oil* (Pittsburgh: The University of Pittsburgh Press, 1980), chapter 5. Also *Latin America Weekly Report*, December 14, 1979.

6. Adapted from Altshuler with Womack and Pucher, *The Urban Transportation System*, 1979.

Bibliography

Books

Abelson, Philip H. (ed.) *Energy: Use, Conservation, and Supply.* Washington, D.C.: American Association for the Advancement of Science, 1974.

Aleman, Miguel Valdes. *La verdad del petroleo en Mexico.* Mexico, D.F.: Biografias Gandesa, 1977.

Altshuler, Alan, with James P. Womack and John R. Pucher. *The Urban Transportation System: Politics and Policy Innovation.* 2nd ed. Cambridge, Mass.: The MIT Press, 1981.

American Association for the Advancement of Science. *Proceedings of the Conference on National Energy Policy.* Washington, D.C., May 17, 1977.

Argentina. Consejo Nacional de Desarrollo. *Plan nacional de desarrollo, 1965-1969.* Buenos Aires, 1965.

Argentina. Consejo Nacional de Desarrollo. *Plan nacional de desarrollo y seguridad, 1971-1975.* Buenos Aires, 1971.

Argentina. *Plan trienal para la reconstruccion y la liberacion nacional, 1974-1977.* Buenos Aires, 1973.

Askari, Hossein, and John Thomas Cummings. *Oil, OECD, and the Third World: A Vicious Triangle?* Middle East Monograph, No. 5. Center for Middle Eastern Studies, University of Texas at Austin, 1978, 1980.

Banco Central de Honduras; Departamento de Estudios Economicos. *Cuentas nacionales de honduras*, 1960-1975.

Banco Central de Reserva del Peru. *Programacion del desarrollo.* Tomo 1 (1963).

Banco Nacional de Comercio Exterior. *Mexico 1976.* Mexico City: Banco Nacional de Comercio Exterior. 1977.

Bermudez, Antonio J. *Doce anos al servicio de la industrial petrolera mexicana.* Mexico, D.F.: Editorial COMAVAL, 1960.

Bermudez, Antonio J. *La politica petrolera mexicana.* Mexico, D.F.: Editorial Joaquin Mortiz, 1976.

Betancourt, Romulo. *Venezuela's Oil.* New York: Allen and Unwin, 1978.

Blair, John M. *The Control of Oil.* New York: Pantheon Books, 1976.

Bohi, Douglas R., and Milton Russell. *U.S. Energy Policy: Alternatives for Security.* Baltimore: The Johns Hopkins University Press, 1975.

Bolivia. Ministerio de Planeamiento y Coordinacion. *Plan nacional de desarrollo economico y social, 1976-1980.* La Paz, 1976.

Bolivia. Ministerio de Planificacion y Coordinacion. *Estrategia socioeconomica del desarrollo nacional 1971-1991.* La Paz, 1970.

Borland, John et al. *Raw Materials and Foreign Policy*. Washington, D.C.: International Economic Studies Institute, 1976.

Brandenburg, Frank. *The Making of Modern Mexico*. Englewood Cliffs, N.J.: Prentice-Hall, 1964.

Brazil. Ministerio do Planejamento e Coordenacao General. *Programa estrategico de desenvolvimento, 1968-1970*. Brasilia, 1969.

Brazil. Presidencia da Republica. *Plano trienal de desenvolvimento economico e social, 1963-1965*. Brasilia, 1962.

Brazil. *Primeiro plano nacional de desenvolvimento—PND: Lei n. 5.727-de-4-11-1971-referenciada*. Sao Paulo, 1971.

Brazil. *II Plano nacional de desenvolvimento, 1975-1979*. Brasilia, 1979.

Brazil. *III Plano nacional de desenvolvimento, 1980-1985*. Brasilia, 1979.

British Petroleum. 1977. *BP Statistical Review of the World Oil Industry*. London.

British Petroleum. 1978. *BP Statistical Review of the World Oil Industry*. London.

British Petroleum. 1979. *BP Statistical Review of the World Oil Industry*. London.

Brookhaven National Laboratory Developing Countries Energy Program. *Energy Needs, Uses, and Resources in Developing Countries*. Upton, N.Y.: March 1978.

Business International Corporation. *Worldwide Economic Indicators, Comparative Summary for 131 Countries, 1981 Annual Edition*. New York: 1981.

Camp, Ai Roderic. *Mexican Political Biographies*. Tucson, Ariz.: University of Arizona Press, 1976.

Castillo, Heberto and Rius. *Huele a gas!: los misterios del gasoducto*. Mexico, D.F.: Editorial Posada, 1977.

Central Intelligence Agency. *International Energy Statistical Review*. Washington, D.C.: June 30, 1981.

CEPAL. *Energy in Latin America: The Historical Record*. Santiago, Chile: The United Nations Press, 1978.

Chile. Oficina de Planificacion Nacional. *Plan nacional indicativo de desarrollo, 1976-1981*. Santiago.

Chile. Oficina de Planificacion Nacional. *Plan nacional indicativo de desarrollo, 1978-1983*. Santiago.

Chile. Oficina de Planificacion Nacional. *Plan nacional indicativo de desarrollo, 1979-1984*. Santiago.

Choucri, Nazli. *International Energy Futures: Petroleum Prices, Power, and Payments*. Cambridge, Mass.: The MIT Press, 1981.

Choucri, Nazli. *International Politics of Energy Interdependence: The Case of Petroleum*. Lexington, Mass.: Lexington Books, D.C. Heath, 1976.

Cline, Howard F. *The United States and Mexico*. Rev. ed. New York: Atheneum, 1965.

Coleman, Kenneth M. *Diffuse Support in Mexico: The Potential for Crisis.* Beverly Hills, Calif.: Sage, 1976.

Colombia. Antioquia Departamento Administrativo de Planeacion. *Sintesis de los planteamientos.* Medellin, 1974.

Colombia. Consejo Nacional de Politica Economica y Planeacion. *Plan general de desarrollo economico y social.* Primera parte; el programa general. Bogota: Departamento Administrativo de Planeacion y Servicios Tecnicos, 1962.

Colombia. Departamento Nacional de Planeacion. *Plan de desarrollo.* Bogota, 1971.

Colombia. Departamento Nacional de Planeacion. *Planes y programas de desarrollo, 1969-1972.* Documento DNP-417, n.p. December 1, 1969.

Colombia. Departamento Nacional de Planeacion. *To Close the Gap: Social, Economic, and Regional Development Plan, 1975-1978.* Bogota, 1977.

Committee for Economic Development. *International Economic Consequences of High-Priced Energy.* New York: CED, September 1975.

Committee on Finance, United States Senate. *Energy Statistics.* Washington, D.C.: Government Printing Office, 1975.

Committee on Foreign Relations, United States Senate, 93rd Congress, First Session. *Energy and Foreign Policy.* Washington, D.C.: Government Printing Office, 1974.

Committee on Interior and Insular Affairs, United States Senate. *The Structure of the U.S. Petroleum Industry.* Washington, D.C.: Government Printing Office, 1976.

Commoner, Barry, Howard Boksenbaum, and Michael Corr (eds.) *Energy and Human Welfare—A Critical Analysis.* Vol. 3. New York: MacMillan Information, 1975.

Costa Rica. Comite de los Nueve Alianza para el Progreso. *Evaluacion del plan de desarrollo economico y social de Costa Rica, 1965-1968.* Washington, D.C.: Union Panamericana, 1966.

Costa Rica. Oficina de Planificacion. *Plan nacional de desarrollo, 1974-1978: estrategia y plan global.* Version preliminar. San Jose, 1974.

Costa Rica. Oficina de Planificacion. *Plan nacional de desarrollo, 1974-1978. Version preliminar.* San Jose, 1973.

Cotta, A. *Energie et transports routiers de marchandises.* Paris: La Federation Nationale des Transports Routiers, May 1980.

Council on Environmental Quality and Department of State. *The Global 2000 Report to the President.* Vol. 1. Washington, D.C.: Government Printing Office, 1980.

Darmstadter, Joel et. al. *How Industrial Societies Use Energy: A Comparative Analysis.* Baltimore: The Johns Hopkins University Press, 1977.

Diaz Serrano, Jorge. *Linea troncal nacional de distribucion de gas natural: El Director General de Petroleos Mexicanos ante la H. Camara de Diputados.* Mexico, D.F.: Petroleos Mexicanos, 1977.

Dunkerley, Joy. *Trends in Energy Use in Industrial Societies: An Overview.* Washington, D.C.: Resources for the Future, Inc., 1980.

Eckstein, Susan. *The Poverty of Revolution: The State and the Urban Poor in Mexico.* Princeton, N.J.: Princeton University Press, 1977.

Ecuador. Junta Nacional de Planificacion y Coordinacion Economica. *Plan integral de transformacion y desarrollo, 1973-1977: resumen general.* Quito, December 29, 1972.

El Salvador. Consejo Nacional de Planificacion y Coordinacion Economica. *Plan de desarrollo economica y social, 1973-1977.* San Salvador, 1972.

Elwell-Sutton, Laurence Paul. *Persian Oil: A Study in Power Politics.* London: Laurence and Wishart, 1955.

Energy Economics Research Ltd. *Statistical Review 1981.* Berkshire, United Kingdom.

Engler, Robert. *The Politics of Oil.* New York: Macmillan, 1961.

European Conference of Ministers of Transport. *Energy and Transport.* Paris: OECD, 1979.

European Conference of Ministers of Transport. *Twenty-Fifth Anniversary of the Foundation of the Conference.* Paris: OECD, 1978.

Exxon Corporation. *World Energy Outlook.* New York: Exxon Corporation, 1978.

Franssen, Herman T. *Towards Project Interdependence: Energy in the Coming Decade.* Washington, D.C.: Government Printing Office, 1975.

Garther, Roscoe B. *Expropriation in Mexico—The Facts and the Law.* New York: Morrow, William, 1940.

Georgescu-Roegen, Nicholas. *Energy and Economic Myths.* New York: Pergamon Press, 1976.

Gonzalez, Alonso Francisco. *Historia y petroleo: Mexico: el problema del petroleo.* Madrid: Editorial Ayuso, 1972.

Gonzalez, Casanova Pablo. *Democracy in Mexico.* New York: Oxford University Press, 1970.

Gonzalez Gorrondona, Jose Joaquin, hijo. *La planificacion economica y su aplicabilidad al caso venezolano.* Caracas: Ediciones del Cuatricentenario de Caracas, 1967.

Grayson, George W. *The Politics of Mexican Oil.* Pittsburgh: The University of Pittsburgh Press, 1981.

Griffin, James M. *Energy Conservation in the OECD: 1980 to 2000.* Cambridge, Mass.: Ballinger, 1979.

Grindle, Merilee S. *Bureaucrats, Politicians, and Peasants in Mexico: A Case Study in Public Policy.* Los Angeles: University of California Press, 1977.

Guatemala. Consejo Nacional de Planificacion Economica. *Plan nacional de desarrollo, 1979-1982.* Guatemala, 1978.

Gutmanis, Ivars, L. Stephen Guiland, Rita A. McBrayer, and Richard P. McKenna. *The Demand for Scientific and Technical Manpower in Selected Energy-Related Industries, 1970-85: A Methodology Applied to a Selected Scenario of Energy Output.* Washington, D.C.: National Planning Association, September 1974.

Haley, K.B. (ed.) *Proceedings of the Eighth IFORS International Conference on Operation Research,* Toronto, Canada, June 19-23, 1978. Amsterdam: North Holland Publishing Company, 1979.

Hansen, Roger D. *The Politics of Mexican Development.* Baltimore: The Johns Hopkins University Press, 1971.

Hicks, Gill V. *Energy Statistics: A Supplement to the Summary of National Transportation Statistics.* Washington, D.C.: Department of Transportation, September 1973.

Honduras. Consejo Superior de Planificacion Economica. *Resumen del plan nacional de desarrollo economico y social, 1965-1969.* Tegucigalpa, 1966.

Honduras, British. *Belizian Seven-Year Development Plan, 1964-1970.* (Belize?), 1964.

Iglesias, Antonio. *Politica petrolera argentina.* Buenos Aires: Leonardo Empresora, S.A., 1980.

Instituto Mexicano del Petroleo. *Energeticos: demanda sectorial, analysis y perspectivos.* Mexico, D.F.: IMP, *Subdireccion de Estudios Economicos y Planeacion Industrial,* 1975.

Instituto Mexicano del Petroleo. *Energeticos: demanda del sector industrial.* Mexico, D.F.: IMP, Subdireccion de Estudios Economicos y Planeacion Industrial, 1976.

Inter-American Development Bank. *Economic and Social Progress in Latin America.* Washington, D.C., 1975.

Inter-American Development Bank. *Economic and Social Progress in Latin America.* Washington, D.C., 1978.

International Energy Agency. *Basic Energy Statistics and Energy Balances of Developing Countries,* Vol. 2. Paris: OECD, 1979.

International Energy Agency. *Energy Conservation in Industry.* Paris: OEEC, September 1979.

International Energy Agency. *Energy Conservation in the International Energy Agency—1978 Review.* Paris: OECD, 1979.

International Energy Agency. *Energy Conservation—Programme of IEA.* Paris: OECD, April 1979.

International Energy Agency. *Energy Policies and Programmes of IEA Countries—1979 Review.* Paris: OECD, 1980.

International Energy Agency. *Energy Research, Development and Demonstration in the IEA Countries: 1979 Review of National Programmes.* Paris: OECD, 1980.

International Energy Agency. *Workshop on Energy Data of Developing Countries*. Paris: OECD, 1979.

International Institute for Applied Systems Analysis. *On Energy and Agriculture: From Hunting-Gathering to Landless Farming*. Laxenburg, Austria: IIASA, December 1979.

International Monetary Fund. *Balance of Payments Yearbook* (various issues).

International Monetary Fund. *International Financial Statistics*. Washington, D.C., 1981.

International Monetary Fund. *IMF Survey*. 1974-1981.

International Road Transport Union. *World Transport Data*. Geneva: Department of Economic Affairs, 1976.

Issachtss, Corrales Jorge. *Las miserias del petroleo*. Mexico, D.F.: Editores Mexicanos Asociados, 1978.

Johnson, Kenneth F. *Mexican Democracy: A Critical View*. Revised ed. New York: Praeger, 1978.

Kash, Don E., and Irvin L. White. *Energy under the Oceans*. Norman, Okla.: University of Oklahoma Press, 1973.

Landsberg, Hans H. *Energy: The Next Twenty Years*. Cambridge, Mass.: Ballinger, 1979.

Latin America and Caribbean Oil Report. Published by the *Petroleum Economist*. London: Nichols, 1979.

Lavin, Domingo Jose. *Petroleo: pasado, presente y futuro de una industria mexicana*. Mexico, D.F.: Fondo de Cultural Economica, 1976.

Lonroth, Mans, Peter Steen, and Thomas B. Johnsson. *Energy in Transition*. Berkeley, Calif.: University of California Press, 1980.

Looney, Robert E. *Mexico's Economy: A Policy Analysis with Forecasts to 1990*. Boulder, Colo.: Westview Press, 1978.

Mancke, Richard B. *Mexican Oil and Gas: Political, Strategic, and Economic Implications*. New York: Praeger, 1979.

Mexico. Secretaria de Patrimonio y Fomento Industrial. *Plan nacional de desarrollo industrial, 1979-1982*. Mexico, 1979.

Meyer, Lorenzo. *Mexico y Los Estados Unidos en el conflicto petrolero, 1917-1942*, second edition. Mexico, D.F.: El Colegio de Mexico, 1972.

Middle East Publications. *International Crude Oil and Product Prices*, Beirut, Lebanon: January 1981.

Ministerio de Planejamento e Coordenacao General. *Programa estrategico de desenvolvimento, 1968-1980*. Brasilia, 1969.

Munasinghe, Mohan. *The Economics of Power System Reliability and Planning*. Washington, D.C.: World Bank, 1979.

Nash, Gerald D. *United States Oil Policy, 1890-1964: Business and Government in Twentieth Century America*. Pittsburgh, Pa.: The University of Pittsburgh Press, 1968.

National Academy of Engineering. *U.S. Energy Prospects: An Engineering Viewpoint*. Washington, D.C., 1974.

National Academy of Sciences. *Energy Consumption Measurement: Data Needs for Public Policy*. Washington, D.C.: Committee on Measurement of Energy Consumption, Assembly of Behavioral and Social Sciences, National Research Council, 1977.

National Academy of Sciences. *Energy for Rural Development*. Washington, D.C., 1976.

National Academy of Sciences. *Materials Technology in the Near-Term Energy Program*. Washington, D.C.: Ad-Hoc Committee on Critical Materials Technology in the Energy Program, 1974.

National Academy of Sciences. *Science and Brazilian Development*. Fourth Workshop on Contributions of Science and Technology to Development, November 1-5, 1971. Washington, D.C.

National Science Foundation. *Energy Research and Technology*. Vol. 1, NSF 74-28. Washington, D.C., July 1974.

National Science Foundation. *Proceedings of the Conference on Energy Conservation in Commercial, Residential and Industrial Buildings*, Ohio State University, Columbus, Ohio, May 5-7, 1974. Washington, D.C., 1975.

National Science Foundation. *Solar Energy School Heating Augmentation Experiment*. Warrington, Virginia: Inter-Technology Corporation, 1974.

National Science Foundation. *Solar Heating Proof-of-Concept Experiment for a Public School Building*. Baltimore: AAI Corporation, 1974.

Nicaragua. *Evaluation of the National Economic and Social Development Plan of Nicaragua, 1965-1969*. Washington, D.C.: Alliance for Progress, 1966.

Oberto, Luis Enrique, and Antonio Casas Gonzalez. *Venezuela y el CIAP*. Caracas: Oficina de Coordinacion y Planificacion de la Presidencia de la Republica, 1973.

Odell, Peter R. *Oil and World Power: A Geographical Interpretation*. London: Penguin Books, 1970.

Office of International Energy Affairs, Federal Energy Administration. *The Relationship of Oil Companies and Foreign Governments*. Washington, D.C.: Government Printing Office, 1975.

Oficina de Planificacion Nacional de la Republica de Chile. *Balances economicos de Chile*, 1960-1970. Santiago: Editorial Universitaria, 1973.

Ojeda, Mario. *Alcances y limites de la politica exterior de mexico*. Mexico, D.F.: El Colegio de Mexico, 1976.

Organization for Economic Cooperation and Development. *Energy Prospects to 1985*. Paris: OECD, 1974.

Organization for Economic Cooperation and Development, International

Energy Agency. *Workshop on Energy Data of Developing Countries*, Vol. 1, 2. Paris: OECD, December 1978.

Organization for Economic Cooperation and Development. *World Energy Outlook*. Paris: OECD, December 1978.

Organization of American States. *Statistical Bulletin of the OAS*. Vol. 1 (January/March 1979).

Organization of Arab Petroleum Exporting Countries. *Oil and Arab Cooperation*. Kuwait: OAPEC (various issues).

Organization of Petroleum Exporting Countries. *Annual Statistical Bulletin*. Vienna: OPEC, 1979.

Organization of Petroleum Exporting Countries. *OPEC Review*. Vienna: OPEC (various issues).

Organization of Petroleum Exporting Countries. Public Information Department. *OPEC Future and World Energy Markets*. London: Macmillan, 1980.

O'Toole, James. *Energy and Social Change*. Cambridge, Mass.: The MIT Press, 1975.

Panama. Direccion General de planificacion y Administracion. *Estrategia para el desarrollo nacional, 1970-1980*. n.p., 1970.

Paraguay. Presidencia de la Republica. *Plan nacional de desarrollo economico, 1971-1975*. Vol. 2. August, November 1970.

Peru. Banco Central de Reserva del Peru. *Programacion del desarrollo*, Vol. 1, 1963.

Peru. Instituto Nacional de Planificacion. *Plan nacional de desarrollo, 1975-1978*. Lima, June 2, 1975.

Peru. Instituto Nacional de Planificacion. *Plan global de desarrollo, 1977-1978*. Lima, April 28, 1977.

Petroleos Mexicanos. *Flota petrolera*. Mexico D.F.: Petroleos Mexicanos, 1975.

Petroleos Mexicanos. *Memoria de labores 1975*. Mexico, D.F.: Petroleos Mexicanos, 1976.

Petroleos Mexicanos. *Memoria de labores 1976*. Mexico, D.F.: Petroleos Mexicanos, 1977.

Petroleos Mexicanos. *El petroleo, 1975*, 14th ed. Mexico, D.F.: Petroleos Mexicanos, 1975.

Petroleos Mexicanos. *El petroleo, 1976*, 15th ed. Mexico, D.F.: Petroleos Mexicanos, 1976.

Petroleos Mexicanos. *Report of the Director General, 1977*. Mexico, D.F.: Petroleos Mexicanos, 1977.

Petroleos Mexicanos. *Report Delivered by the Director General*. Mexico, D.F.: Petroleos Mexicanos, 1978.

Petroleum Economist. *Latin America and Caribbean Oil Report*. London, 1974.

Pindyck, Robert S. *The Structure of World Energy Demand*. Cambridge, Mass.: The MIT Press, 1979.

Powell, J. Richard. *The Mexican Petroleum Industry*. New York: Russell and Russell, 1956.

Price, James D., Peter Troop, and Harvey W. Gershman. *Potential for Energy Conservation through the Use of Slag and Flay Ash in Concrete*. Washington, D.C.: Department of Energy, December 1978.

Purcell, Susan Kaufman. *The Mexican Profit-Sharing Decision: Political in an Authoritarian Regime*. Los Angeles: University of California Press, 1974.

Reyna, Jose Luis, and Richard S. Weinert (eds.) *Authoritarianism in Mexico*. Philadelphia, Pa.: Institute for the Study of Human Issues, 1977.

Ripply, Merrill. *Oil and the Mexican Revolution*. Leiden, Netherlands: E.J. Brill, 1972.

Russell, Philip. *Mexico in Transition*. Austin, Tx.: Colorado River Press, 1977.

Sampson, Anthony. *The Seven Sisters: The Great Oil Companies and the World They Made*. London: Hodder and Stoughton, 1975.

Schurr, Sam H., Joel Darmstadter, et al. *Energy in America's Future: The Choices before Us*. Baltimore: The Johns Hopkins University Press, 1979.

Secretaria de Patrimonio y Fomento Industrial. *Plan nacional de desarrollo industrial, 1979-1982*. Mexico, 1979.

Secretaria de Programacion y Presupuesto, Coordination General del Sistema Nacional de Informacion. *Matriz de insumo—producto de Mexico ano 1970*. Tomo 2, Industria Manufactura. (New York): UNDP, (1970).

Smith, Peter S. *Oil and Politics in Modern Brazil*. Toronto: Macmillan, 1976.

Smith, Ralph Stuart. *The United States and World Energy*. A discussion paper. Washington, D.C.: Department of State, 1977.

Statistical Bureau of the Ministry of Economic Development. *Economic Survey of British Giuana (Guyana), 1965*. Georgetown: Government Printery, 1966.

Stern, Claudio. *Las regiones de Mexico y sus niveles de desarrollo socio-economico*. Mexico, D.F.: El Colegio de Mexico, 1973.

Stevens, Evelyn P. *Protest and Response in Mexico*. Cambridge, Mass.: The MIT Press, 1974.

Stout, B.A. *Energy for World Agriculture*. Rome: U.N. Food and Agriculture Organization, 1979.

Subcommittee on Energy Research of the Committee on Science and Technology, U.S. House of Representatives. *Energy Facts II*. Washington, D.C.: Government Printing Office, 1975.

Tomazinis, Anthony R. *An Assessment of the Interface between Energy Requirements and the Transportation Sector for Egypt: 1975, 1985, 2000.* Philadelphia, Pa: The University of Pennsylvania, June 5, 1978.

Transportation Research Board. *Energy Effects, Efficiencies, and Prospects for Various Modes of Transportation.* National Cooperative Highway Research Program Report no. 43. Washington, D.C.: National Academy of Sciences, 1977.

Transportation Research Board. *Strategies for Reducing Gasoline Consumption through Improved Motor Vehicle Efficiency.* Special Report 169. Washington, D.C.: National Academy of Sciences, 1975.

Tugwell, Franklin. *The Politics of Oil in Venezuela.* Stanford, Calif.: Stanford University Press, 1975.

Turner, Frederick C. *The Dynamic of Mexican Nationalism.* Chapel Hill, N.C.: University of North Carolina Press, 1968.

United Nations. Center for Natural Resources, Energy, and Transport. *State Petroleum Enterprises in Developing Countries.* New York: Pergamon Press, 1980.

United Nations. *1978 Demographic Yearbook.* New York: United Nations, 1979.

United Nations. *Demographic Yearbook: Historical Supplement.* Special Issue. New York: United Nations, 1979.

United Nations. Department of International Economic and Social Affairs. *1979 Yearbook of World Energy Statistics.* New York: United Nations, 1981.

United Nations. *The Economic Commission for Europe and Energy Conservation: Recent Experience and Prospects.* Geneva: ECE, 1980.

United Nations. Statistical Office. *1950-1974 World Energy Supplies,* Series J, no. 19, 1975.

United Nations. *Transport Modes and Technologies for Development.* New York: United Nations, 1980.

United Nations. *Yearbook of World Energy Statistics.* New York: United Nations, 1979.

United Nations Economic Commission for Latin America. *1978 Statistical Yearbook for Latin America.* Santiago, Chile: United Nations Press, 1979.

U.S. Department of Commerce. *Possible Contributions of Cement and Concrete Technology to Energy Conservation,* NTIS PB 295-584. Washington, D.C.: Department of Energy, May 1979.

U.S. Department of Commerce. *Standards of Photovoltaic Energy Conversion Systems.* Washington, D.C., Department of Energy, Division of Solar Technology, May 1979.

U.S. Department of Transportation, Federal Aviation Administration. *Potential Closure of Airports,* Report of the Secretary of Transportation to the U.S. Congress. Washington, D.C., January 1978.

Uruguay. Comision de Inversiones y Desarrollo Economico. *Plan nacional de desarrollo economico y social, 1965-1974.* Montevideo, 1965.

Venezuela. *V (Cinco) Plan de la nacion, 1976-1980.* Decreto 1.454. "Gaceta oficial de la republica de Venezuela." Caracas, March 11, 1976.

Venezuela. Oficina Central de Coordinacion y Planificacion. *Plan de la nacion, 1965-1968.* Caracas, 1967.

Vernon, Raymond (ed.) *Public Policy and Private Enterprise in Mexico.* Cambridge, Mass.: Harvard University Press, 1964.

Weil, Thomas E., et al. *Area Handbook for Haiti.* Washington, D.C.: The American University Press, 1973.

Williams, Edward J. *The Rebirth of the Mexican Petroleum Industry.* Lexington, Mass.: Lexington Books, 1979.

Wilson, Carroll L. *Coal: Bridge to the Future.* Report of the World Coal Study Group at MIT. Cambridge, Mass.: Ballinger, 1980.

Wilson, Carroll L. *Energy: Global Prospects 1985-2000.* Report of the Workshop on Alternative Energy Strategies at MIT. New York: McGraw-Hill Book Company, 1977.

World Bank. *Energy in the Developing Countries.* Washington, D.C., August 1980.

World Bank. *World Development Report.* Washington, D.C., 1979, 1980, 1981.

World Bank. *World Tables 1980.* Washington, D.C., 1980.

Wright, Harry K. *Foreign Enterprise in Mexico.* Chapel Hill, N.C.: University of North Carolina Press, 1971.

Wyant, Frank R. *The United States, OPEC, and Multinational Oil.* Lexington, Mass.: Lexington Books, D.C. Heath, 1977.

Yergin, Daniel (ed.) *The Dependence Dilemma: Gasoline Consumption and America's Security.* Cambridge, Mass.: Harvard University, Center for International Affairs, 1980.

Articles and Monographs

Alfaro, Orfelia. "Requeza petrolera: ?A quien beneficiara?" *Excelsior* (January 2, 1977), p. 7A.

American Chamber of Commerce of Mexico. *Quarterly Economic Report* (January 1979). Mexico City.

American Embassy, Mexico. "Industrial Outlook Report—Chemicals." *Airgram* (August 1976). Mexico City.

American Embassy, Mexico. "Industrial Outlook Report—Chemicals." *Airgram* (September 1977). Mexico City.

American Embassy, Mexico. "Pemex Petrochemical Projects." *Airgram* (1978). Mexico City.

American Society of Civil Engineers. "Transportation and Energy." *Proceedings of Urban Transportation Division, Specialty Conference* (May 1978). Washington, D.C.

Argentina, Secretary of State of Transportation and Public Works. "Consumption and Costs of Energy in the Transportation Sector in the Republic of Argentina." Presented at "Seminario 'Impacto del Costa de la Energia en el Sector Transporte,' " December 1-3, 1980, Bogota, Colombia.

Argentina, Secretary of State of Transportation and Public Works. "Studies for the Formulation of a National Transport Plan." Presented at "Seminario 'Impacto del Costa de la Energia en el Sector Transporte,'" December 1-3, 1980, Bogota, Colombia.

Aroche Parra, Miguel. "Pemex y el sindicato." *Excelsior* (January 23, 1978), p. 7A.

Aviles, Alejandro. "Penacho hispanico y petroleo oscuro." *Proceso* (October 7, 1977), pp. 33-34.

Bank of London and South America Review. "Energy Prospects in Latin America." Vol. 14 (May 1980), pp. 98-112.

Bank of London and South America Review. "Latin America: After the Oil Crisis." Vol. 13 (December 1979), pp. 708-709.

Bank of London and South America Review. Vol. 14 (February 1, 1980), p. 4.

Bennett, Douglas, and Kenneth Sharpe. "The State as Banker and Entrepreneur: The Last Resort Character of the Mexican State's Economic Intervention, 1917-76." *Comparative Politics* (January 1980), pp. 165-189.

Berg, Charles A. "Energy Conservation through Effective Utilization." *Science*, vol. 181 (July 13, 1973), pp. 128-137.

Berg, Charles A. "Process Innovation and Changes in Industrial Energy." *Science*, vol. 199, pp. 608-614.

Berkoz, Esher Balkan. "Optimum Building Shapes for Energy Conservation." *Energy and Architecture.* Vol. 30, pp. 25-30.

Blair, Calvin P. "Economic Policy in Mexico: Retrospect and Prospect." Testimony to the Joint Economic Committee, U.S. Congress, January 1977. Mimeographed.

Blair, Calvin P. "Mexico: Some Recent Developments and the Interdependency Relationship with the United States." Statement before the Joint Economic Committee, U.S. Congress, January 1977. Mimeographed.

Blanco Sanchez, Javier. "Bloqueos a Pemex: dano a la economia." *Excelsior* (July 12, 1978), p. 7A.

Bodansky, David. "Electricity Generation: Choices for Near-Term." *Science*, vol. 207, pp. 721-727.

Borrell Navarro, Eduardo. "Agricultura y petroleo." *Excelsior* (January 11, 1978), p. 7A.

Briggs, Don, Larry Bruno, and Giner Levin. "An Analysis of U.S. National Transportation Policy Alternatives." *Transportation Research*, vol. 14A (1980), pp. 255-261.

Brown, N.L., and J.W. Howe. "Solar Energy for Village Development." *Science*, vol. 199, pp. 651-656.

Busch, Daniel A. Personal letter to Dr. James R. Schlesinger to the attention of Mr. Les Goldman, March 4, 1977, Tulsa, Okla.

Bussiere, Jane (ed.) "The Future of Energy in OECD Countries." *OECD Observer*, no. 73 (January-February 1975).

de Cacer, Guillermo. "Questionamientos del Partido Accion Nacional." *Economica* (November 16, 1977), pp. 38-40.

Campbell, Colin, and Thomas Reese. "The Energy Crisis and Tax Policy in Canada and the United States: Federal-Provincial Diplomacy vs. Congressional Lawmaking." 1976. Mimeographed.

Carlson, Sevinc. "Mexico's Oil: Trends and Prospects to 1985." Center for Strategic and International Studies, Georgetown University, 1978.

Castillo, Heberto. "La CIA informa: Mexico proveera hasta 4.5 milliones de barriles diarios de petroleo en 1985." *Proceso* (October 31, 1977), pp. 12-17.

Castillo, Heberto. "El gas a Texas a pesar de todo." *Proceso* (August 15, 1977), pp. 33-34.

Castillo, Heberto. "El gasoducto a Texas: ?Opcion patriotica?" *Proceso* (September 12, 1977), pp. 34-35.

Castillo, Heberto. "Heberto Castillo ante el gasoducto: '!Como deseo estar equivocado!' " *Proceso* (October 3, 1977), pp. 6-9.

Castillo, Heberto. "Pemex en evidencia." *Proceso* (January 2, 1978), pp. 34-35.

Castillo, Heberto. "Petroleo y gas, ?Vender mas para perder mas?" *Proceso* (November 14, 1977), p. 33.

Castillo, Heberto. "Sobre el documento de la CIA." *Proceso* (November 7, 1977), p. 33.

Castner, Stephen, and John Stone. "Heat and Fuel: Cutting Our Mexican Connection." *New West* (November 8, 1976), p. 15.

CELADE. *Boletin Demografico*, vol. 13 (July 1980), pp. 10-12.

Chavez, Elias. "Los diputados, convencidos por Diaz Serrano." *Proceso* (October 31, 1977), pp. 10-11.

Chavez, Elias. "Manzanilla Schaffer: 'Volere a disentir cuando conciencia y Dignidad lo Exijam.' " *Proceso* (January 9, 1978), pp. 10-13.

Choucri, Nazli. *Energy in Latin America: Transportation, Development and Public Policy*, prepared for the Seminario "Impacto del Costa del Energia en el Sector Transporte, December 1-3, 1980, Bogota, Colombia.

Choucri, Nazli. "The Arab World in the 1980s: Macro-Politics and Economic Change," *Journal of Arab Affairs* (in press).

Choucri, Nazli. "OPEC: Calming a Nervous World Oil Market." *Technology Review* (October 1980), pp. 36-45.

Colombia, National Institute of Transportation. "Colombia: Effect of Prices of Hydrocarbons on Transport." Presented at "Seminario 'Impacto del Costa de la Energia en el Sector Transporte,' " December 1-3, 1980, Bogota, Colombia.

Colson, R.F. "Brazil: The Proalcool Programme—A Response to the Energy Crisis." *Bank of London & South America Review*, vol. 15 (May 1981), pp. 60-70.

Comercio Exterior. "The Gas Pipeline: Polemics about a Tube." December 1977, pp. 475-485.

Comercio Exterior. "Reflections on the Need for Fiscal Reform in Mexico." Editorial. June 1978, pp. 243-248.

Comercio Exterior. "The Role of the Public Debts in the Mexican Economy." December 1977, pp. 465-470.

Congressional Budget Office, Congress of the United States. "The Current and Future Savings of Energy Attributable to Amtrak." A Staff Draft Analysis for the Natural Resources and Commerce Division. Washington, D.C., May 1979.

Congressional Budget Office, Congress of the United States. "Preliminary Projections of Fuel Savings and Revenues Associated with Increased Taxes on Motor Fuels." Technical Note. Washington, D.C., December 14, 1979.

Congressional Budget Office, Congress of the United States. "Projected Composition of Sales for New Cars." Technical Note. Washington, D.C., March 17, 1980.

Congressional Budget Office, Congress of the United States. "Technical Note on the Potential Savings of Petroleum by Different Modes of Urban Transportation." Washington, D.C., December 3, 1979.

Congressional Budget Office, Congress of the United States. "Urban Transportation and Energy: The Potential Savings of Different Modes." Washington, D.C., December 1977.

Cornejo, Angeles Sarahi. "Crisis de energeticos: y todo a media luz." *Los Universitarios*. Mexico, D.F.: UNAM, December 31, 1973.

Courturier, Edith B. "Mexico." In *Latin American Foreign Policies: An Analysis*. Edited by Harold Eugene Davis and Larmar C. Wilson. Baltimore: The Johns Hopkins University Press, 1975.

Croll, Donald O. "Search for New Oil Reserves." *Petroleum Economist*, vol. 44 (September 1977), p. 349.

Cruikshank Garcia, Jorge. "Nuestro comercio exterior y la lucha por la independencia nacional." *El Universal* (January 13, 1976), p. 4.

Deppen, Robert W. "The Wise and Careful Use of Hv/AC." *Building Research*, vol. 10, pp. 21-23.

Diaz Serrano, Jorge. "Carece de base afirmar que el petroleo es mas caro en Mexico." *Excelsior* (January 11, 1978).

Diaz Serrano, Jorge. "Informe de Petroleos Mexicanos." *El Mercado de Valores* (March 28, 1977).

Diaz Serrano, Jorge. "Inquisicion de los 4 Partidos." *Economica* (November 16, 1977).

Diaz Serrano, Jorge. "Panama petrolero de Mexico." *El Mercado de Valores* (April 25, 1977).

Diaz Serrano, Jorge. "El papel de Pemex en el estado de Tabasco." *El Mercado de Valores* (September 25, 1978).

Diaz Serrano, Jorge. "Presupuesto de egresos para 1979." *El Mercado de Valores* (December 11, 1978).

Diaz Serrano, Jorge. "Programa de inversiones de petroleos Mexicanos." *El Mercado de Valores* (January 17, 1977).

Diaz Serrano, Jorge. "La tecnologia mexicana a la altura de la Shell y la Standard Oil." *Economica* (November 16, 1977).

Dietz, Albert G.H. "Materials for Solar Energy Collectors." In *Solar Energy Application in Buildings*. Edited by A.A. Sayigh. New York: Academic Press, 1979.

Dovali, Antonio Jaime. "Hacia la autosuficiencia." *El Mercado de Valores* (December 17, 1973).

Drake, Paul W. "Mexican Regionalism Reconsidered." *Journal of Inter-American Studies*, vol. 12, pp. 401-415.

Economica. "Revista de la Quincena." November 16, 1977, pp. 10-16.

El Salvador, Superintendent of Energy. "Energy Analysis of the Transportation Sector in El Salvador." Presented at "Seminario 'Impacto del Costa de la Energia en el Sector Transporte,' " December 1-3, 1980, Bogota, Colombia.

Elizondo, Gaspar. "Escandalo en la Camara." *Proceso* (January 9, 1978), p. 36.

Estrategia. "Energeticos, capitalismo y contradicciones de clase." Vol. 2 (May 25, 1975), pp. 35-46.

Estrategia. "La industria petroquimica en Mexico." Vol. 2 (January 25, 1976), pp. 24-28.

Estrategia. "Petroleo, fuente prodigiosa." Vol. 3 (September-October 1977), pp. 60-69.

Estrategia. "Los trabajadores petroleros." Vol. 1 (September 20, 1975), pp. 46-52.

European Conference of Ministers of Transport: "Transport and the Economic Situation." From the *Sixth International Symposium on Theory and Practice in Transport Economies*, held in Madrid, September 22-25, 1975. Paris: OECD, 1975.

Excelsior. "Saqueo a PEMEX." November 14, 1977, p. 6A.

Executive Intelligence Review. "Response to Schlesinger Blackmail: Mexico Breaks Off Gas Negotiations with U.S." Vol. 5 (January 10, 1978), pp. 1-2.

Ezra, Arthur A. "Technology Utilization: Incentives and Solar Energy." *Science*, vol. 198 (February 28, 1975), pp. 707-714

Fagen, Richard R. "The Realities of U.S.-Mexican Relations." *Foreign Affairs*, vol. 55 (July 1977), pp. 685-700.

Fagen, Richard R., and Henry Nau. "Mexican Gas: The Northern Connection." Prepared for a conference on the United States, U.S. Foreign Policy, and Latin American Regimes, Washington, D.C., March 1978. Published in *United States Foreign Policy and Latin America*. Edited by Richard R. Fagen. Stanford, Calif.: Stanford University Press, 1979.

Felix, David. "Income Inequality in Mexico." *Current History* (March 1977), pp. 111-114.

Fisher, John C. "Energy Crises in Perspective." *Physics Today* (December 1973), pp. 40-49.

Fitzgerald, E.V. "Mexico: A New Direction in Economic Policy?" *Bank of London & South American Review* (October 1978), pp. 528-538.

Fitzgerald, E.V.K. "Some Aspects of the Political Economy of the Latin American State." *Development and Change*, vol. 7 (1976), pp. 119-133.

Fitzgerald, E.V.K. "The State and Capital Accumulation in Mexico." *Journal of Latin American Studies*, vol. 10 (1978), pp. 263-282.

Flores Caballero, Romeo. "Mexico in the International System and Its Relations with the United States." *Proceedings of the Pacific Coast Council on Latin American Studies*, vol. 4 (1975). San Diego.

Garabito Martinez, Jorge. "El gasoducto beneficiara a Monterrey: PAN." *Economica* (November 16, 1977).

Garcia Soler, Leon. "Petroleo sin politica equivalente a suicidio." *Excelsior* (October 28, 1977), p. 6A.

Garcia Colin-Scherer, Leopoldo. "La ciencia y la tecnologia del petroleo: situacion actual y Perspectivas futuras en Mexico." *Foro Internacional*, vol. 18 (April-June 1978), pp. 678-690.

Garcia Sainz, Ricardo. "Presupuesto de egresos para 1979." *El Mercado de Valores* (December 11, 1978).

Garibay, Ricardo. "Petroleo: dignidad nacional." *Excelsior* (October 17, 1974), p. 6.

Garrett, Hoke M. "Energy Conservation by U.S. Cement Industry." *Pit and Quarry* (April 1976), pp. 106-112.

Goldenberg, J. "Brazil: Energy Options and Current Outlook." *Science*, vol. 200 (April 14, 1978), pp. 153-158.

Gordon, David. "Mexico: A Survey." *The Economist* (April 22, 1978), pp. 1-34.

Gordon, R.L. "The Hobbling of Coal: Policy and Regulatory Uncertainties." *Science*, vol. 200 (April 14, 1978), pp. 153-158.

Grayson, George W. "Mexico's Opportunity: The Oil Boom." *Foreign Policy*, no. 29 (Winter 1977-1978), pp. 65-89.

Green, Rosario. "Deuda externa y politica exterior: la vuelta a bilateralidad en las relationes internacionales de Mexico." *Foro Internacional*, vol. 18 (July-September 1977), pp. 54-80.

Grey, J., G.W. Sutton, and M. Zlotnick. "Fuel Conservation and Applied Research." *Science*, vol. 200 (April 14, 1978), pp. 135-142.

Griffith, J.W. "Energy Criteria for Resource Optimization." *Building Research*, vol. 10 (July-December 1973), pp. 9-12.

Grindle, Merilee S. "Policy Change in an Authoritarian Regime: Mexico under Echeverria." *Journal of Inter-American Studies*, vol. 19 (November 1977), pp. 523-555.

Gross, James, and James H. Pielert. "Building Standards and Codes for Energy Conservation." *Energy and Architecture*, vol. 30 (February 1977), pp. 54-57.

Gustavson, M.R. "Limits to Wind Power Utilization." *Science*, vol. 204 (April 6, 1979), pp. 13-18.

Gutierrez Santos, Luis E. "Algunas reflexiones sobre los criterios de exportacion a corto plazo." A position paper. Mexico, D.F. (April 20, 1977). Mimeographed.

Gutierrez Santos, Luis E. "Framework for Investment." Mexico City (no date). Mimeographed.

Gutierrez Santos, Luis E., and Michael G. Webb. "Comentarios sobre la evaluacion de proyectos con referencia al sector energetico mexicano." *El Trimestre Economico* (April-June 1977), pp. 371-388.

Guzman, Eduardo J. "Exploration by Petroleos Mexicanos." In *The Role of National Governments in Exploration for Mineral Resources*. Edited by William E. Bonin et al. Ocean City, N.J.: The Littoral Press, 1964.

Hafele, W. "IIASA's World Regional Energy Modelling." *Proceedings of Conference on Energy Systems Analysis*, The Netherlands, October 9-11, 1979. Laxenburg, Austria: IIASA, 1979.

Hafele, W., and W. Sassin. "The Global Energy System." *Annual Reviews*, 1977.

Hafele, W., and W. Sassin. "Resources and Endowments: An Outline on

Future Energy Systems." Prepared for NATO Science Committee Twentieth Anniversary Commemoration Conference, Brussels, April 11-13, 1978.

Hammond, A.L. "An Interim Look at Energy." *Science*, vol. 199 (February 10, 1978), pp. 607-613.

Handler, Heinz. "Oil Revenues—Their Implications for an Industrial Economy." *Finance and Development*, vol. 13 (December 1976), pp. 16ff.

Hannon, Bruce. "Energy Conservation and the Consumer." *Science*, vol. 189 (July 11, 1975), pp. 95-102.

Harte, J., and M. El-Glasseir. "Energy and Water." *Science*, vol. 199 (February 10, 1978), pp. 623-633.

Hillman, Jimmey S. "Statement before the Joint Economic Committee, Subcommittee on Inter-American Economic Relations." Washington, D.C., January 24, 1977.

Hinojosa, Juan Jose. "Conata de dignidad en el Congreso." *Proceso* (January 9, 1978), p. 35.

Hirst, Eric, and Bruce Hannon. "Effects of Energy Conservation in Residential and Commercial Buildings." *Science*, vol. 205 (August 17, 1979), pp. 656-662.

Holdren, J.P. "Fusion Energy in Context: Its Fitness for the Long Term." *Science*, vol. 200 (April 14, 1978), pp. 168-180.

Holguin, Romero A., and Veras G. Holguin. "Considerations on the Impact of Rise of Energy Costs in Transport Sector in the Dominican Republic." Presented at "Seminario 'Impacto del Costa de la Energia en el Sector Transporte,' " December 1-3, 1980, Bogota, Colombia.

Huey, John. "No Fiesta Ahead: Despite Rising Wealth in Oil, Mexico Battles Intractable Problems." *Wall Street Journal* (August 30, 1978), p. 1.

International Energy Angency. "Summary of Discussions and Technical Papers." *Proceedings of Workshop on Energy Data of Developing Countries*. Vol. 1. Paris: OECD, 1979.

Jakubiak, Henry E., and M. Taher Dajani. "Oil Income and Financial Policies in Iran and Saudi Arabia." *Finance and Development*, vol. 13 (December 1976).

Johnson, Timothy E. "Performance of Passively Heated Buildings." *Energy and Architecture* vol. 30 (February 1977), pp. 16-20.

Kakela, Peter J. "Iron Ore: Energy, Labor and Capital Changes with Technology." *Science*, vol. 202 (December 15, 1978), pp. 1151-1156.

Katz, Julius L. "Energy and the World Economy." News Release. Washington, D.C.: Department of State, Bureau of Public Affairs, Office of Media Services, January 5, 1977.

Kelley, H. "Photovoltaic Power Systems: A Tour Through the Alternatives." *Science*, vol. 199 (February 10, 1978), pp. 634-643.

Knochenhauer, Guillermo. "Espejismo petrolero: comercio y politica." *Excelsior* (January 6, 1978), p. 6A.

Knochenhauer, Guillermo. "Incongruencias: endeudamiento externo." *Excelsior* (November 3, 1977), p. 6A.

Knochenhauer, Guillermo. "El petroleo, riqueza social." *Excelsior* (January 3, 1978), p. 6A.

Knowles, Ralph. "Solar Energy, Building and the Law." *Energy and Architecture*, vol. 30 (February 1977), pp. 62-67.

Kritz, Mary M., and Douglas T. Gurak (eds.) *International Migration Review*, issue entitled "International Migration in Latin America." Vol. 13 (Fall 1979).

Labra, Armando. "Mexico, ?Un modelo agotado?" *Economica* (November 16, 1977), pp. 75-78.

Latin America Economic Report. "Gas Deal Expected from Carter's Visit to Mexico." February 9, 1979, p. 45.

Latin America Economic Report. "Mexico Launches Ambitious Programme to Create Jobs." June 30, 1978, p. 200.

Latin America Economic Report. "Mexico Likely to Limit Growth in Oil Production." January 26, 1979, p. 28.

Latin America Economic Report. "Mexico Shy about Oil Abundance." March 28, 1975, pp. 49-50.

Latin America Economic Report. "Oil Masks Weakness in Mexico's Payments Balance." March 10, 1978, pp. 76-77.

Latin America Economic Report. "PEMEX Still the Big Spender in Mexico's 1979 Budget." December 8, 1978, p. 377.

Latin America Political Report. "Mexico: Be My Valentine." February 9, 1979, pp. 45-46.

Latin America Political Report. "Mexico: Educating Yankees." February 23, 1979, pp. 57-59.

Latin America Political Report. "Mexico: Fallen Angel." February 9, 1979, p. 41.

Latin America Weekly Report. 1979, 1980, 1981.

Latin America Weekly Report. "Special Report: Latin America and Middle East Draw Closer." December 7, 1979, pp. 68.-69.

Laviada, Inigo. "Esfuerso de una minoria." *Diario de Yucatan* (January 12, 1978), p. 3.

Lipinsky, E.S. "Fuels from Biomass: Integration with Food and Materials Systems." *Science*, vol. 199 (February 10, 1978), pp. 644-651.

Lopez Portillo, Jose. "First State of the Nation Report." Supplement to *The News*. Mexico City (September 2, 1977).

Lopez Portillo, Jose. "La tarea para los mexicanos es ahora mas facil, pero mas delicada." *Hispano*. Mexico City (September 11, 1978).

Los Angeles Times. "Playing Rough with Mexico." June 13, 1979.

Macrakis, Michael S. "Energy: Demand, Conservation and Institutional Problems." In *Proceedings of a Conference Held at MIT under National Science Foundation Grant GI-36476, February 12-14, 1973.* Edited by Michael S. Macrakis. Cambridge, Mass.: The MIT Press, 1974.

Mancke, Richard B. "Mexico's Petroleum Resources." *Current History* (February 1979), pp. 74ff.

Mansfield, Edwin. "Major Issues Concerning U.S. Technology Policy." In *Economic Issues of the Eighties.* Edwin Mansfield. Baltimore: The Johns Hopkins University Press, 1979, pp. 185-198.

Marchetti, Cesare. "From the Primeval Soup to World Government: Essay on Comparative Evolution." Laxenburg, Austria: IIASA, March 1976.

Marshall, Harold E. and Rosale T. Ruegg. "Energy Conservation Through Life-Cycle Costing." *Energy and Architecture*, vol. 30 (February 1977), pp. 42-53.

Martre, Gonzalo. "Grito en la Camara: !Somos ricos!" *Excelsior* (November 3, 1977), p. 6A.

Maza, Enrique. "Los derechos indigenas y el petroleo." *Proceso* (December 5, 1977), pp. 38-39.

Maza, Enrique. "Petroleo, Manzanilla y los elegidos." *Proceso* (January 9, 1978), pp. 34-35.

McBride, Robert. "U.S.-Mexican Relations." *Princeton Alumni Weekly* (March 13, 1978), pp. 23-25.

Meisen, Walter A. "Energy Conservation in the General Service Administration." *Building Research*, vol. 10 (July-December 1973), pp. 34-40.

Mejias, Jose Luis. "Petroleo." *El Universal* (February 27, 1977), p. 1.

El Mercado de Valores. "Prestamos internacionales para el sector publico." April 24, 1978, pp. 309-310.

Metz, William D. "Mexico: The Premier Oil Discovery in the Western World." *Science*, vol. 202 (December 22, 1978), pp. 1261-1265.

The Mexican Investor. Mexico's Oil Future. Mexico City (April 4, 1977).

Mexican Newsletter. "Development of Energy Resources." Vol. 62 (April 30, 1976), pp. 2-3.

Mexican Newsletter. "The State Petrochemical Industry in 1971-1975." *Mexican Newsletter.* May 31, 1976, pp. 6-11.

Mexico Special Report. "Latin America." March 1977.

Middle East Economic Survey, 1976-1981.

Meyer Cosio, Lorenzo. "El auge petrolero y las experiencias mexicanos disponibles: los problemas del pasado y la vision futuro del *Foro Internacional*, vol. 18 (April-June 1978), pp. 577-596.

Michel, Marco Antonio and Leopoldo Allub. "Petroleo y cambio social en el sureste de Mexico." *Foro Internacional*, vol. 18 (April-June 1978), pp. 691-709.

Montenegro, Manuel Roberto. "Gasoducto a EU: a mayor gloria imperial." *Excelsior* (September 15, [no year]), p. 6A.

Montenegro, Manuel Roberto. "Tabasco y petroleo: negra corte de milagros." *Excelsior* (November 14, [no year]), p. 7A.

Morales, Isabel. "Olga Pellicer de Brody: exporter petroleo no es la solucion." *Proceso* (December 5, 1977), pp. 16-17.

Morawetz, David. "Import Substitution, Employment and Foreign Exchange in Colombia: No Cheers for Petrochemicals." In *The Choice of Technology in Developing Countries.* C. Peter Trimmer et al. Cambridge, Mass.: Center for International Affairs, Harvard University, 1975.

New York Times, 1979-1981.

New York Times Magazine. January 11, 1981, pp. 22-25, 56, 58, 59.

Niering, Frank E., Jr. "Argentina: Private Capital Aids Oil Drive." *Petroleum Economist*, vol. 46 (October 1979).

Niering, Frank E., Jr. "Brazil: Open-Door Policy to Oil Search." *Petroleum Economist*, vol. 47 (November 1980).

Niering, Frank E., Jr. "Ecuador: Continued Obstacles to Development." *Petroleum Economist*, vol. 48 (February 1981), p. 53.

Niering, Frank E., Jr. "Peru: Latin America's New Oil Exporter." *Petroleum Economist*, vol. 46 (July 1979).

Niering, Frank E., Jr. "Venezuela: On Course for the 21st Century." *Petroleum Economist*, vol. 47 (May 1980).

Nugent, Jeffrey B. "Contemporary Issues in Development Economics." In *Economic Issues of the Eighties.* Jeffrey B. Nugent. Baltimore: The Johns Hopkins University Press, 1979, pp. 262-270.

Oil and Gas Journal. Dennwell Pub. Co., Tulsa, Ok., January 1981.

Oil and Gas Journal. "Mexico Eyes Gas-Starved U.S. as Outlet for Surplus." Denwell Pub. Co., Tulsa, Ok., June 22, 1977, pp. 63-65.

Ojeda, Mario. "El poder negociador del petroleo: el caso de Mexico." *Foro Internacional*, vol. 21 (Julio-Septiembre 1980), pp. 44-64.

Ojeda, Mario. "Mexico ante los Estado Unidos en la coyuntura actual." *Foro Internacional*, vol. 18 (July-September 1977), pp. 32-53.

Ojeda, Mario. "Mexico: The Debate over the New Oil Resources." 1978. Mimeographed.

Organization for Economic Cooperation and Development. "Register of Development Research Projects in Latin America." In *Liaison Bulletin Between Development Research and Training Institutes.* Paris: OECD, 1979.

Ortiz, H.E., and G. Rene. "Workshop on Energy and Development: Increasing Third World Collective Self-Reliance." *OPEC Press Communique*, no. 11 (July 9, 1980).

Ortiz Pinchetti, Francisco. "Carestia, crecimiento disordenado y con-

taminacion Fisica y moral." *Proceso* (June 19, 1978), pp. 16-19.
Ortiz Pinchetti, Francisco. "Leandro Rovirosa Wade: El Petroleo, Fortuna de Tabasco pueda ser su ruina." *Proceso* (October 31, 1977), pp. 18-19.
Ortiz Pinchetti, Francisco. "Tabasco, tierra de platano, cacao y petroleo." *Proceso* (November 14, 1977), pp. 18-19.
Ortiz Priego, Luis. "La nacion no escatimara su apoyo: PRI." *Economica* (November 16, 1977).
O'Shaugnessy, Hugh. "Oil in Latin America." *The Financial Times*. London, 1976.
Oteyza, Jose Andres. "Acuerdos industriales con Brasil." *El Mercado de Valores* (January 1, 1979).
Oteyza, Jose Andres. "El programa sexenal petroquimico." *El Mercado de Valores* (November 27, 1978).
El Partido Popular Socialista. "El Partido Popular Socialista y el Petroleo de Mexico." *Excelsior* (March 3, 1978).
Pellicer de Brody, Olga. "Mexico in the 1970s and Its Relations with the U.S." In *Latin America and the U.S.: The Changing Policy Realities.* Edited by Julio Cotler and Richard R. Fagen. Stanford, Calif.: Stanford University Press, 1974, pp. 314-333.
Petroleos Mexicanos. "Annual Report, 1975." *Mexican Newsletter* (Separata), no. 36 (March 18, 1976).
Petroleos Mexicanos. "Datos relevantes illustrativos del crecimiento y mejoria de la productividad de Petroleos Mexicanos." *Excelsior* (December 30, 1976).
Petroleos Mexicanos. "Expansion de la oferta de energeticos." *El Mercado de Valores* (January 10, 1977).
Petroleos Mexicanos. "PEMEX Report, 1974." *Mexican Newsletter*, no. 30 (March 18, 1975).
Petroleum Economist. "Mexico Emerging as a Major Exporter." August 1977, pp. 311-312.
Petroleum Economist. "Mexico: PEMEX's Activities in 1976." May 1977, p. 195.
Petroleum Economist. "PEMEX Plans Big Expansion." March 1977, pp. 94-96.
Petroleum Economist. "Rapid Rise in Oil Exports." July 1976, pp. 260-261.
Petroleum Economist. 1979-1981.
Petroleum Intelligence Weekly. 1978-1981.
Pimentel, David, L.E. Hurd, A.C. Bellotti, et al. "Food Production and the Energy Crisis." *Science*, vol. 182 (November 2, 1973), pp. 443-450.
Pimentel, David, Elinor C. Terhune, et al. "Land Degradation: Effects on Food and Energy Resources." *Science*, vol. 194 (October 8, 1976), pp. 149-156.

Pindyck, Robert S. "The Critical Issues in U.S. Energy Policy." In *Economic Issues of the Eighties*. Baltimore: The Johns Hopkins University Press, 1979, pp. 135-145.

Platt's Oilgram News. May 1, 1981, p. 1.

Platt's Oilgram News, 1980, all issues.

Poitras, Guy. "Mexican Oil Policy." 1976. Mimeographed.

Polanco, Milciades Perez. "Transport in the Dominican Republic." Presented at "Seminario 'Impacto del Costa de la Energia en el Sector Transporte,' " December 1-3, 1980, Bogota, Colombia.

Porter, Lanning M., Capt. "Special Report, Mexican Petroleum." Mexico City, Mexico: Embassy of the United States of America, Office of the Defense Attache, 1976.

Powell, J. Richard. "Labor Problems in the Mexican Petroleum Industry, 1938-1950." *Inter-American Economic Affairs*, vol. 6 (1952), pp. 3-50.

Proceso. "PEMEX: Investigadores del IPM; contra precios atados del gas." November 7, 1977, p. 29.

Proceso. "PEMEX: vender petroleo, como vender tomate: Diaz S." August 22, 1977, pp. 22-24.

Proceso. "Petroleo: Exigen indemnizaciones justas a Pemex." November 28, 1977, p. 27.

Puente Leyva, Jesus. "La critica ha sido desinformada y dolosa: PRI." *Economica* (November 16, 1977).

Punto Critico. "La 'reprivatizacion' de PEMEX." Ano 6 (May 1977), p. 11.

Purcell, John F.H., and Susan Kaufman. "The State and Economic Enterprise in Mexico: The Limits of Reform." *Nueva Politica* (Mexico), vol. 1 (April-June 1976), pp. 229-250. Mimeographed.

Quinlan, Martin. "Refineries: New Projects and Extensions." *Petroleum Economist* (September 1977), pp. 337-340.

Reveles, Jose. "El Consejo de Administracion de Pemex. La discusion interna sobre el gasoducto." *Proceso* (October 31, 1977), pp. 6-9.

Reveles, Jose. "El Petroleo Mexicano, reserva de EU ante la OPEP." *Proceso* (February 6, 1978), pp. 10-11.

Riding, Alan. "Mexico Keeps Plenty of Aces in the Hole." *New York Times* (March 9, 1980).

Rippy, Merrill. "Mexico's PEMEX: A Successful Nationalized Industry." Paper presented at the Western Social Science Association meeting in Tempe, Arizona, May 1976. Mimeographed.

Risser, Hubert E. "The U.S. Energy Dilemma: The Gap between Today's Requirements and Tomorrow's Potential." *Illinois State Geological Survey*, no. 64 (July 1973).

Rivera, Miguel Angel. "Chiapas y Tabasco: PEMEX destruye mucho y paga poco." *Proceso* (January 9, 1978), pp. 19-20.

Rivlin, Alice M. "Statement on Feasibility and Possible Impacts of Increasing the Fuel Economy Standards for Cars Produced after 1985." Presented before the Subcommittee on Science, Technology, and Space, Committee on Commerce, Science, and Transportation, U.S. Senate. Washington, D.C., May 14, 1980.

Rodriquez Otal, Ezequiel. "Ante todo, mantener la independencia nacional: PPS." *Economica* (November 16, 1977).

Ross, March H., and Robert H. Williams. "The Potential for Fuel Conservation." *Technology Review*, vol. 79 (February 1977).

Roush, Larry F. "Energy Conservation for Public Office Buildings." *Building Research*, vol. 10 (July-December 1973), pp. 5-8.

Salinas Rios, Francisco. "Contratistas particulares extraeran petroleo y gas en la zona norte: PEMEX." *Excelsior* (November 30, 1977), p. 1.

Salinas Rios, Francisco. " 'Enormes yacimientos' de petroleo y gas en 3 estados: PEMEX." *Excelsior* (August 31, 1977), p. 1.

Sanchez Gavito, Vicente. "Invitacion que nunca llegara." *Excelsior* (May 25, 1976), p. 6A.

Sandeman, Hugh. "PEMEX Comes Out of Its Shell." *Fortune* (April 10, 1978), pp. 45-48.

Sanders, Thomas G. "The Economic Development of Tabasco, Mexico." *Field Staff Reports*, North America Series, vol. 5, no. 8. New York: American Universities Field Staff, 1977.

Sansing, Bill. "Mexico's Oil, Gas Plans Good for U.S." *Tulsa Tribune*, June 17, 1977, p. 1C.

Santana, G.P. "Considerations on the Transport Sector and Energy Consumption in Venezuela." Prepared for the Seminario "Impacto del Costa de la Energia en el Sector Transporte," 1-3 December 1980, Bogota, Colombia. Trans. Massachusetts Institute of Technology, Cambridge.

Secretaria de Programacion y Presupuesto. "Presupuesto de egresos de la federacion para 1978." *Proceso* (January 9, 1978).

Sepulveda, Isidro. "Pensamientos sobre el proceso de interdependencia Mexico-Norte Americano y el futuro del sistema mexicano." Paper presented at an international symposium on the problems of migratory workers in Mexico and the United States, Guadalajara, Mexico, 1978. Mimeographed.

Serrato, Marcela. "Las vicisitudes del plan energetico de Carter." *Foro Internacional*, vol. 18 (April-June 1978), pp. 549-576.

Severo, Soares Cloraldino. "The Energy Problem and Transport: The Brazilian Experience." Prepared for the Seminario "Impacto del Costa de la Energia en el Sector Transporte," December 1-3, 1980, Bogota, Colombia. Trans. Massachusetts Institute of Technology, Cambridge.

Skelton, Max B. "1978 to be Year of Uncertainties for Oil Industry." *Dallas Times Herald* (January 1, 1978), p. G7.

Smil, Vaclav, and William E. Knowland. "Energy in the Developing World." *American Scientist*, vol. 67 (September 1979), pp. 522-532.

Smith, Peter H. "Continuity and Turnover within the Mexican Political Elite, 1900-1971." In *Contemporary Mexico: Papers of the IV International Congress of Mexican History*. Edited by James W. Wilkie, Michael C. Meyer, and Edna Monzon de Wilkie. Los Angeles: University of California Press, 1976.

Stein, Richard G. "Observations on Energy Use in Buildings." *Energy and Architecture*, vol. 30 (February 1977), pp. 36-41.

Streadman, Philip. "Energy and Patterns of Land Use." *Energy and Architecture*, vol. 30 (February 1977), pp. 62-67.

Swabb, L.E. Jr. "Liquid Fuels from Coal: From R&D to an Industry." *Science*, vol. 199 (February 10, 1978), pp. 619-622.

Taborga, Pedro N. "Forecasting Railway Traffic Demand: Lessons from Cross-Country Comparisons." Presented at World Conference on Transport Research, London, April 1980.

Toureilles, Francisco A. "The Effects of Energy Price Changes on the Transportation Sector in Latin America—List of References." Cambridge, Mass.: Massachusetts Institute of Technology, September 5, 1980.

Toureilles, Francisco A. "Network and Financial Data for the Transport Sector, Various Countries: Argentina, Brazil, Chile, Mexico and U.S.A." Cambridge, Mass.: Massachusetts Institute of Technology, February 6, 1978.

Toureilles, Franciso A. "Transportation Perspectives in Developing Countries." Cambridge, Mass.: Massachusetts Institute of Technology, February 5, 1978.

Trechsel, Heinz R. "Research in Energy Conservation." *Energy and Architecture*, vol. 30 (February 1977), pp. 31-33.

Turrent Diaz, Eduardo. "Petroleo y economia: costos y beneficios a corto plazo." *Foro Internacional*, vol. 18 (April-June 1978), pp. 623-654.

United Nations. "Centroamerica: evaluacion del impacto de la crisis de energia en el transporte automotor." New York: United Nations, 1975.

U.S. Agency for International Development. "Natural Resources: Energy, Water and River Basin Development." Prepared for the United Nations Conference on the Application of Science and Technology for the Benefit of the Less Developed Areas, vol. 1. Washington, D.C.: Superintendent of Documents, 1973.

U.S. Central Intelligence Agency. "The International Energy Situation: Outlook to 1985." Washington, D.C., April 1977.

U.S. Department of Energy. "Energy Efficient Electric Motors." Fact Sheet DOE/CS-0163. Oak Ridge, Tennessee: May 1980.

U.S. Department of the Interior. "U.S. Energy through the Year 2000." Washington, D.C., December 1972.

U.S. Department of State. "Energy and Foreign Policy," no. 69. Washington, D.C.: Bureau of Public Affairs, June 1979.

U.S. Energy Policy and Planning Office. "The National Energy Plan." Washington, D.C., April 1977.

U.S. General Accounting Office. "The United States and International Energy Issues." Report to the Congress of the U.S., EMD 78-105. Washington, D.C., December 18, 1978.

Valdez, Fernando. "Exportacion de hidrocarburos: a la larga, problemas." *Excelsior* (December 8, 1977), p. 6A.

Valdez, Fernando. " '?Exportar a todo costa?' Peligros del petroleo." *Excelsior* (September 22, 1977), p. 7A.

Vicaino, Roberto. "Ustedes tienen petroleo y nosotros lo necesitamos." *Proceso* (January 14, 1977), pp. 14-16.

Del Villar, Samuel I. "Solo diez anos de reserva petrolera." *Excelsior* (July 29, 1976), p. 6A.

de Villegas, Maria Adriana. "Migration and Economic Integration in Latin America: The Andean Group." *International Migration Review*, vol. 11 (Spring 1977), pp. 59-76.

Villecco, Marguerite. "Energy Conscious Design in Schools of Architecture." *Energy and Architecture*, vol. 30 (February 1977), pp. 6-10.

Wagstaff, H. Reid. "Petroleum in Latin America." *Proceedings of the Arizona Latin American Conference.* Tempe, Ariz.: Center for Latin America Studies, Arizona State University, 1975.

The Wall Street Journal, 1980-1981.

Weisz, Paul B., and John F. Marshall. "High-Grade Fuels from Biomass Farming: Potentials and Constraints." *Science*, vol. 206 (October 5, 1979), pp. 24-30.

White, David C. "Energy Choices for the 1980s." *Technology Review*, vol. 82 (August-September 1980), pp. 30-40.

Whitehead, Laurence. "Petroleos y bienestar." *Foro Internacional*, vol. 18 (April-June 1978), pp. 655-677.

Williams, Edward J. "The Agricultural Sector, Unemployment, and Petroleum Earnings in Mexico: Policy Prospectives for the Medium Range." *Proceedings of the Rocky Mountain Council on Latin American Studies Conference.* Missoula, Mont.: May 1978.

Williams, Edward J. "Mexican Hydrocarbons Export Policy: Ambition and Reality." In *International Energy Perspectives: A Comparative Approach.* Edited by Robert Lawrence and Martin Heisler. Lexington, Mass.: Lexington Books, D.C. Heath, 1979.

Williams, Edward J. "Oil in U.S.-Mexican Relations: Analysis and Bargaining Scenario." *Orbis*, vol. 22 (Spring 1978), pp. 201-216.

Williams, Edward J. "Petroleum and Political Change in Mexico." Unpublished paper.

Windheim, Lee Stephen. "A Systems Morphology for Examining Energy Utilization in Buildings." *Building Research*, vol. 10 (July-December 1973), pp. 29-33.

Wilson, S.S. and N.D.C. Tee. "Energy Economics and Transport." Presented at a meeting of the Urban Transport Studies Group, University of Warwick, March 28, 1974. Paris: OECD, 1974.

Wishart, R.S. "Industrial Energy in Transition: A Petro-Chemical Perspective." *Science*, vol. 199 (February 10, 1978), pp. 614-618.

World Bank. *Ownership and Efficiency in Urban Buses*. Working Paper no. 371. Washington, D.C., February 1980.

World Bank. *Transportation Sector Working Paper*. Washington, D.C., January 1972.

World Business Weekly. "Survey: Latin America, A Continent at Odds with Itself." August 24, 1981.

World Business Weekly, July 6, 1981.

World Business Weekly, August 3, 1981.

World Oil. "Reforma Trend Reserves May Exceed Prudhoe Bay." June 1976, pp. 101-102.

Yunez Naude, Antonio. "Politica petrolera y perspectivas del desarrollo de la economia mexicana." Un ensayo exploratorio. *Foro Internacional*, vol. 18 (April-June 1978), pp. 597-622.

Index

About the Author

Nazli Choucri is professor of political science and associate director of the Technology Adaptation Program at Massachusetts Institute of Technology. She received the M.A. and Ph.D. degrees from Stanford University. Dr. Choucri has written extensively on problems of international development, specifically with respect to conflicts that arise from resource issues. Her major interest is analysis of conflicts resulting from differentials in resource endowments, population characteristics, or technological development. Dr. Choucri's most recent book, titled *International Energy Futures: Petroleum Prices, Power, and Payments*, was published by the MIT Press in 1981.

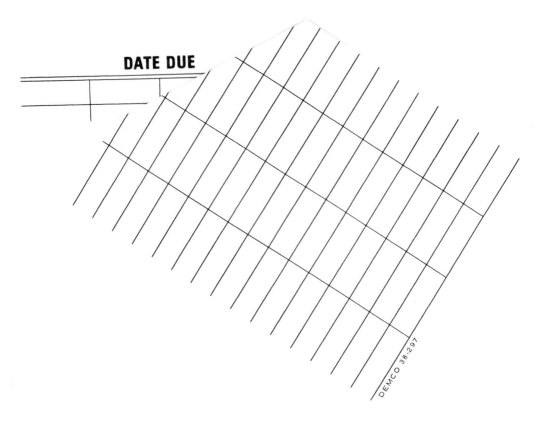

DATE DUE

DEMCO 38-297